RUSSIA OBSERVED

Advisory Editors
HARMON TUPPER   HARRY W. NERHOOD

A SUMMER ON THE YENESEI
1914

Maud D. Haviland

ARNO PRESS & THE NEW YORK TIMES
New York • 1971

Reprint Edition 1971 by Arno Press Inc.
LC 70-115543
ISBN 0-405-03081-9

Russia Observed
ISBN for complete set 0-405-03000-2

Reprinted from a copy in
the Pennsylvania State Library

Manufactured in the United States of America

A SUMMER ON THE YENESEI

The Antonoffs' House and Dog Sledge.

A SUMMER
ON THE YENESEI

(1914)

BY

MAUD D. HAVILAND
AUTHOR OF "THE WOOD PEOPLE AND OTHERS"

ILLUSTRATED

LONDON
EDWARD ARNOLD
1915

[*All rights reserved*]

PREFACE

ANYONE who writes about the birds of Yenesei, nowadays, does so with diffidence, for the recollection of the *Birds of Siberia* is always present with him, like a critic standing at his shoulder. But the journey down the river is shorter than it was in Seebohm's time, and therefore there is less opportunity to observe the birds and men who live along the banks; for *taigà* and tundra slide past as quickly as at a kinematograph show. There is more scope at Golchika, and there, if wishes might have found place, I should like to have woven a little of the spell of the tundra into these lines of print—the voices of the wild-fowl calling up the summer, the poppies above the snowdrifts, the smell of driftwood fires, and the squelch of the reindeer's little hoofs in the moss. But this book has no pretension to such art. It contains merely some pages from the journal of a season spent among birds, which, for the most part, are known in this country only on migration or as vagrants.

The scientific names employed are those used in the *Hand-List of British Birds* (1912), except for certain species not included in the British lists, for which the nomenclature is that of H. E. Dresser's *Manual of Palæarctic Birds*.

PREFACE

I must again express my best thanks to Miss M. A. Czaplicka, by whose energy and enterprise the expedition was organised, for permission to join the party. My thanks are also due to Mr. H. L. Popham, who kindly gave me much information about the Yenesei, both before and after the trip.

MAUD D. HAVILAND.

CONTENTS

CHAPTER I

The "Gillissy"—Departure from London—Warsaw—Contretemps at Moscow—Krasnoyarsk—Vassilli Ivanovitch—We embark for the north—The Angara River—Yenesiesk—The *Oryol* and her captain—Fellow-passengers—The "wide water"—Nasimorokoya—Vorogovo—The Kamin Pass—Midnight in the forest 1

CHAPTER II

A ramble in the forest—Verkne Imbatskaya—The Ostiaks of the Yenesei—The black-throated ousel—The romance of the telegraph—Difficulties on the voyage—Monastir—Bird's-nesting at Turukhansk—The pale thrush—The Kureika—The Yenesei cuckoos—Lost in the forest—The willow island—Igarka 23

CHAPTER III

The *taigà*—The dusky ousel and the little bunting—The Tungus—Platina—Women merchants—Dudinka—The first sight of the tundra—Krestova—The Yenesei fisheries—Breokoffsky Ostrov—Stormbound—Arrival at Golchika—First impressions—A Good Samaritan—Michael Petrovitch Antonoff . 45

CHAPTER IV

A morning theft—Cockroaches—Spring at Golchika—A dog sledge—A trip to Och Marino—A Siberian household—The Eastern golden plover—A change in the weather—Rough water on the Yenesei—Return to Golchika 68

CONTENTS

CHAPTER V

People of Golchika—Protyvik—Antonoff and his household—The Prokopchuk family—Sylkin the Samoyede—His sayings—His religion—The natives at Golchika—Their manners and customs—The need for medical missions—The colonisation and future of Siberia 90

CHAPTER VI

The birds of Golchika—Seebohm—Popham—The effect of the season—The curlew-sandpiper—The grey phalarope—The red-necked phalarope—The little stint—The Temminck's stint . 119

CHAPTER VII

The Eastern golden plover—The bar-tailed godwit—The distribution of birds at Golchika—The dotterel—Some other birds—The Siberian herring-gull—The long-tailed duck—The king-eider—The wild swan—The black-throated diver—The red-throated diver—The white-fronted goose—The red-breasted goose—The migration of geese—Scarcity of birds of prey—The blue fox—Some smaller birds—The Lapland bunting—The red-throated pipit—The autumn migration—Young bluethroats 142

CHAPTER VIII

First days at Golchika—The coming of the steamers—Our hut—The commissariat—A home-made sundial—The *Lena*—A disturbance in the Prokopchuk family—"The Alcohol King"—Mosquitoes—Native fishermen—The people of the balagan—An unwilling ferryman—The spell of Golchika . . 163

CHAPTER IX

Bird's-nesting on the Golchika—A morning call—Grey phalarope—Dunlin—A Dolgan—Red-throated divers—Pintail duck—Richardson's skua—Peregrine falcon—Sylkin's perplexity—Willow-grouse—*Vino*—A fish hunt—White-fronted geese—Grey plovers—A narrow escape—A bird pirate—Plovers' eggs 188

CONTENTS

CHAPTER X

The charm of the tundra—The reindeer sledges—"Into the tundra"—A wet drive—The sense of locality—A difficult passage—The *choom*—A wet night—The Dolgan family—Sunshine on the tundra—Photographing the Eastern golden plover—A goose hunt—Good-bye to the tundra 204

CHAPTER XI

Swerifskye—Its reputation—We go there—*Mnogie vino*—A stroll on the tundra—A night in the open air—Walk to Och Marino—Mirage—A search-party—Birds and men at Och Marino . 228

CHAPTER XII

A native postman—An invitation—We go to Kazachye—A midnight visit—Simeon Prokopchuk and his family—Mezenchyne—The long-tailed skuas—A night on the river-bank—The tragedy of the balagans—The flowers of the tundra—The return to Golchika—Appeasing Gerasim Androvitch . 240

CHAPTER XIII

The fall of the year—The departure of the *chooms*—The arrival of the *Yenesiesk* — First news of the war — Packing up — A dinner with the Antonoffs—Church parade at Golchika—The *Turukhansk* and *Lena* arrive — Stormbound — News of home — The *Oryol* again — Joseph Gerasimvitch — Disappointed hopes—The English steamers—A native wedding—Nosonovsky Ostrov 256

CHAPTER XIV

Nosonovsky Ostrov—The English expedition—Our party is broken up—The *Ragna* and the *Skule*—A cosmopolitan crew—A heavy cargo—Homeward bound—The last sight of Golchika—Dickson Island—In the ice—A narrow escape—Wireless news—A Government scandal—Novaya Zemlya . . 280

CONTENTS

CHAPTER XV

PAGE

The Kara Gates—Sir Hugh Willoughby—The magic of the Arctic—Captain Wiggins—The Kara Sea route—Ingoe—A storm—Bird passengers—Midnight off North Cape—Hammerfest—Rumours of war—Tromsoe—Sidelight on German mobilisation—From Bergen to Newcastle—War-fever—London again   303

INDEX   323

LIST OF ILLUSTRATIONS

The Antonoffs' House	} Frontispiece
Dog Sledge	

	FACING PAGE
Yenesiesk	14
Krestova	40
The Taiga by the Kureika	40
Native Children	102
Sylkin and his Son, Nerobi	102
Eastern Golden Plover (*Charadrius d. fulvus*)	142
Lapland Bunting (*Calcarius l. lapponicus*), immature plumage	142
Little Stint (*Erolia minuta*)	142
Blue Fox	156
Yurak Boots	164
A Dolgan Cap	164
A Native Fisherman	182
Natives Fishing by the Yenesei	182
Willow Grouse (*Lagopus albus*)	194
Eggs of Grey Plover (*Squatarola squatarola*)	194
Eggs of Curlew-Sandpiper (*Erolia ferruginea*)	194
Reindeer Grazing	214
Dotterel (*Charadrius morinellus*)	222
Grey Phalarope (*Phalaropus fulicarius*)	222
Temminck's Stint (*Erolia temminckii*)	222

LIST OF ILLUSTRATIONS

	FACING PAGE
THE NESTING-PLACE OF THE CURLEW-SANDPIPER	234
SIBERIAN GULLS (*Larus f. antelius*)	234
FOXTRAP ON THE TUNDRA	234
BALAGAN FOLK	250
CHOOMS AT GOLCHIKA	258
VASSILLI SOTNIKOFF AND HIS REINDEER	258
A YURAK GRAVE	278
A SAMOYEDE DOLL	278
S.S. *SKULE* IN THE ICE	298
"PANCAKE" ICE IN THE KARA SEA	298

A SUMMER ON THE YENESEI

CHAPTER I.

The "Gillissy"—Departure from London—Warsaw—Contretemps at Moscow—Krasnoyarsk—Vassilli Ivanovitch—We embark for the north—The Angara River—Yenesiesk—The *Oryol* and her captain—Fellow-passengers—The "wide water"—Nasimorokoya—Vorogovo—The Kamin Pass—Midnight in the forest.

THE first allusion to the Yenesei River that I can find in literature dates from 1595. In that year Willem Barentz, the Dutchman, sailed up to the Kara Sea, and while his ship was fast in the ice, some Muscovy hunters came on board. They told him a tale how that each summer ten small smacks sailed eastwards from Kholmorgori on the White Sea, "through the Sea of Tartary right past the river Obi, to another river, the Gillissy," where they carried on a trade in cloth and other stuffs.

Now Willem Barentz, that practical old adventurer, knew well enough from the quaint charts of his day that the Gillissy River flowed into the northern ocean from the land of Cathay, where the sands were golden, where spices grew on all the bushes, and where silks and furs might be had for the asking. Therefore, in the following year, he tried to reach it by the coast of Novaya Zemlya, but the ice was against him, and he was forced to return unsuccessful.

After Barentz' time, very many men tried to reach the "Gillissy" from the north. A few succeeded, and many more failed, and by degrees it came to be known that the river flowed from no ready-made El Dorado, but merely through a wilderness of vast and undeveloped resources. During the latter part of the last century, several Englishmen penetrated as far east as the Yenesei. As far as I know, the first of these to write a popular account of his travels in Siberia was the great ornithologist, Henry Seebohm. In 1877, Seebohm travelled down the river, and afterwards described his experiences in that most fascinating book, *The Birds of Siberia*. From an ornithological point of view his trip was a failure in some respects. Owing to a series of accidents, he did not reach the river mouth until late in the summer, and consequently little was known of the bird life of the Lower Yenesei, until, in the nineties, Mr. H. L. Popham made three expeditions down the river. Among other rarities Mr. Popham found the nests of the curlew-sandpiper, red-breasted goose, bar-tailed godwit, and grey plover. But since then, partly because of the distance and the difficulty of reaching the estuary early in the summer, no other English ornithologist has visited the country. Nevertheless, for naturalists, the banks of the Yenesei still hold something of the romance of an ornithological land of Cathay. They are the certain summer haunt of great rarities, and have even greater possibilities. You never can tell what you might find there, said the wise men. Wherein doubtless lies much of the romance of the region. Therefore I considered myself very fortunate, when, in the spring of 1914, an opportunity of visiting the country unexpectedly presented itself. Miss Czaplicka, the well-known Polish anthropologist of Oxford University, was about to travel down the river from Krasnoyarsk to Golchika in order to study the native tribes that live along the banks, and I gladly accepted the offer to join her expedition.

There were four of us who travelled east together. Tireless energy and a most winning address, even apart from her intellectual gifts and knowledge of the world, marked Miss Czaplicka's striking personality. Then there was Miss Dora Curtis, an artist. A better comrade for such a journey it would be impossible to find. Always in good spirits, and keen for either work or play, always the very soul of good nature and kindness, she was the life of the party, and later on contributed much to its material as well as to its mental well-being, as one who has had the good fortune to taste her cookery can testify. The third of my travelling companions was an American gentleman, Mr. H. U. Hall, who was interested in the aborigines of Siberia.

Miss Curtis, Mr. Hall and I left London on 28th May—a still spring day with a promise of rain—and travelling by Flushing and Berlin, we reached Warsaw forty-eight hours later. Here we spent a few hours in seeing the sights of the ancient city. Fine as they were, we should have looked upon them with tenfold interest had we but guessed at the titanic battle which only four months later was to be fought under its walls. But even at the time, one sight struck me forcibly, and in the light of after events I recall it vividly. We were driving down one of the shady streets, when our carriage drew up to allow a regiment of Cossacks to pass. There were some hundreds of them, returning from manœuvres outside the city. They were all small men, and sat well up on their horses' withers, as you may see our English jockeys ride. As they rode by they sang some monotonous marching song to the clash of cymbals and the thud of their horses' feet. Our companion, a Polish gentleman, drew attention sarcastically to their dusty accoutrements and careless ranks, but for the moment I could not look at those things. What struck me, even in that fleeting vision of ochre and scarlet and thumping cymbals, was the virility of the corps. Here was no war machine, but a living force— the stuff with which battles must be won. . . . Their voices rose and fell in abrupt barbaric cadence, as they streamed away down the sunny road, and turned towards the Vistula.

In the evening we left Warsaw for Moscow, where we were to meet Miss Czaplicka. The rather tedious journey across the plains of Poland would have been wearisome no longer if we could have foreseen the part that the country was so soon to play in the greatest war in the world.

At Moscow, a disaster occurred. Our luggage, which had been registered correctly from London, and which we had seen safely through the customs at Alexandrovo, had not arrived. It was absolutely necessary that we should leave on the morrow for Krasnoyarsk if we wished to catch the first steamer down the Yenesei; and in spite of the assurances of the station officials that the luggage would follow next day, we went out in despondent mood to look at the Kremlin, and the wonderful view of Moscow that lay below its terraces.

However, morning brought all the luggage except a box of cartridges, which, owing to the blunder of a carrying agent, had been detained *en route*. I had no time to wait for it to overtake me, and the delay was the more annoying as so much of my work depended upon it. There were only a couple of hours in which to make good the deficiency, and in Russia the sale of firearms and ammunition is fenced in with much red tape. The first gunsmith refused to supply me, but the second was more amenable, and agreed to sell some cartridges on the production of the gun, and the official letter of introduction, with which, in addition to the regulation passport, each member of the party was provided. While I was unpacking the gun case in the hall of the hotel, the two lift-boys peeped round the door.

Said the first lift-boy: " What has she there ? "

Second lift-boy: " Weapons ! "

First lift-boy: " What does she want with them ? "

Second lift-boy: " I do not know."

Opinion of both lift-boys: " Now without doubt these are Suffragettes ! " (*Suffragettski*).

There was only an hour and a half before the train left, but the gunsmith, whom I shall always remember with gratitude, turned on all his men to loading cartridges, and in addition I bought materials for reloading, which, with economy, were sufficient to last me during my stay in Siberia.

The journey across Asia by the Trans-Siberian Railway can never be anything but unspeakably tedious. We had missed the International Express by twenty-four hours, and were therefore obliged to go on to Krasnoyarsk by one of the daily post trains, which is a slower, but also a less expensive way of travelling. After the first thirty-six hours, the novelty of running out to bargain for the daily provisions at the buffet wore off, and there was nothing left to do but lean from the window and watch the little line of shining railroad which wound away into the west behind the train, just as a snail crawls across a garden path and leaves a shining trail of slime behind it.

We reached Krasnoyarsk at midnight on 8th June, to find that again our luggage, which we had seen safely on to the train at Moscow, had been delayed somewhere *en route*, and had not arrived. Things looked serious for our enterprise, for the steamer which we were bound to take if we wished to reach Golchika by the beginning of July was to leave on the following day. Hopes were held out that the baggage might come by a post train at 2 a.m., but, alas, the cases that were turned out of the van were not ours, but the property of some mining engineers who were travelling up the river to Minnusinsk, and our spirits sank.

At Krasnoyarsk, rooms had been taken for us at the hotel, and other arrangements made, by an acquaintance of Miss Czaplicka—Mr. Gunnar Christensen

—a very agreeable young man, who was the Yenesei agent of the Siberian Steamship Company. To his energy and foresight much of the subsequent comfort of our trip was due. We went to bed at sunrise and tried to snatch a few hours of sleep.

But when the train from the west came in next morning, there was still no luggage. It was therefore arranged that at noon we three women should go on to Yenesiesk, and that Mr. Hall should wait for the baggage, which had been delayed at the frontier, and was due to arrive on the following day. Mr. Hall was to travel after us by a steamer which left a day later than ours did.

Krasnoyarsk has profited by the coming of the railway, and is now the largest of the three principal towns of the Yenesei. It takes its name from the colour of the sandstone cliffs around, for *Krasno* in Russian means red. The city has still that mixed appearance of crude rawness and rising prosperity that is characteristic of most Siberian towns. Some of the houses are of stone, but more are built of timber, with broad streets and squares of unkept ground between them. There are five schools, museum, etc., a large cathedral dedicated to the Nativity, and an automatic ferry, a thousand yards long, across the river. But, as I have said, to our regret we had no time to see all these things.

At Krasnoyarsk our party received two additions. One was a young black-and-white setter named Jest, who at the last moment was lent to us for the summer by Mr. Christensen. The other was a servant, Vassilli

Ivanovitch. A Siberiak who is guaranteed neither to steal nor drink is a precious possession, but as a matter of fact his excellent recommendations were true of Vassilli. He was wont to declare virtuously that the mere sight of a drunken man made him feel quite ill; and although while he was in our service he had plenty of opportunity of obtaining liquor, we never saw him drunk, and as far as I know, he never stole anything. His vices were laziness and conceit. Whenever he was found fault with, he merely twisted his moustaches and replied pityingly, "How could I know how you wished it to be done? I am not used to service. I have always lived in my own house."

However, like all Siberiaks, he was a handy man with tools, could row a boat, cook passably, and described himself as an *Ohotnik*—a hunter—which in plain language meant that he could shoot ducks. The only thing about which he was really energetic was his desire to learn English. At all times of haste or anxiety, we were driven sometimes to exasperation, and sometimes to laughter, by his irrepressible, "Pa Russki thus and thus: pa Angliski . . . ?" And when the answer was given, it was immediately written down as he conceived that we pronounced it in Russian script in a very ragged pocket-book. We never had the opportunity of looking at this pocket-book, but it must have been a curiosity in phonetics.

It must be confessed that our prospects when we embarked at Krasnoyarsk were not of the brightest. We started down the river with literally nothing but the clothes that we stood up in, and these were already sufficiently travel-stained by ten days and nights spent in the train. Miss Curtis and I could speak not a word of Russian; Miss Czaplicka had never visited Siberia before. We left behind us a companion, who, in his turn, could speak nothing but English, and were in considerable uncertainty as to whether our luggage would arrive in time to allow him to overtake us at Yenesiesk.

On the quay we were introduced to a Mr. Peacock, one of the merchants who trade on the Yenesei. This man and his brother, although they were Siberian born and had never been east of Moscow, were of English descent, and were both exceedingly proud of their British nationality. Mr. Peacock had only just reached Krasnoyarsk from the north, and told us that below the Kureika the ice had not yet broken up on the river.

The journey from Krasnoyarsk to Yenesiesk occupied thirty hours. For the greater part of the way, the river ran between low banks clothed with pine trees, and which here and there were honey-combed by sand-martins' nesting-holes. Once or twice we stopped for an hour or two at a riverside village, and the peasants in their brightly coloured clothes crowded down to the bank to look at the first north-ward-bound steamer of the year, for it was Sunday, and they had no work to do. Late in the evening, while we were sitting alone at supper, we stopped at such a village. Presently a half-drunken man lurched into the saloon and began to shout to us, until the steward who was passing turned him out. But for the most part we had very little unpleasantness of this kind during the whole trip.

At one o'clock on 9th June, we passed the Angara, the first of the three great tributaries of the Yenesei. The steamer stopped at Trotzska, a small wooden village at the mouth of the river, and we went ashore for an hour to stretch our legs and give our poor dog a run, for she was already very tired of her cramped quarters on board the steamer. A few white wagtails and house-sparrows were pecking on the rubbish-heaps that surround every Russian village, and the banks of the river were buzzing with sand-martins. Vassilli brought me two of the latter birds that he caught upon their nests, but it was evidently still too early for eggs.

After it had received the waters of its mighty tributary, the Yenesei widened out to almost double its former size. All the afternoon we steamed along between low-lying pine woods, and, later, came abreast of a forest fire which threw a lurid banner of smoke across the river. It may have been the atoms of ash in the atmosphere which made the sunset so gorgeous that evening. The sun went down behind the trees in a blaze of clouds, and the steamer seemed to travel through blue and orange fire. Even the stolid Siberiaks on deck paused in their incessant nut-cracking to stare at the sky.

We reached Yenesiesk on the evening of 10th June, and after travelling for 217 miles through virgin forests, it was strange to come suddenly upon a large town with schools, churches, museum, *and a picture palace* in the middle of the wilderness. Before the railway came to Krasnoyarsk, Yenesiesk was the principal town on the Yenesei and a great centre of the gold-mining trade. It stands among wide, low meadows, and its mellow-toned wooden houses and shady grass-grown streets are much more picturesque than the blatant newness of Krasnoyarsk. As we steamed down the river on a fine summer's evening, its timbered houses, dominated as usual by the green and white cupolas of the church, looked curiously barbaric and Byzantine.

We went ashore at once to the post-office, where, to our relief, we found a telegram from Mr. Hall at Krasnoyarsk to say that the luggage had arrived, and that he expected to join us on the following day. I had been given a letter of introduction to Mr. Stephan Vassillievitch Vostratine, the member of Duma for the Yenesiesk Government, but we had already been told at Krasnoyarsk that he was in St. Petersburg. However, Miss Czaplicka had an introduction to his brother, Mr. Vassilli Vassillievitch Vostratine, who, with his wife, showed us the greatest kindness during our stay at Yenesiesk.

From an ornithological point of view, the neighbourhood of Yenesiesk is full of interest, and I was sorry that I had no opportunity of spending a day out in the country; but we had only two days to pass in the town, and much of the time was taken up in many final preparations for our journey to the north. Yenesiesk was full of the bustle of the coming of summer, and the quay was humming with life. Stacks of timber, hundreds of fish barrels, boats, sacks of flour, household goods—in fact, every conceivable thing that the riverside population could need for the whole year—were heaped beside the steamers and barges, for the northern season is short, and there are only three months in which supplies can be taken down the river.

After we had settled our business, our first thought was to have a bath—a luxury which we had not enjoyed since we left England. Accordingly we walked along the quay and out of the town to the bathhouse, which stood by the bank of the river. It was very hot out of doors, and hotter still in the bath-rooms. We waited while the mystified attendants scrubbed down the little cubicles, and then, ordering all the buckets and all the hot water that could be prepared, we had a kind of compromise between a Russian vapour bath and a soap-and-water English one.

After we had thus ridded ourselves of some of the dust of travel, I went for a ramble outside the town. It was a beautiful summer's evening, and although it was scarcely a month since the snow had melted, the leaves and grass were at their prime. It was my first introduction to the birds and flowers of Siberia, and I still like to remember a cock bluethroat who was singing among some white clematis, as if a golden pea leaped and vibrated in the pipe behind his gaudy bib. The brilliance of these northern birds in their breeding plumage is a revelation to those who hitherto have seen them only on their winter visits to Britain. Under the clematis were pink primulas, cranesbill, and honeysuckle, and there were marsh marigolds which might have been picked in the ditches of the Thames.

It was my first walk alone in Asia, and perhaps I should not have been surprised if a red-throated thrush or a blue-rumped chat had crossed my path. But here were willow-warblers talking English with only a slight foreign accent, and reed-warblers, and a couple of magpies who cursed in their familiar jargon when a hand was thrust into their nest. The bluethroat was the only stranger, and even his song was in the dialect of the nightingale. Soon, however, the mosquitoes fairly drove me out of the thicket. If Siberia is ever in need of a national emblem, she cannot do better than to quarter her arms with a cloud of mosquitoes rampant. I think the number of mosquitoes in the Yenesei valley alone must outnumber the insects in all the rest of the world put together! They swarmed not only in the swamps, but likewise in the town. Along the riverside a number of brown-faced boys were fishing. Even they were tormented by the plague, and by each rod burnt a little green-wood fire to smoke away the insects.

At five o'clock next morning Mr. Hall arrived with the luggage. He had had a very uncomfortable time on the journey, for, at the last, he had been unable to find a place on the steamer herself, and was obliged to travel on the lighter that she towed behind her. Here he found that he was expected to share a cabin with some fisher-folk who had the poor Russian's usual dislike to fresh air, and accordingly he had preferred to sleep when and where he could on deck.

A good deal of the forenoon was taken up in readjusting our luggage and in looking at the **Museum**.

In the latter my companions found much that was of interest to them, such as the weapons and tools of the different races that inhabit the Yenesei. I went to look at the natural history section, but unfortunately this was in a state of great confusion. The tottering and dusty specimens were not classified; in many cases neither sex nor locality were given; and birds from other parts of Siberia were mixed indiscriminately with the local species. It seems a pity that the museum of the chief town of a country full of ornithological interest should be thus neglected, for with a little care a most valuable and interesting collection might be formed. After this I was the more sorry that I had not been able to see the museum at Krasnoyarsk, which was said to be well worth a visit.

In the evening Mrs. Vostratine took me for a drive along the Yenesei. I was a little disappointed not to spend an extra hour or two among the birds, but it was impossible to refuse so kind an invitation, and indeed it is worth going far to see the Yenesiesk meadows in June. The lush-grass was in its first freshness, but under the birch trees it was almost hidden by sheets of orange trollia, pink bird's-eye primroses, and forget-me-nots. On every bush a yellow-breasted bunting, as bright as the flowers, poured out his monotonous little song, and the thickets were filled with the racket of jays and woodpeckers, and half a dozen more, whose notes I could not identify. We returned along the main high road between Krasnoyarsk and Yenesiesk, which was nothing but a turf track full of holes into which the wheels bumped and swung perilously. I was

YENESIESK.

obliged to cling ignominiously to my seat to avoid lurching out altogether, and envied the composure of my companion, who never even swayed as we banged over the ruts. The people of Yenesiesk do not concern themselves much with roads, for nature has already given them the finest highway in the world, and one, moreover, which needs no cost of upkeep. This is the noble Yenesei, along which, by boat in summer or sledge in winter, they can travel either to the north or to the south.

In the evening we took coffee with Mr. and Mrs. Vostratine, and while we were at their house, we were introduced to one of the largest merchants of the Yenesei —Mr. Kutcherenkoff. This gentleman took a most good-natured interest in Miss Czaplicka's enterprise, and it was a great deal owing to his kindness that our way was made so smooth for us at Golchika.

About nine o'clock we went down to the quay, and found most of the town assembled there to see the start of the first northward-bound steamer. The decks were crowded with household goods and children, and down below, the crush was even greater. In the forepart of the ship, and even in the narrow passage on each side of the engine-room, the sleeping-benches were arranged so closely side by side that it was almost impossible to step between them. After much bustle and shouting we swung out into midstream, and amid the flurry of paddle-wheels and cheers from the quay we started on our fifteen-hundred-mile journey to the north.

The steamer *Oryol*, in which we travelled down the Yenesei, was owned by a private company, and from what we saw, she was the most comfortable of the steamers that ply up and down the river. She formed one of a fleet of European boats which the Russian Government bought in 1905, and sent out to the Yenesei *via* the Kara Sea, in order to carry foodstuffs to the starving people of Siberia, who were reduced to great want owing to the Russo-Japanese War. The *Oryol* had been used for passenger work on the Clyde, and her old Scottish name, *Glenmore*, still appeared on her bell and buckets. She had accommodation for a few first-class passengers aft, but forward she was crowded during the whole trip. The third-class berths were divided into "numbered" and "unnumbered." The passengers in the first division paid a little more, and were certain of a sleeping-place each night. Those in the second slept where they could, and it was almost impossible to move about between decks, for every corner was occupied by bundles of bedding, kegs of butter, cooking utensils, or sleeping children. The older people sat about in groups and drank *tchai* steadily all day long, or else cracked sunflower seeds and the nuts of the Siberian cedar (*Pinus cembra*). Not only was the steamer herself thus crowded. Behind her, she towed a barge as large as Noah's Ark, and almost as unwieldy as that commodious vessel must have been. Every nook in it was thronged with poor Siberians, and on deck was piled a medley of goods—empty fish barrels, fishing skiffs, spars, and flour sacks; and among them all a great Russian cross in cheap white wood, evidently destined for some distant trapping station, and ordered during the previous autumn when the last steamer went down to the south. Behind the barge was tied a scow loaded with barrels, and two or three boats. It needed no little skill to manœuvre all these clumsy craft inshore, especially when the wind was at all strong or the riverbed shallow.

Captain Otto Ello of the *Oryol* was a Finn. He was an exile from his own country, but his banishment was self-imposed. In his youth he had shirked his term of military service, and dared not now return lest he should be arrested as a deserter. He had settled in Siberia, and married a most kindly Russian wife, who accompanied him on his voyages. He spoke excellent English, and had accompanied Mr. H. L. Popham when that distinguished ornithologist travelled down the river in 1897.

The *Oryol's* small saloon was almost as crowded as the deck. Besides the four members of our own party, there were two merchants who were travelling down the river to inspect graphite mines on the Kureika, and a Yenesiesk trader called Kitmanoff, one of the owners of the steamer. There was also on board a very influential person, an official of some kind in the province of Yenesiesk. He was a morose, ugly little man, with a goatee beard, who spent much of his time in drinking tea and eating dutch cheese, which he kept in a tin box in his cabin—a frugal custom that we, after a perusal of the steward's tariff card, resolved to imitate. Our attention was first called to him at Yenesiesk, where a deputation of the officials of the town waited to receive him at the gangway; and when we left the place two days later, the same deputation brought offerings to him. The Influential Person was very pleased with the gifts, which were small but practical, and consisted of a jar of honey and a green pocket-handkerchief.

With Yenesiesk, we left some of the formalities of life behind us. Nicolai, the saloon steward, who, for four broiling days, had endured a crumpled white shirt front as a sort of insignia of office, now ran about in collarless comfort for the rest of the trip; and Captain Ello paced the bridge in a sort of semi-lay attire, something like that of a Wesleyan minister.

Now that the last of the towns was left behind, it became a little easier to realise this wonderful river down which we were travelling. The Yenesei—"the wide water" as it was called by its first navigators (beetle-browed and hairy-jerkined folk, who launched their catamarans upon its upper reaches when history was dim)—is the fifth longest river in the world. It is the second of the three stately rivers that flow northwards from the central watershed of Asia, and drains an area of 970,000 square miles. The sources of the Yenesei, the Bei-Kem, Khua-Kem, and the rest, rise in the mountains of Mongolia and flow for 3000 miles before they reach the Arctic Ocean. All the great tributaries—the Angara, which comes from Lake Baikal, the Podkammenaya Tunguska, and Lower Tunguska—enter it from the east. Even at Yenesiesk, the great river is a verst in width, and it gradually grows, until just below Dudinka it sweeps out into one of the most magnificent estuaries in the world. What energy, as it seems, is here poured profitlessly into the Arctic

Ocean! The strength of all these billions of tons of moving water is scarcely harnessed sufficiently even to turn a sawmill. And if the waste were twenty times as great, it would be almost useless to exploit it, for during the half of each year the Yenesei is securely locked away under ice. Marvellous must be the power of the frost that can bind such a volume of running water. But strong though the frost is, the strength of the thaw is greater still. Seebohm,[1] who watched the break-up of the ice on the Lower Yenesei, gives a graphic account of a display of force which "dwarfs Niagara into insignificance. . . . Some idea of what the pressure must have been may be realised by the fact that a part of the river a thousand miles long, beginning with a width of two miles, and ending with a width of six miles, covered over with three feet of ice, upon which was lying six feet of snow, was broken up at a rate of a hundred miles a day. . . . On several occasions we stood on the banks of the river for hours, transfixed with astonishment, staring aghast at icebergs, twenty to thirty feet high, driven down the river at a speed of ten to twenty miles an hour."

When we left Yenesiesk the heat was intense, and mosquito netting was stretched over all the portholes. About midday we stopped for an hour at Nasimorokoya, a large settlement on the left bank of the river. This was the terminus of the high road from Krasnoyarsk. From here, the only communication with the north is down the river or else by telegraph. We went ashore and walked about the village with interest, for it was

[1] *Birds of Siberia*, p. 331.

the first of its kind that we had seen. All the villages of the Yenesei are built after the same plan. They vary only in size. Each consists of a manure heap with a few wooden huts on the top. Sometimes it is a small manure heap with one or two huts, and such a place smells only a little. Nasimorokoya was a large manure heap with about fifty huts, and it smelt a great deal. It was very hot, so we went into a little shop to buy something to drink. They brought us *quass* from an underground store. It was a kind of small beer distilled from bread, and I thought that the taste was very bitter and nasty, but my companions liked it. When we returned to the ship, we found that the crew were in the act of slaughtering two young calves beside the gangway. Somehow none of us felt inclined for the veal that came on to the table for supper!

That night it was so hot that we could scarcely sleep, but on the following morning we awoke to find weather like that of an English March, with a chilly northerly breeze. In the course of the day we went ashore at Vorogovo, another village that almost deserves the name of town in this part of the world. I went for a ramble along the banks of a long-stagnant backwater which lay between the river and the forest. It was the haunt of innumerable reed-warblers, and also of innumerable mosquitoes. A great spotted woodpecker popped his scarlet poll round a stump, and a widgeon duck malingered beside a willow-grown island. In the meadows at the back of the village a flock of fifty common gulls were resting on their journey to the north, all turned heads to wind in ranks like a squad of soldiers. The commonest birds were the yellow-breasted buntings, which swarmed everywhere. Although it was the middle of June, a female that I shot contained eggs not yet ready for extrusion. I fancy that they must breed rather late, and Mr. Popham also informs me that he did not procure any eggs. Cuckoos were calling in the forests on the other side of the backwater, and I shot a short-eared owl in a thicket. There was a curious medley of east and west in the bird calls, for while the redwings were making the woods ring, and I heard the low, plaintive note of a yellow-browed warbler among the willows, the dominant voices were those of a pair of starlings, who were breeding in an ivied tree-trunk hard by. The mosquitoes were as bad here as at Yenesiesk, and fairly drove me back to the ship at last.

We left Vorogovo in the afternoon, and a few hours later entered the Kamin Pass. This is the only reach of the river between Krasnoyarsk and the sea which is conventionally beautiful. Elsewhere, the stream is so wide and the banks are so flat, that the interest of the landscape lies in its immensity, and even this is so panoramic that the eye cannot grasp it properly. But just here, the Yenesei narrowed to half its usual width, and wound between steep fir-clad hills and crags. A dark, hump-backed island, called Monastirskiy, lay in mid-channel, and the river was divided into bewildering creeks and inlets. A little village was perched on a crag at the edge of the forest, and the hills and woods were limned so sharply in the placid water that substance and reflection might have changed places, and the landscape would have lost nothing of its clearness. A number of black-throated divers were swimming in front of the steamer, and their melancholy cries seemed quite in keeping with the loneliness of the place. It seemed almost like a sacrilege to drive our noisy, smoky little boat through a scene of such profound peace, and smash the still images of the hills into a thousand ripples in our wake.

In an hour we left the pass behind, and the riverbanks flattened out into their usual monotony. In the small hours of the morning we stopped at a little station in the forest to take in fuel for the engines. The wood was already stacked at the waterside, so that there was no delay, and the crew went to work at once to fill the bunkers. The bank was overgrown with white flowering shrubs, and by climbing to the top it was possible to escape from the steamer and step into the peace of the forest. The place had recently been on fire, and little wreaths of smoke hung among the tree-tops. It was still dark, but somewhere a long way off a thrush praised the dawn that was coming. One of the ship's boys made a pipe from an alder cane, and its plaintive lilt was in harmony with a scene whose spell even the laughter and chatter of the woodcutters could not break. We seemed to stand at the edge of an enchanted land.

CHAPTER II.

A ramble in the forest—Verkne Imbatskaya—The Ostiaks of the Yenesei—The black-throated ousel—The romance of the telegraph—Difficulties on the voyage—Monastir—Bird's-nesting at Turukhansk—The pale thrush—The Kureika—The Yenesei cuckoos—Lost in the forest—The willow island—Igarka.

BETWEEN Yenesiesk and Turukhansk, the stoppages of the steamer were much fewer and shorter than those later on when we neared the river's mouth, and this obliged me to leave a great deal of most interesting country unexplored. It was very tantalising to see mile after mile of forest slipping past with all its wealth of bird life, and not go ashore there.

On the following day, 13th June, I could not land until the afternoon, when we stopped at a firewood station. Vassilli came with me and brought his gun, for the size of our weekly bill had startled us, and we found that it was cheaper to furnish our own pot than to live upon *stchee* from the steamer's kitchen. Before leaving, I asked how long the steamer waited, and was told one hour.

Vassilli and I went along the waterside. Several times we tried to penetrate into the forest, but the trees here were saplings growing so closely together that a man could scarcely force his body between them, and we were obliged to keep to the river-bank. In an English woodland, if one pauses for a minute, some bird or other is certain to betray himself—a robin flits across a clearing, titmice squabble overhead, or else a blackbird rushes chuckling from his stronghold, but by the Yenesei, small birds seemed oddly scarce. Vassilli shot a hazel hen (*Rabchik*, the Russians call them), and forthwith teased me until I had taught him the English for " horoshie myaso," which means " good meat." A cuckoo flitted before us into the forest, and a great spotted woodpecker hammered a stump. Inside the forest sounded the voices of tits and willow-wrens, and down by the waterside a pair of common sandpipers were nesting. This was the most northerly place at which I heard the insistent monotonous little song of the yellow-breasted bunting.

It was rather a disappointing walk on the whole, and in the hope of finding better things I pushed on rather farther than I intended. Consequently we were still more than a mile from the ship when the hoot of her departure blared into the forest. When we arrived, excessively hot with running, it was to find Captain Ello whistling to us from the bridge, and all the gangways up ready to start, while we had to run the gauntlet of the highly flavoured comments of the passengers of the barge, who leaned over the rail to watch us hurry past. Often on that trip down the river I was reminded of Epictetus' parable of the man who, while on a sea voyage, goes ashore to gather shells and nuts, and thereby is in danger of losing the ship altogether. I always made a point of finding out how long a stop was expected in a given place, but the answer was generally an hour beside the truth. It was annoying to hurry back to the steamer from some promising place only to find that her departure had been delayed for some reason, and that I might have put in an hour of extra work.

During the afternoon we passed the post boat from Turukhansk to Yenesiesk. In the summer, the mails are sent by the river and forwarded from village to village. The little boat was scudding along at a fine pace, with her square sail set to the southerly breeze, and we were told that letters sent in this way reach headquarters more quickly than if they were carried by the steamers. We also saw a small boat towed along the shore by dogs. A man and woman sat in it at their ease, while the dogs ran along the bank. The latter were harnessed very clumsily, as it seemed to me, by a trace fastened to a girth round the middle of the body, so that all the strain came upon the animal's loins. The sledge dogs of the Yenesei are fine fellows, something like a Scotch collie, only more stoutly built, with prick ears and tremendous furry coats. The native dogs, on the other hand, are much smaller, and are not used for haulage but only for hunting and for herding the reindeer.

In the evening, we reached Verkne Imbatskaya, but the steamer did not stop long enough to allow me to do any bird's-nesting there. Here for the first time we saw some Ostiaks by the waterside. Half a dozen of their boats, clumsy but ingenious contrivances, built like a punt with a barrel on the top, were moored in a backwater beside the village. The owners, who were living in two very dirty *chooms* on the bank, were timid, especially the women. At the approach of strangers they all dived into their primitive house-boats, and hid there until tempted out by the offer of kopecks, the value of which they quite realised.

The Yenesei Ostiaks are of very great interest ethnologically, and are said to be unlike any other tribe in Siberia. One scholar has even put forward the hypothesis that they belong to the same race as the short-skulled people who lived in Northern Europe before the Germanic immigration. Philologists, however, have given good reasons for supposing that the Ostiaks are nearly related to the present inhabitants of Thibet; and there seems no doubt that in very early times they immigrated to the middle Yenesei from the south-east, or at least from the south. Formerly they were a fine and warlike race, and gave their Slavonic invaders much trouble before they were subdued. But during the last two hundred years, their strength has declined, and now they are a quiet and inoffensive people, miserably poor, and decimated by the diseases that they have acquired from the white men. At one time there used to be a great annual fair at Imbatskaya, to which hundreds of Ostiaks came to sell fish and furs; but now the race has dwindled to such an extent that the total number of the whole tribe probably does not now exceed a thousand souls. Soon, no doubt, like other primitive races, they will totally disappear before the advance of Western civilisation.

Mr. Popham found both the black-throated thrush

(*Turdus atrigularis*) and the pintailed snipe breeding near Imbatskaya, and I was therefore disappointed that I had no opportunity of bird's-nesting there. However, on the following day, I went ashore for an hour or two in the evening at Markova, a small fishing village farther down the river. A pair of oyster-catchers, the only ones that I saw on the Yenesei, were paddling about, almost in the street. A thrush whose note was then unknown to me was singing among the thick willows, and I spent about half an hour out of a precious two hours in trying to stalk it, but in vain. I afterwards knew it to be the Siberian thrush (*T. sibiricus*). I then left the willow thicket, and went into the spruce woods at the back of the village. Redwings were breeding there in some numbers, but there was little undergrowth for other small birds, and those that there were had gone to roost. Presently, however, a thrush that was no redwing bounced out of a low spruce tree. I shot her as she fluttered through the branches, and was pleased to find that she was the black-throated thrush, a species whose eggs were first taken on the Yenesei by Mr. Popham.[1] The nest was built between four and five feet from the ground, close to the trunk of a low spruce tree, and was stoutly made of twigs, dry grass, and mud, like that of a blackbird. It contained five eggs. A little farther on another pair of the birds were evidently breeding, but they kept out of shot, and while I was looking for the nest, the steamer hooted its hideous warning, and I had to give up the search.

[1] H. E. Dresser, *The Ibis*, July 1901.

At Markova, as at all these riverside villages, a broad lane was hewn through the forest parallel with the river to make a way for the single line of telegraph wire which connects Turukhansk and Vorogovo with Yenesiesk. The trees and saplings were just lopped off, and lay where they fell in an avenue some thirty yards wide and five hundred miles long. When you walked beneath it in the dusk of a Siberian midnight, and listened to the wind buzzing round its insulators, that telegraph had a peculiar romance of its own. Here were two intense patches of human life, set down hundreds of versts apart in the wilderness, and this wire seemed such a slender, inconsequent sort of thing to bind them together. How many messages must in the course of the year travel thus through the heart of the forest all unknown and unsuspected by the birds who fly across the clearing, and the beasts who hunt through the thickets hard by!

The voyage between Vorogovo and Turukhansk was made difficult for us by the illness of the only member of our quartet who could speak Russian. The conversation of the other three was limited to authoritative requests for tea and bread and butter, and as our only other linguistic asset was an inquiry as to how long the steamer would wait at the next stopping-place, the situation would have been very inconvenient if it had not been for the kindness of everybody on board the *Oryol*. All, from Captain Ello, who was the only person with whom we could converse, to Nicolai, the good-natured steward, did their best to help us. Even the Influential Person dashed out of his cabin to rebuke a fellow-passenger who disturbed the patient by slamming a door; and another traveller, a little merchant of Monastir, hearing that we were trying to obtain oranges, brought a dozen that he was taking home as an especial treat for his wife, and offered half of them for the invalid. Nevertheless there were awkward moments, and neither I nor one of my companions will forget one critical evening when ice became a necessity and the dictionary was mislaid. Then we took the law into our own hands, and went in person to those mysterious and odorous regions whence our food came. The galley door was open. Inside, the cook stood with his back to us, unawares. His face was buried in the soup tureen which was tilted to his thirsty throat. My companion and I looked at each other meaningly; and then, unperceived, we slunk past on tip-toe to the storeroom. It was locked, but some grinning third-class passengers, who thoroughly entered into the joke, showed us a trick, the knowledge of which was evidently common property, by which the padlock might be slipped aside. We entered like conspirators among the butter-kegs, pickled cabbage, and gory carcases which would furnish our future meals; and in haste chipped off illicit chunks of ice and stored them in a thermos flask. When we turned round, we found that we had been caught *in flagrante delicto* by the chiefs of the commissariat department of the ship, who were too speechless at our audacity to interfere.

We were due to arrive at Monastir on 15th June, and we were most anxious to reach this town, as we hoped to find a doctor for our companion, who was seriously ill. In the ordinary course, we should have arrived at midday, but at 11 a.m. the wind rose so much that for the sake of the barge, the steamer was obliged to anchor for two hours. Behind the barge was towed a scow full of empty fish barrels, and as the river grew choppy, these began to shift about perilously. Half a dozen men went off in the dinghy to make them fast, but before they could reach the spot, some of the cargo had rolled off, and floated away gaily down the Yenesei. Then some spars on the deck of the barge were blown bodily overboard, and there was some confusion before all was made secure. At length the boat returned, but the crew were in such a hurry to scramble aboard out of the rain, that they omitted to make fast the painter, and two minutes later the boat was seen to follow the barrels down the river. The steamer had then to slip the cable and go off to pick up the boat. Altogether we did not arrive at Monastir until after seven o'clock.

We lost no time in inquiring for the doctor. He came on board at once, and was able to reassure us about our companion, whose illness had fortunately taken a turn for the better during the day. We were lucky to find him at home; for his district includes a million square versts of country, and it must take a good deal of travelling to cover it all, if indeed he ever succeeds in doing so.

I did not see much of Monastir, and that not under the most favourable conditions; but, on the whole, I do not think that I have ever seen a more dreary-looking place. Miss Curtis and I went ashore late in the

A SUMMER ON THE YENESEI

evening. It was bitterly cold, and there was scarcely a living thing to be seen except a few dogs who were prowling over the mixens by the landing-stage. The main street was like an open sewer-ditch, spanned by a broken plank; and as we balanced ourselves precariously above the mud, it began to sleet heavily enough to make us look for winter gloves—a woeful change from the heat at Yenesiesk, where we had sat about in cotton shirts and talked of bathing.

Monastir is now the capital of the Turukhansk district. Until a few years ago, Turukhansk, on the little river Turukhan, held that position; but recently the Government buildings were burnt down by a raid of criminal exiles, and it was decided to move the seat of officialdom to Monastir. Turukhansk was founded in 1662, when Mangaseya, the great trading town on the Taz, was burnt down by the Yuraks; and until 1822, when its importance declined, it was the largest town in this part of the north. Each year a great fair was held there, and was visited by numbers of people who came partly to buy and sell, and partly to worship in the church of the Monastery of Svyato-Troitskiy (*i.e.* the Holy Trinity), which contains the sarcophagus of St. Vassilli of Mangaseya, which, so the legend says, was brought there by miraculous aid from the Taz in the seventeenth century. Now it is nothing but a miserable hamlet; for what little prosperity official peculation has left to this part of the country has been transferred to the neighbouring village of Monastir.

We went to the little post-office at the top of the

town to buy stamps; and the magnitude of our purchase fairly staggered the postmaster, who had probably never before sold letter stamps by the dozen. Afterwards we tried to buy biscuits, but it was after midnight, and the houses were all shut up. However, at last we found a little shop, whose owner was not only awake, but could also talk German. He seemed to take great interest in us, and asked us to drink a glass of tea with him, but we had to decline with thanks, for the steamer was about to start. A great deal of this was kindly Siberian hospitality, but there was besides a certain amount of curiosity. Our party was a matter for wonderment all along the river. The most popular explanation of our presence on the Yenesei was that we were Suffragettes who had been exiled there by the British Government! But if that had really been the case, it would have been doubly kind of the Monastir shopkeeper to ask us to tea.

We went to bed at 2 a.m., and awoke next morning to find that the *Oryol* was anchored at Old Turukhansk, about thirty versts farther on. It was a fine bright morning, and I lost no time in going ashore. Turukhansk stands on some rising ground in the middle of water meadows. Behind it lie miles and miles of broken country, of pasture, marsh, and forest, all swarming with bird life. I saw the little bunting here for the first time. This was one of the nests that I was most anxious to photograph while on the Yenesei, and I spent a considerable time in searching for one; but the birds were still coquetting in pairs along the woodside, and did not seem to have begun to breed yet. Seebohm took his first nest on 23rd June, and that was a full week later than the date on which I first saw the bird.

Behind the village there was a stretch of marshy lake, and the debatable land between woodside and water teemed with birds. Redwings, fieldfares, and the graceful yellow-headed wagtail were breeding, but the willow-warblers were still courting in the tree-tops, so it seemed to me. I saw *Phylloscopus borealis*, *P. tristis*, and *P. superciliosus*. The latter was very common, and its little monotonous song tinkled on without ceasing from every bush. Here, for the first time, I saw the love flights of the pintailed snipe. Half a dozen of the birds were buzzing over the forest. They rose in circles to a great height, uttering a sharp single note not unlike the *kek* of the common snipe, and then made a tremendous perpendicular dive earthwards. Dresser[1] describes the noise as being like the bubbling of water, but I found that this was rather misleading. The sound when heard at close quarters is a hollow roar, extraordinarily loud and deep. I should not compare it to water at all, unless it has a remote resemblance to the noise made by filling up quickly a vase with a narrow neck. Two pairs of wood sandpipers were honeymooning among the rushes. Their voices were happy: *taludle taludle lirra lirra taludle*, and from a birch tree fell a shower of the most liquid notes that are heard in the Yenesei forests—the song of the Siberian thrush. But *Turdus sibiricus* is the wariest of a wary family; and when he spied me among the bushes, he dropped out of sight with a low *chuck-chuck*, for all the world

[1] *A Manual of Palæarctic Birds.*

like a blackbird who dives into the laurels when you surprise him on the shrubbery path. To an amateur in bird-watching, it is a constant interest and pleasure to notice among the birds of another country the little actions and ways that he has learned to know so well in their kindred in Britain.

In the scrub birch wood at the back of the village, I shot a pine grosbeak. He was like a flash of red sunshine as he flew through the wood, and when I had him in my hand, I was sorry, because sunshine is scarce. I wonder why a bird is beautiful even when it is dead. A dead beast is always ugly and generally repulsive. *White as pearls are his teeth,* was said of the dead dog in the legend, and it was all that even perfect Compassion could say. I once saw a dead fox who looked beautiful, but then he was curled up as if in life with the sunshine on his ruddy pelt, and all the hateful consequences of death were hidden. But a bird's dead body keeps some grace, and why this should be so I do not know, for, when in life, it is so much the incarnation of all that is joyous and vital that symbolically, if not actually, it seems as if it ought to be doubly repellent in death.

Close to this spot I found a wood sandpiper brooding over three fresh eggs in an old fieldfare's nest, built in a low spruce tree. In Europe the wood sandpiper breeds in a hollow in the ground; and it was Mr. H. L. Popham who first pointed out that on the Yenesei, in four cases out of five, the site chosen was the deserted nest of some other bird. The sandpiper sat so closely that he almost allowed himself to be pushed off the nest, and if a camera had been at hand it would have been easy to photograph him as he peeped over the brim.

On my way back to the ship I passed through the village of Turukhansk, which was even more desolate and poverty stricken than that of Monastir. All the inhabitants were down by the waterside, unloading flour sacks and revelling in the excitement caused by the arrival of the first steamer of the summer. We understood this excitement better when we had lived for two months on the river without news of the outer world.

In the course of the afternoon we weighed anchor and proceeded down the river, putting into a firewood station in the evening. I went ashore with Vassilli, but it was a cold, wet night, and there were hardly any birds to be seen. I walked for more than a verst into the forest and saw nothing but a few bramblings and one cuckoo. Presently, however, a thrush, which at first sight I took to be a redwing, dived off a nest built in the angle of a fir-tree branch about twelve feet from the ground. A minute later, and both birds were fluttering round me. I shot one, and to my surprise found that it was a cock pale thrush (*Turdus obscurus*). I climbed up to the nest, which contained four eggs lying on a grass lining like that of a redwing. As time was short, I could not wait to secure the other bird, but hastened back to the ship. On the way I met Vassilli, who brought a nest and five eggs similar to those I had found, and also a female pale thrush, which he had shot at the nest. Vassilli had been using duck-shot and had fired at a fifteen-foot range, so that it was impossible to make a skin of the mangled corpse that he produced for my inspection, but it was quite recognisable enough for identification. Shortly afterwards, while waiting for the gangway to be raised, I heard another bird singing on a larch tree close to the river bank. The song, what there is of it, is sweet and very characteristic of the thrush family; but as it consists only of a few notes and then a semibreve rest, it is not to be compared with that of our own throstle.

The following morning, 17th June, I turned out at 7.30 a.m., and found that we were at anchor a couple of versts south of the river Kureika. This must always be one of the most interesting parts of the river to the ornithologist, associated as it is with Seebohm's account of his explorations in 1877, and I went ashore at once with Vassilli.

The shore was littered with whitening branches, the dead bones of the forest flung hither and thither by the spring floods. A pair of ringed plovers—those cheerful cosmopolitans — had staked their claim to a patch of the beach, and some sandpipers had already prepared their nest in the sand. There were many cuckoos flying about the river bank. The Kureika was the most northerly point at which I saw these birds, and they puzzled me a good deal. There were, so it seemed, two distinct kinds. One, when on the wing, appeared to be identical with our common cuckoo (*Cuculus canorus*). The other, which was of about the same size, was constantly seen in company with the grey bird, but it had plumage which was as dark as that of a nightjar. These Yenesei cuckoos had two distinct notes. One was the familiar cuckoo call; the other was a weird *hoo-hoo-hoo*, which rang for miles in the forest. I was not well acquainted with the cuckoo family, and hastily jumped to the conclusion that the new call belonged to the dark birds. I made several attempts to secure one of the latter, but always failed to do so. When I returned to England, Mr. Popham kindly allowed me to see nine skins that he obtained on the Yenesei some years ago. These skins were formerly identified as *Cuculus canorus*, but they have recently been re-examined by Mr. H. F. Witherby, who pronounces that all but two belong to an allied species, *C. optatus*, which ranges eastwards from the Yenesei to China, and southwards to the Himalayas. It differs from our bird in note, and also in the cream-coloured underwing- and undertail-coverts, and in the broader markings on the breast. Among these *C. optatis* are two examples of the red or hepatic variety of plumage. I have not much doubt but that the dark birds that I saw belonged to this type. If so, it is common on the Yenesei, for I reckoned that one-third of all the cuckoos seen belonged to this form.

We walked along the beach, and about half a mile from the ship, where the covert was densest, I heard a little crackle of brushwood. There, hidden among the willows, were two little Ostiaks, gathering firewood and chattering together as they worked. In their brown hide dresses they looked as much children of the primitive forests as wild fawns or hares, and they were nearly as timid. At the rustle of our passing, they looked up, startled, with their gentle, inquiring faces turned to the spot whence the sound came, and then in panic-stricken silence they slipped away into the bushes.

Presently we reached the junction of the Kureika and the Yenesei, and I could scarcely believe that I was actually standing beside the river of which Seebohm wrote, and perhaps in the very spot where he went bird's-nesting. With the recollection of the *Birds of Siberia* in my mind, I was rather disappointed in the Kureika. Perhaps, in a sort of subconscious way, one expected to find ruby-throated warblers or red-tailed fieldfares on every bush. As it was, I walked for two miles up the tributary and saw nothing at all except two wood sandpipers, scores of willow-warblers, and some pintail duck. By and bye I thought of taking a short-cut back to the ship, through the forest, and as Vassilli took kindly to the idea, we turned off among the trees. I knew quite well that it was necessary to be careful, and I generally wore a compass on my watch chain, but that morning by some oversight it had been left behind, and as we had only to cross the open angle formed by the two rivers, it did not seem possible to lose the way. The trees grew very close together, with long tags of lichen-like sparse hair waving from their twigs. The moss underfoot deadened the footfall like a blanket, and every now and then the foot slipped down into the heart of a tree that had been buried out of sight under the rotting pine needles of hundreds of summers. Here there were even fewer birds than by the riverside. Once or twice I heard the harsh *chee* of a brambling, or a defiant spasm of song from a wandering chiff-chaff, but, for the most part, the forest was as silent as a church, and nearly as uninteresting from an ornithological point of view.

I had reckoned that in order to hit off the steamer we ought to walk in a south-westerly direction, but after we had wandered on for more than an hour I began to be rather anxious, and appealed to Vassilli. He, however, was quite confident, and explained by signs that the steamer was ahead of us. Wherever he goes, a man is taken at his own valuation. Vassilli rated himself very highly indeed, and consequently, at first at all events, we had much respect for his judgment and capabilities. Accordingly I followed him for another mile towards the south-west, although with increased misgivings. Twice I tried a southerly direction, but each time he insisted with emphatic gestures that we ought to walk straight ahead. The forest was undulating, and at each ridge I expected to see the Yenesei, but each time only another immense vista of tree-tops met the eye. Vassilli began to lag and cast doubtful glances round him, and when I next turned to him he merely shrugged his shoulders and threw up his eyes in despair. I then realised that we had fairly lost our bearings in a forest some seven thousand versts long by fifteen hundred wide. I think that the faculty of direction, or orientation, or whatever one may call it, must fill a very large place in the human mind, because, when it is lost, the feeling is one of such utter helplessness. You pooh-pooh the idea that you have really gone astray, but at the same time you have an insane wish to go on walking somewhere, no matter where, just so that you may keep on the move. Your instinct declares so emphatically that you are all wrong that you are tempted to believe it, and turn right about, although your reason says that you are all right. I knew, of course, that we could not be so very far from the ship, and that if the worst came to the worst we could retrace our steps with a reasonable chance of hitting off either one or the other of the rivers; but this would have meant spending several hours in the forest, and, besides, we had twisted about so much among the trees that I was by no means certain that I was right. The question was, would it be best to wait until the steamer hooted her departure, and trust to hearing the siren, or should we go and look for her? But sound did not carry far under the trees, and there was the possibility that we might have wandered beyond the range of the whistle. Therefore, as Vassilli had no suggestions to offer beyond the futile one that we should continue to walk towards the south-west, I turned back, and, much against his will, went off at an angle to our former course. After we had gone for a couple of miles we heard the sound of running water, and soon came across a little ravine with a brook at the bottom. Guessing that this stream must run into the Yenesei, we followed it up, and soon came out on the river bank. The *Oryol*—welcome sight—still lay two or three versts downstream. Vassilli was delighted, said, "I told you so" in dumb show, and insisted on writing down the Russian and English words for "steamer." This little adventure gave me a fright, and I did not venture again upon promiscuous explorations

KRESTOVA.

THE TAIGA BY THE KUREIKA.

in the forest, but always followed up the river-bank, or walked beside some watercourse, which in the end would guide me back to the ship.

The steamer stopped at the mouth of the Kureika to set down two merchants who were prospecting for graphite about sixty miles up the river. Their venture, however, turned out very badly. They entered into a contract for the shipment of the graphite to Europe *via* the Kara Sea, but the contractor very prudently insisted that his money should be paid in advance. When the European War broke out, the merchants wished the contract to be void, but the contractor held them to their bargain. The unfortunate men lost their money, and, for all I know, their graphite is still lying beside the Kureika.

After we had crossed the Arctic Circle we came in for a spell of stormy weather. Late in the evening, after we had passed the Kureika, the wind rose, and, for the sake of the barge, we were obliged to lie to under a willow-grown island. A regular blizzard was driving over the river, and all the leafless trees by the waterside moaned and rattled their branches together like dancing skeletons. Most birds were hidden out of sight. Those who were in evidence included a party of mealy redpolls (*Carduelis linaria*) in the adult frosted-roseleaf plumage, and a terek sandpiper who jumped up from a clutch of fresh eggs under a fallen tree-trunk. Fieldfares were breeding in the willows, and I saw a bluethroat and a little bunting. Vassilli went off to shoot ducks for the pot, and secured a widgeon, a teal, and a tufted duck, while I wasted a lot of time in trying to stalk a bird which turned out to be my alert friend, the Siberian thrush, again. I was climbing up to what appeared to be a fieldfare's nest, when, unexpectedly, a long beak like a bee's sting darted over the brim, and instead of the original architect, the grey poll of a wood sandpiper popped up. Near the same place Vassilli found a clutch of eggs of the same species laid upon the ground. In all the nests found by Mr. Popham the male bird was on the eggs; but in this case Vassilli shot the sitting bird for identification, and it turned out to be the female, thus proving that the hen does take some part in the work of incubation.

The following day — 19th June — was cold and squally, with a southerly wind. We travelled past miles and miles of willow forests. The banks were shaved away sharply by the recent floods, and the roots and branches of broken trees stuck through the débris. All along the Yenesei nothing is more striking than this prodigal litter of driftwood. Scores of acres of forest must be washed away every year and carried down to the sea. Much of the flotsam is stranded on the beaches and islands of the estuary, but more drifts into the Arctic Ocean, and after travelling to and fro for months or years is finally thrown up on the coasts of Novaya Zemlya, or else carried in the ice right across the Pole to Greenland. At midday we stopped for half an hour at Igarka, a typical riverside settlement. The place was a trapping as well as a fishing station, and a man came on board with fox and martin skins for sale. A few immature common gulls and a

A SUMMER ON THE YENESEI

dozen arctic terns were flying round the landing-stage —perhaps in anticipation of the pickings that would be theirs by and by. In the forest behind the houses, the snow lay more thickly than at any place that we had yet seen, and a flock of redpolls were feeding in the drifts in front of the huts as confidently as sparrows. This was the destination of the white cemetery cross from Yenesiesk, for although there were not half a dozen houses in the place, yet there was a well-filled graveyard beside them. Two or three pallid children peeped at us from the doorways, and although the settlement did not seem as poor as many that we had seen, yet it had a look of unutterable dreariness that even the cheerful twittering of the redpolls among the tombstones could not dispel.

What a strange big-little horizon must compass the folk who live in these pioneer settlements! Their outer world is almost boundless—*taigà* and *taigà* and *taigà* again for three thousand miles. But their inner view is limited by the price of fish and foxskins, and the change of the weather. Often as I watched these lonely spots slip behind us, I wished that I could spend a year in pilgrimage on these waters, to work with the people for a little while and live as they lived. Later on we learned something of their precarious lives, but even there we saw them only as a man sees players moving on the stage, and criticised and applauded with a certain detachment. What sort of people are they? Very simple, very powerful, very crude, but not brutal any more than children or animals are brutal, and not so much immoral as unmoral. It is only in the lees of cities that human nature becomes wholly debased : men who live in the wilderness keep some saving grace, however small. At least the air that they breathe is pure, and the sights that they see, save those of their own making, are clean. But life such as this is a great leveller. Many of the old settlers sink back to the state of the aborigines. From year to year, they almost forget a stranger's speech and gradually relapse into the native dress and customs. On the Yenesei, there are more half-breeds in the *choom* than in the Russian hut. Face to face with the primitive life and the primitive country, the native strain soon quenches the European blood.

At one time this region must have been much more densely populated than it is at present. In 1824 there are said to have been forty-six Russian homesteads north of Turukhansk, whereas in 1863 there were only twenty-seven. According to Dr. Nansen,[1] who quotes an old map of the Yenesei estuary, " there was a fairly dense population the whole way, especially along the east side of the Yenesei, from Dudinka northward, right up past Dickson Island, and eastward to the mouth of the Pyasina." Of late years, there has of course been a renewed flow of immigration, but it will be a long time before the traffic along the lower reaches of the river is equal to what it used to be in the past.

[1] *Through Siberia*, p. 180.

CHAPTER III.

The *taigà*—The dusky ousel and the little bunting—The Tungus—Platina—Women merchants—Dudinka—The first sight of the tundra—Krestova—The Yenesei fisheries—Breokoffsky Ostrov—Stormbound—Arrival at Golchika—First impressions—A Good Samaritan—Michael Petrovitch Antonoff.

As we travelled northwards, the trees on the river bank became smaller, and the snow patches between them grew larger. It seemed as if for every day, spring was retarded for one week. Outside Platina, which we reached on 19th June, the steamer made a long stop to take fuel on board, and I was able to take a walk in the forest. The snow here lay so thickly that it was possible to blunder waist-deep into a drift, but where the thaw had left the moss black and bare, the crisp crimson leaf-buds of the wild rhubarb were uncurling in the sunshine, and the whole forest rang with the tinkle of little rills of melting snow. Although the calendar made the season mid-June, the air was that of a jocund English March. Yellow heartsease were in bloom beside the snow, and wild garlic at the waterside. All day divers passed the ship on their journey down the river—either singly or in pairs. In the spring most birds go north in couples, but they return in the autumn in troops. The cook of the *Oryol* caught a red-throated diver—a *ga-garra* as he called it—and brought it home alive, writhing and striking like a snake in his hands. Besides the divers, geese were on the move, and flocks continually flew gag-gaggling overhead. But all these I hoped to meet again farther north, and the small birds of the *taigà* were more appealing at that time. Of these the little bunting was the most in evidence, and this was the most northerly spot at which I observed this elegant and charming species. On the whole, the buntings are a homely family, well tricked out perhaps, but, all the same, a little clumsy of build and a little scanty of song. There are, however, two over whom I could find it in me to become poetical. One is the trim reed-sparrow of our Berkshire osier beds, and the other is the little bunting under the Yenesei cedars. The birds had not yet begun to breed, but males and females were keeping company together in little parties consisting of two and three couples in the forest where the undergrowth was thickest, and where one might have only a glimpse of their dainty mottled plumage through a lattice of twigs. The song, unlike most bunting music, is a distinctive and pleasant little warble, and the manner of its delivery is not like that of most buntings. The corn-bunting and the yellow-hammer, for instance—their European cogeners—make a serious business of song, and will not interrupt it either for food or for battle. But the little bunting, like the warblers, weaves his music into his common round, until it seems as spontaneous as the rustle of the wind in the leaves overhead.

That afternoon the silence of the *taigà* was more absolute than anything that I have ever known. It was even more impressive than the silence of the tundra, for, still as it was, one felt as if a life in which one had no share was going on around. All the dense vegetation, grass and undershrub and tree, seemed to be engaged in a desperate battle for light and air. You saw the results of this tremendous wrestling bout in the rotten branches that cracked in the moss underfoot, and in the vigourous young undergrowth above them, until you felt oppressed and stifled, as if you were a trespasser in this tense and secret place.

I had walked for a mile before I realised that I was not the only living thing in the forest. A pair of dusky ousels (*Turdus fuscatus*) were breeding in a spruce fir-tree beside a watercourse, and their harsh clamour of alarm disturbed the stillness rudely. The nest was built about five feet from the ground, and contained four eggs, which, to a casual eye, would not be distinguishable from those of a blackbird. When Seebohm visited the Yenesei in 1877 he found the nest of this thrush, but it contained young birds. Later on, Mr. Popham took a number of nests with eggs. "These," he writes,[1] "were generally placed in small isolated trees, and rarely on the ground, though none were more than two feet from it." In 1914 I took two nests, both of which were built, exceptionally perhaps, at least five feet from the ground. The song of the dusky ousel as I heard it in the *taigà* is loud and clear, though rather broken in phrasing, something like the song of our own missel-thursh. When their breeding-ground is invaded, both birds clamour like fieldfares. The dusky ousel is

[1] *Ibis*, 1898, p. 493.

the most northerly in range of the Yenesei thrushes. I found it at the Breokoffsky islands, beyond the limit of forest growth.

At this firewood station a Tungus came down to the steamer to sell red foxskins. The Tungus inhabit the *taigà* on the east bank of the Yenesei round the basins of the Nishni Tunguska and Kamina Tunguska, as far east as the watershed of the Lena. It is said that, unlike the more northerly races, the Tungus, even when offered unlimited vodka, seldom become helplessly drunk. However, this Tungus must have been a decadent specimen, for, unluckily for himself, as soon as he came on board, he fell into the clutches of a merchant from Yenesiesk, who plied him with drink until he was quite stupid, and then persuaded him to barter all his winter's catch of foxskins in exchange for a bottle of vodka. This Tungus had brought a little girl with him, and while he was carousing on the deck of the *Oryol*, the poor child crouched in the canoe, staring bewildered at the files of shouting woodmen who ran between the gangway and the forest. Evidently she had never before seen so much bustle and confusion on the river bank, and when I tried to photograph her as she sat in the boat, the poor little thing covered her face timidly. When we last saw the pair, the man was waving his bottle and shouting lustily, while the child in the bows tugged patiently at the oars and rowed him out of sight round a promontory.

In the course of the evening we passed Platina. At this settlement there was one house which was of much better appearance than the rest. It stood in a good situation, and had an unwonted look of comfort and neatness. A couple of cows and a horse grazed near, and it had some attempt at a garden beside it. On inquiry we heard that this house belonged to a widow woman who had set up a small store there, and conducted her business with such prudence and economy that she outstripped all the masculine traders of the district. Judging from what we saw on the Yenesei, the women of Siberia are fully a match for the men in the field of commerce. One of the passengers on the *Oryol*—a certain Madame Nerotova—was the manager for a large merchant in Dudinka. She was an intelligent-looking, dark-eyed woman of middle age, and as her employer could neither write nor read, she had control of all his business, and many thousands of roubles passed through her hands annually. Whenever the steamer stopped at a fishing station, she went ashore to look after the interest of her firm; and for the credit of our sex we were glad to see that her fishing tenants, both native and Siberian, were on the whole happier and more prosperous looking than their neighbours.

We reached Dudinka on 21st June. Although it is only half the size of Monastir, this town is of some importance on the Yenesei, for it is the focus of all the trade and traffic of the tundra from as far east as the Khatanga and Anabara Rivers. Twice a year, in spring and autumn, the natives come with their reindeer to buy and sell, and the merchants of Dudinka are reputed to be the wealthiest in the whole country. Here we left the forest behind, and the only trees were a few meagre larches, not more than ten feet high. Dudinka itself stood upon rising ground, and the country around was open and rolling, although, owing to the melting snow-drifts, it was impossible to walk straight for two hundred yards in any direction. But in between the patches of snow were thickets of scrub willows which were just *blazing* with birds. The word may sound exaggerated, but anyone who has seen the edge of the tundra at the end of June will know what is meant by it. Here I met with many species that were new to me. Red-throated pipits were very abundant, and on all sides they parachuted down into the willows in a cascade of song. The Lapland bunting was the next commonest species. These birds were in pairs, and I shot a female who was toying with a feather. I also saw a yellow-headed wagtail, who was trailing a wisp of grass as long and as unmanageable as her own tail. The willow bushes held bluethroats and a number of small green furtive things—*Phylloscopus tristis* and *P. borealis* so my gun told me. How charming these little warblers are, and how exactly, both in form and colouring, they harmonise with the willow leaves among which they hide! At Dudinka, for the first time, wading birds became common. I heard several golden plover on the tundra, and shot a great snipe in the snow. Red-necked phalaropes were abundant, and flocks of ruffs constantly flew overhead. From a half-frozen creek came harsh the cries of some long-tailed ducks—*coal an' can'le licht*, as the Scotch syllable the call—and a dozen arctic terns were fishing in a flood pool. I did not see the pintailed snipe here, although it had been common in the marshy parts of the *taigà* and was afterwards observed as far north as Pustoy.

I did not visit the town (*sic*) of Dudinka. It is said to contain thirteen houses, which annually consume a hundred barrels of vodka between them. In fact, we were told on good authority that there were only two men in the place who did not drink, and both of these were political exiles. Two of the merchants, following what we found was the usual custom both here and at Monastir, came into the saloon of the *Oryol* and ordered dinner, but before the meal was half finished, both worthies were lying fast asleep across the table. On the Yenesei the women traders have the men at a disadvantage, for the former do not lose half of their wits and their roubles in the vodka bottle.

As we steamed on our way, we saw a smart little motor-boat lying inshore. This was the patrol boat *Omul* belonging to the Government. Dr. Nansen travelled up the river in her in 1913.

Next morning — 22nd June — I went ashore at Krestova, and explored the marshy banks of a small lake. Here for the first time I saw the Temminck's stint. Numbers of these gay little waders were hovering like butterflies overhead while they uttered their gay trilling call. The willow bushes were full of chiffchaffs, but as far as I know there were no willow-warblers to be seen. The specimens that I secured were all *Phylloscopus tristis*. There were also a number of redpolls, and I found two nests, containing respectively one and two eggs. The nests were full of snow, and of course the eggs were discoloured and rotten, for they belonged to the previous summer. All the redpoll skins that I brought back from the Yenesei have been pronounced to be those of *Carduelis linota*, but Mr. Popham obtained specimens of *C. h. exilipes* also. Besides warblers and redpolls, the willows contained yellow-headed wagtails, red-necked phalaropes, and Lapland buntings. I also saw a dusky ousel and a great snipe, and shot a long-tailed duck—one of a couple, who were preening themselves on a cake of ice in the lake. Four red-throated divers were swimming in Indian file down the river, and ringed plovers were as common as usual.

Although the ice had not long broken up on the river, and blocks as big as cottages were piled up on the bank, fishing had already begun. There were three or four Yurak *chooms* on the foreshore, and as I returned to the steamer, I paused to watch how the natives hauled a good catch on to the sand.

The Yenesei fisheries are yearly becoming more valuable, as more regular steamboat communication is established on the river. In 1908, there were two thousand men fishing on the Lower Yenesei, and 188,000 pouds, or three thousand tons, of fish were caught. The output is probably still greater nowadays, although no exact figures have been published, but the trade might be enormously developed if it was properly organised. As it is, the fish is bought from the fishermen, both native and Siberian, by merchants who sell it again in Yenesiesk, and in spite of the cost of freight, etc., they make a very good profit. For instance, the price of omul per poud at the fisheries is about one rouble and a half, but the same fish is sold in Yenesiesk at three to five roubles. The fishermen are obliged to sell at the traders' price, for they have no other market for their fish, and as there are no Trades Unions on the Yenesei, they have not even the remedy of a strike to help them to obtain better wages. The methods of catching and preserving the fish are also very primitive. With the introduction of modern appliances and modern ways of curing, the Yenesei might supply half Europe with fish.

The principal fish caught are the sturgeon (*Acipenser bæri*), the nyelma(*Stenodus nelma*), the omul (*Coregonus autumnalis*), the muksun (*C. muksun*), and the seld (*C. merki*). These fish come up the river every year from the Arctic Ocean. The sturgeon and nyelma move as soon as the ice breaks up in May and June. The muksun and seld follow three weeks later, and the omul goes up stream about the middle of July. But a good many sturgeon remain in the pools all the year round, and at the settlements on the estuary, omul and muksun are caught under the ice in the winter. The Siberiaks say that these winter fish are fatter than those taken in the summer.[1]

In the afternoon, we went ashore at Bieliy Pesok (White Sand) for an hour. Two friendly Siberian puppies, who were quite impervious to such snubs as a pebble pelted at their heads, took it for granted that I should take them for a walk. They quartered the ground zealously for a hundred yards on either side of me, and as the tundra was full of birds, our advance made a deal of commotion. This was the last place

---

[1] For these and other interesting notes on the fisheries of the Yenesei, I am indebted to Dr. Nansen's account of his journey, *Through Siberia*.

where I heard the willow-wren in song, but the chiffchaffs ranged as far north as Breokoffsky. An oddly assorted pair were hawking over the foreshore. One was a pomatorhine skua, the first that I saw on the Yenesei, and the other was a small hirundine of some kind—probably the Siberian house-martin (*Chelidon lagopoda*). There was a regular colony of common snipe here, and among them were some pintail snipe. The latter rise much more slowly than our nimble bird. In fact, when they flipped up out of the willows, they looked as big and dark as woodcock. I shot a male, and managed to secure him before my self-constituted retrievers could reach the spot. Then the *Oryol* began to whistle, and the retrievers and I had to run back through the swamp. However, there was some hitch about sending off a boat, and my friends, who had been visiting some *chooms* in the neighbourhood, sat down on the sand to wait. Presently the owner of the principal hut in the place came out and asked us to take a cup of tea with his family. We entered the house by a dark, covered passage, which served both as a storeroom and to keep the living-room warm in winter. Inside the kitchen was clean and well furnished. There were actually pots of flowers on the window-sill, and an armchair. We sat on the big square bed in the corner while our kindly brown-faced hostess plied us with tea and excellent *pirog*. The latter is a kind of pasty or turnover made with fish, meat, or sauerkraut. These people were Tatars from the south, and like most of their hardy, frugal race in this part of the world, they seemed to be more prosperous than their Russian neighbours.

Late on the same evening, Captain Ello called me to the bridge to look at Lukovoi Protok, where in 1895 Mr. Popham found the red-breasted goose breeding. The *Oryol* did not stop at the place, but in the distance could be seen the row of cliffs, still speckled with snow, at the foot of which the nests were found.

After we passed Dudinka, the steamer and the barge began to empty fast. Every few versts there was a balagan, *i.e.* a low, turf-roofed hut, and here a whole family, with children, nets, and cooking pots, would go ashore with a boat and half a dozen barrels of salt and a sack of flour. Some of these folk travelled a thousand versts down the river and back again each summer, just for the sake of the fishing season, which lasts only for six weeks. Some of the Yenesei fisheries belong to the Government, and some to the natives. The fishing at the latter is free, and consequently the Siberians prefer to settle there rather than at the Government stations where a rent must be paid. But this is rather hard on the poor Yuraks and Samoyedes, who are thus gradually ousted from their ancient rights.

Below Krestova, the river suddenly opens out into the magnificent estuary which is here over forty miles from shore to shore. The low, bleak coast appears as little more than a distant horizon, and where the wind meets the water, a nasty choppy sea can spring up in an hour or two. And so indeed we found it, for on 22nd June the weather changed, and for forty-eight hours we were storm bound. In the evening, some fishermen were sent ashore. They managed to put up a wooden hut, but all the driftwood was sodden by the rain, and they could not light a fire. On the second morning some of the crew tried to take food ashore to these unfortunate people, but the ship's clumsy boat could not be beached in the surf on the open strand, and the sailors were obliged to return, wet to the skin.

This delay was very trying to everybody on board, from Captain Ello, who wanted to finish his voyage to Golchika and return to the south, to our dog, the "Sabaka," as she was nicknamed by common consent, who lived in a makeshift kennel in the stern of the steamer. The poor thing found her quarters very cramped, although whenever it was possible we took her ashore for a run. She was cunning enough to find this out, and as soon as she heard the rattle of the anchor chains, she used to yelp dolorously until she was taken for a walk, or until she heard the paddle wheels thrash the water again, and knew that the hope of release was over for the day.

The wind did not go down until 25th June. Then the *Oryol* began to pant her fussy way down the river again, stopping every ten or twenty miles to land fish barrels. We grew heartily tired of watching the crowded boats creep ashore, and the equally leisurely unloading of their contents. These halts delayed our progress very much, and were seldom long enough to allow me to do any serious work on shore, except at Breokoffsky, which we passed on 26th June.

We anchored off an island on the eastern side of the archipelago, at ten o'clock at night. The water was so shallow that the *Oryol* could not approach within a mile of the bank; and as there were two or three families to send ashore, they had to be taken over in small boats, a slow and tedious work. At the head of a broad, shallow creek, there were three or four small balagans. They had not been occupied since the previous season, and were half full of snow; but the people did not seem to mind their damp and chilly quarters at all, and went off in the best of spirits to their summer's work.

A number of ruffs had evidently hit upon the neighbourhood of these balagans as a suitable place for the foolish sham combats in which they indulge during the spring. Every few minutes, about a dozen of these doughty, bedizened warriors would flop on to the grass, and posture about, and "square up" to each other, with truculent thrusts of their harmless pink bills. In this attitude, with their gaudy plumage and curling ruffs, they reminded me irresistibly of the "Mignon" gallants of the reigns of the Valois. Now and then a passing man would step almost in between the combatants. Then the whole party would flounce off and alight to settle their absurd rivalries on some other hillock. The reeves were seldom seen, for they would soon begin to breed in the long herbage, even if they had not already begun to do so.

When Seebohm visited Breokoffsky in the middle of July 1877 he complained of the heat and the swarms of mosquitoes. When I saw the place in 1914, it was very different, for there were still three feet of snow in many of the swamps, and although the sun was shining gloriously all night, the wind was cold enough to freeze the breath on one's lips. The ground on the banks of the *kurias* was thawed and marshy, but inland, round the lakes, there was much snow, and most of the time I was splashing over the knees in half-melted sludge. The willows in this wind-swept country were so stunted and twisted that they all seemed to lie along the ground in one direction from south to north, as if the most prevalent gales blew down the river instead of up from the sea, as indeed I afterwards heard was the case. It was easy enough for a man to walk into such a thicket, but it was quite another thing for him to go back again, for as soon as he turned, the slanting tops of the branches confronted him like fixed bayonets, and held him a prisoner. You may see the same device in the throat of the cuckoo-pint flower, where the little flies creep into the corolla to steal the honey, and then find that their retreat is cut off by a palisade of hairs, that springs into position behind them.

It was unfortunate that the Siberian birds did not share the Siberian men's indifference to time. No matter how brightly the sun was shining, they went to roost at midnight in the orthodox way—all, that is, except a few ardent spirits who were too intent upon their nuptials to take covert. Hence it was difficult to make an exact ornithological census of the place. Chiff-chaffs, red-throated pipits, bluethroats, redpolls, and Lapland buntings were very common, especially the former, whose *chivet-chivet* note could be heard all night long; and I saw two dusky ousels among the willows. It was probably this thrush and not the redwing that Seebohm found breeding here in 1877. Common snipe continually bleated overhead, and the lakes were full of red- and black-throated divers. Temminck's stints were abundant, but I did not see the little stint above Golchika, and this is probably its most southerly breeding-place on the Yenesei.

I saw a pretty sight beside a pool. A pair of red-necked phalaropes, male and female, were standing on the snow with their dainty little blue feet just dabbled in the water, while they mutually preened each other's neck plumage with a loving concern that was very amusing to watch. Of course my wretched human intrusion broke up the picture. There was a cry of alarm, and then nothing but a circle of ripples to show that two beautiful and contented creatures had been there only a moment before. How often does the bird-watcher wish that he owned the cap of darkness of the fairy-tale that made its wearer invisible.

I was disappointed not to find the mountain accentor at this place, but on the return journey in the autumn I saw several birds. Breokoffsky is one of the known breeding-places of the Bewick's swan upon the Yenesei, and presently six of these magnificent birds flew leisurely across the island. I was watching the play of the sunlight on their huge wings, when a gun was fired near at hand and drove them down the creek at the rate of eighty miles an hour. I turned my glasses on the place, and discovered a sporting-looking individual whom I had no difficulty in recognising as the ship's cook, who had been last seen at Turukhansk, with his face in the soup tureen. He had been out to shoot for the pot, and was carrying a couple of long-tailed ducks.

The steamer was timed to start at 2 a.m., so we walked back to the balagans, where the people were busily shovelling snow out of their summer lodgings. The bones of a beluga, or white whale, lay on the shore. These creatures come up the river in the summer after the omul and seld, and are sometimes caught in the seine nets. The hide is valuable for making sledge harness, and the flesh is cut into strips, dried, and sold to the natives, who are very fond of it.

As usual there was no sign of a boat, and for half an hour the cook and I wandered disconsolately up and down the bank, for we were both about three times as wet and six times as cold as we liked to be. Then luckily a boat full of Yuraks paddled past, and we persuaded them to take us back to the steamer.

At midday on 28th June the *Oryol* anchored off the Golchika River. The coast was full of sandbanks, and therefore the steamer dared not approach within a mile of the shore. Our first view of the place where we were to live for the next two months was therefore a distant one, but it was none the less dreary for that. In the background lay a range of low hills, overhung by heavy snowstorms, and still streaked with white drifts. A turbid, coffee-coloured river flowed through them, and between the hills and the shores of the Yenesei was a long stretch of low marshland, partly covered with floods and partly with snow. The position of the Yenesei and its tributary at Golchika

A SUMMER ON THE YENESEI

reminded me of a capital letter Y. The stem of the letter represented the Golchika River, which, just before its junction with the Yenesei, forked on either side of a flat delta island.

There were but three permanent houses at Golchika, and two of them were built upon this island. Almost as soon as the *Oryol* cast anchor, boats put off and the inhabitants came on board. Siberiaks in *shubas* and fur caps strolled into the saloon, and natives in *sakooy* pattered round the decks. Captain Ello introduced us to the two principal men in the place. The first was a short, stout Siberiak with a good-natured, clean-shaven face and a bluff manner. He was Michael Petrovitch Antonoff, and he lived in the largest of the houses on the island. He seemed disposed to be friendly to us; but when Captain Ello, who was shocked at the idea of us camping out in the snow, asked whether there was not some place where we could sleep for that night, he replied evasively that he must ask his wife.

The other merchant, Prokopchuk, was the agent of Mr. Kutcherenkoff, who had given Miss Czaplicka an introduction to him. He was a very imposing-looking personage in a fine reindeer-skin coat, and his manner was cordial to the verge of effusiveness. He lived on the mainland, about a verst up the left bank of the Golchika River, and he was insistent that we should go home with him until we found a suitable camping ground.

Meanwhile all our baggage had been stowed away in the boat with the fish barrels; and as there was no room for us all to go with it, our new acquaintance immediately suggested that we should follow with him in his boat in about an hour's time. Accordingly, Mr. Hall and Vassilli went ashore at once, while Miss Czaplicka, Miss Curtis, and I sat down to wait.

At the end of an hour, we met the merchant, who was just coming out of the captain's cabin. His manner was even more expansive than before as he explained that he had been taking tea with Madame Ello, and that he would not detain us for more than a minute while he transacted a little business on the barge. Captain Ello was standing by the rail.

"Are you going back with Prokopchuk?" he asked in his careful English.

We answered that we were.

"You should not do so," said the captain.

"Why not? Hasn't he a family?"

A smile that was nearly as suggestive as a nudge in the ribs spread over the captain's face. "Oh yes," he answered in his slow way, "Prokopchuk has a wife— *even two!*"

We began to think that perhaps Prokopchuk's patronage might not be as disinterested as it appeared. However, it was too late to draw back, and we could only wait with what patience we could muster.

We waited for another hour: we waited for an hour and a half. Then the boat came alongside, and we got into it. Ten minutes later, its owner appeared. It could be seen at a glance that he had been drinking something else besides Madame Ello's tea. He did not fall overboard, because it is as difficult for a Golchikan, however drunk, to fall out of a boat, as it is for a cat to fall out of a tree, but it was certainly a wonder that he did not upset us all into the river. Then he shouted for a barrel to be brought, and when it came, he insisted that it should be placed in the stern, and that he and I should sit upon it back to back. It was flattering to me, no doubt, but I should have liked to have had more than a small fifth of the diameter of the barrel for a seat, especially as the boat was bobbing about in a disconcerting manner!

The distance between the steamer and the island was not more than a verst, but it took us nearly an hour and a half to cover it. A long tongue of current swept out of the Golchika River into the Yenesei. Lumps of ice and pieces of driftwood were floating about in it, and the water was very choppy. At any time it would have been difficult to cross it. In our case it was impossible, because Prokopchuk was much too drunk to steer straight, and consequently we meandered aimlessly about the river. A big raw-boned woman in a sad-coloured shawl crouched on the bottom of the boat and shouted exhortations and reproaches. We supposed that she must be one of the two wives. Of the two men at the oars, one was an ordinary little Siberiak in a *shuba*, but the other, whom I took for a servant, was of a different type. His size would have made him remarkable anywhere: here, among the little spindle-shanked natives, and stunted fisher-folk, he seemed gigantic, for he was not only tall, but also finely proportioned. He wore no cap, and his thick, curly hair, which was blown out round his head like a halo, seemed to add to his height. He did most of the work of pulling the clumsy boat along; but he did not seem to resent this, nor the noisy antics of the old debauchee in the stern. He just rowed uncomplainingly in a sort of stolid, ox-like way.

But even his strength could not struggle alone against that stream, and after tossing to and fro for some time, the boat ran aground on a cake of ice, and spun round on her keel like a beetle on a pin. This occasioned a great deal of shouting, and nearly capsized us altogether. The only advantage of the situation was that the ice had grounded on a long spit of sand on the island side of the river; and it was obviously impossible that we should cross the flood to Prokopchuk's house on the mainland, which, since the captain's warning, we had been very unwilling to do. But the big man took the painter, and, stepping overboard, he waded shorewards, towing the boat after him. I think that it was then, when we saw him striding along with the water foaming up to his thighs, that we gave him the nickname that afterwards stuck to him—the Giant.

We were very glad to be on land again, even though we were uncertain whether we could find a night's lodging. Our cases were piled up by the landing-stage, and very forlorn they looked. Everywhere the snow lay knee-deep, and the wind was bitterly cold. I know now what it feels like to be a tramp—and there was not even a Casual Ward at Golchika!

There was, however, something much better, and that was a Good Samaritan. As we walked up the beach, Mr. Hall came to meet us, accompanied by a good-looking young man, whom he introduced as Mr. Peacock, a brother of the merchant of that name whom we had seen at Krasnoyarsk. Like his brother, Mr. Peacock spoke excellent English, and was exceedingly proud of his status as a British subject.

"No," he said in reply to a question; "I was born in Siberia, and have never seen England, but it is the wish of my life to visit my own country some day."

It was humiliating to think of the hundreds of Britons upon whom the obligations of their nationality sit so lightly, while this young Anglo-Siberiak, although he had not so much as seen the cliffs of Dover, made a boast of his English birth. Mr. Peacock had been staying at Golchika on business, and was returning to the south in the *Oryol*. Meanwhile, hearing from Mr. Hall of our houseless plight, he had visited the stout merchant, Antonoff, and had persuaded him to allow us three women to sleep there, at any rate for one night, while he arranged that Mr. Hall and Vassilli should go to the house of his agent, Protyvik. While we were still discussing the matter, out came Michael Petrovitch himself to invite us to enter, and to grant us the use of one of his sheds in which to house our baggage. He had not liked to ask us himself, he said, "because he had such poor lodging to offer!" Antonoff's house stood beside the little battered church, which was only opened once a year when the pope came down from Dudinka. There were many graves around it, all marked with the double cross, but there was no boundary between the cemetery and the rest of the swamp. The living walked where they liked among the graves, and in some way this was symbolical of the attitude of those simple people towards death. About a score of great sledge dogs bounded to meet us as we entered the wooden house, much to the dismay of poor Jest. The porch opened into an outer storeroom, and on the left hand was the house door. We passed through it into the long low kitchen, and thence into the parlour, which was filled with the cheerful din of a gramophone.

The room seemed wonderfully warm and cheerful after the snowy waste outside, although it was small and contained little furniture except a table apiece for the gramophone and *samovar*, and a few chairs. In the far corner hung an elaborate ikon, surrounded by a wreath of wax flowers, and a sewing-machine stood on the window-sill. A sewing-machine and a gramophone at Golchika! We felt that we were not so much beyond civilisation as we had thought.

Madame Antonoff was preparing the *samovar*. She was a plump, sweet-faced woman, some years younger than her husband. With her were her two sisters, Nura and Tania, girls of fourteen and fifteen years old.

After tea she explained that there was an empty room which would be at our disposal, and took us out to look at it. As we passed through the kitchen we saw the big curly-haired man, who sat on a stool in the corner, while his wet clothes dripped into a pool on the floor. He looked so patient and humble that we were surprised to learn that he was not a hired servant, but the eldest son of Prokopchuk—Joseph Gerasimvitch.

We passed through the storeroom to the back of the house, and by a low door we entered the bakery, which was almost filled up by a big brick oven. Along one side there was a settle upon which two huge workmen were snoring in chorus, but Madame Antonoff explained that in future they should sleep elsewhere. Leading out of the bakehouse by an opening in the wall was a fair-sized empty room. It had a window and a wooden floor, and after the night in the snow that we had anticipated it seemed a palace of luxury. When we had fixed up a curtain over the doorway and spread out the sleeping-bags, it looked quite comfortable. So much so, that when, in the midst of our preparations, we heard the distant whistle which announced the departure of the *Oryol*, we scarcely sent a glance after her as she steamed back to the south.

CHAPTER IV.

A morning theft—Cockroaches—Spring at Golchika—A dog sledge—A trip to Och Marino—A Siberian household—The Eastern golden plover—A change in the weather—Rough water on the Yenesei—Return to Golchika.

WE were awakened next morning by a stealthy movement at the window, followed immediately by a loud clatter. Jumping out of bed, we found that one of the Siberian sledge dogs had thrust his shaggy head through a broken pane of glass, and had tried to capture an egg which lay on the table just beyond his reach, by insinuating his long red tongue beneath it. Of course the egg had rolled on to the floor, and the smash had so alarmed the thief that, in his guilty effort to escape unobserved, he had knocked over the kettle and half a dozen tin plates. This incident aroused us effectually, and we hastened to dress and prepare breakfast, the latter a task of some little difficulty on this first morning, as there was no stove in the room, and most of our goods had been left in the shed on the river-bank, owing to lack of space. It was now that we observed something that on the previous evening we had been too tired to notice—namely, that both the bakery and our own room swarmed with cockroaches. Half a dozen of the creatures scuttled out of my sleeping-bag when I went to roll it up, and several times, while we were at breakfast, inquiring antennæ peered over the edge of the table, or else made tentative excursions into the sugar. Later on we found that most of the balagans along the Yenesei were infested with cockroaches, and sometimes with worse vermin. At first the appearance of a "black-beetle" in the beds was greeted with shrieks of horror, but before the day was out, we ceased to exclaim, and by the morrow we scarcely even troubled to kill the intruders. It is curious how quickly one becomes accustomed to such small discomforts. I well remember that not two weeks before we had been discussing our disgust at various insects, including beetles. One of the party told the story of a traveller who, sleeping at a wayside inn in the East, had put his hand under his pillow in the morning and drawn out a fistful of cockroaches. At the time this anecdote had evoked shouts of disgust, and now here we were doing the same thing. Indeed, in three days' time I found that I could squash cockroaches quite callously, and even stamp on them with feet shod only in felt slippers. The latter was a great test of courage, but it is only fair to say that the cockroaches of Golchika were of a less lusty type than the inhabitants of English kitchens. They seemed, in fact, to be a sort of bantam race of beetle!

As we sat down to breakfast Mr. Hall came in. He did not say much about his night's rest, but we gathered from his reticence that his lodging had not been so comfortable as ours. Later on it turned out that, by way of celebrating the arrival of the steamer,

Protyvik had kept late hours. When at length the older members of the family had gone to bed, the little Protyviks had awakened up, and played hide-and-seek about the room, until, in despair, Mr. Hall had risen and left the house.

After breakfast I went out to explore the island. All that I previously knew of Golchika was from the little vignette in Seebohm's book, and it was very interesting to try and trace the resemblance; but it was not until I had been for some time in the place that I found the point from which this picture had evidently been made.

The island of Golchika, which is really the delta of the Golchika River, is a flat swamp about a verst in diameter. It stands upon natural piles, for, since countless ages, the Yenesei has carried down timber from the forests and stranded them on the mud. Then the Golchika has in its turn brought down soil from the tundra and buried the tree-trunks; and so, built alternately of layers of wood and layers of earth, an island has gradually been formed. On one side flows the Yenesei, and the other two sides are bounded by the two mouths of the Golchika. At this time the place was all under snow. Deep drifts, besmirched with refuse and trampled upon by the pack of dogs, lay waist deep round the house, and the surrounding marshes were still white, spangled only here and there by icy pools. It was impossible to walk a yard without plunging almost over one's boots in the half-melted sludge. The Antonoffs' house stood about a hundred yards back from the river-bank. A path led from the door to the landing-place, where already, in preparation for the fishing season, sheds and sorting houses had been built beside the stacks of fish barrels; and here and there were one or two turf-roofed balagans which would soon be tenanted for the summer. But in spite of the grey lowering sky and the snow-covered swamps, there was an indefinable air of bustle and stir about the settlement on that cold June morning. Down by the waterside men were hard at work, repairing boats and mending fish nets. The air was full of the clapper and rasp of hammer and saw, and from the Antonoff kitchen I heard Anastasia singing over her pots and pans.

And it was not only human beings who worked and sang because summer was coming. Every snowdrift and every muddy pool was full of birds, dibbling daintily in the ooze. Such birds too! There were stints—the little stint (who is such a personality that I wish that our ornithologists would give him a more individual name) and the Temminck's stint, his cousin —the querulous, red-necked phalaropes, intent upon their fussy courtships, the delicate white wagtail, a splendid snow-bunting or two, and Lapland buntings with perky guinea-pig colouring—black and white and tortoiseshell. All these and more, newly arrived from the south, were feeding and fighting and courting and playing by the waterside, scarcely troubling to flutter out of the way of the lazy sledge dogs who roamed round the house. And as I watched I saw more birds flying down the river—ducks, geese, and waders. They were the rearguard of that great and eager host of birds, which, every spring when the ice breaks up on the Yenesei, pours northwards to Dickson, to Solitude, and to the far Taimyr, all in haste to make the most of the short arctic summer and rear their young before the ice should close down, and, like an iron hand, force them southwards again. In spite of the bleak grey skies overhead, there was something infectious in all this activity and gaiety. It seemed as if the soul of spring—the awakening of new life—was in the air. I forgot all about the dismal prospects of the previous night, and felt as happy and as glad of life as any of the birds who sought so diligently by the waterside.

That day I had no opportunity of going over to the mainland, for presently our host, Michael Petrovitch, came out smiling all over his jolly face, and told us that in the evening he was going to visit one of his fishing stations about thirty versts farther down the river, and suggested that we should go too. Needless to say we were only too glad to accept this proposal, and it was arranged that we should start at six o'clock.

In the meantime Michael Petrovitch showed us his team of dogs, of which he was exceedingly proud. On the Yenesei, a good sledge dog is worth a hundred and sixty roubles, but they are very difficult to obtain, for a dog is not reckoned to be of much use for draught purposes unless he has been reared by his owner. A dog bought after he has grown up can never be relied upon to find his way home as readily as one which has lived in the same surroundings since puppyhood; and as this homing faculty may often be of inestimable service to his owner, if the latter loses his bearings on the open tundra, the Siberiaks seldom buy a new dog unless for breeding purposes. Michael Petrovitch had bought the parents of his team from a merchant of Turukhansk who was leaving the country. Although one or two had been crossed with a hound strain, they were a magnificent pack. Each sledge with eight dogs could carry a weight of forty pouds of goods and two men, and Mars, the gigantic leader, could by himself draw five pouds, *i.e.* two hundred pounds' weight, on the sledge. Michael Petrovitch used his dogs in the winter time when he went down the river to visit his white-fox traps. He told us that on a good surface they could travel as much as a hundred versts in three hours. He gave us a ride down to the river bank and back, and I must say that it was great fun. The dogs appeared to enjoy it as much as we did, and seemed as delighted to show off as dogs generally are. They were guided entirely by the driver's voice as he shouted: "*Port*," i.e. "right," or "*Maneh*"—"left," as the case might be; and "*touss-touss*" (go on) was obeyed by these zealous servants as readily as the "*ta-ta*" which meant "stop." Antonoff's dogs lived in a lean-to shed behind the bakehouse. Some dog owners do not feed their dogs in the summer, and allow them to roam about and pick up what they can find, but Michael Petrovitch wisely held that to keep his team in health it was worth while to spend a little trouble on them all the year round. He said, however, that the dogs ate more in the summer when they were idle than in the winter when they were in full work. Our "Sabaka," who at first had been cowed into abject terror by the pack, not only speedily shook off her alarm, but in a day or two became a regular termagant. Even the huge Mars fled in a most undignified fashion when she caught him purloining a trifle from her kennel, and not one of his fellows dared to face the little bully. The only member of the pack who could hold her own with Jest was a large canine matron with an uncertain temper; but even she was not permitted to set paw inside an invisible, but none the less strictly defined boundary, which Jest had ordained must extend for six feet round our doorstep.

It had been arranged that we were to start on our trip down the river at six o'clock. Meanwhile the clouds, which had looked so threatening during the forenoon, had cleared away. The wind had fallen, and the Yenesei was like a sheet of glass, tinted softly with opalescent blue and rose. It was to all appearances a halcyon evening. Nevertheless, following Michael Petrovitch's advice, we took with us a certain amount of food, for the weather on the lower Yenesei is fickle, and sometimes a change in the wind may mean a delay of several days. The party consisted of our four selves, of Michael Petrovitch, who took the steering paddle, and of our Vassilli, and Nill, the sturdy, red-haired servant of the house. From the outset we knew that the boat was low in the water, but as the weather was so fine we thought that a little overcrowding might not matter. Opposite Golchika, the Yenesei is some ten versts wide, and we crossed it at once in order to reach the shelter of the farther bank. The stream was with us and our oarsmen had easy work. Even Vassilli, who hated exercise, was quite contented, and sang blissfully as he rowed.

Och Marino, whither we were bound, is, I should think, one of the forlornist outposts of the world. Even now, when I look at my old school map of Asia, I can recognise the place and lay my compass point upon it exactly. The estuary of the Yenesei, which widens out so enormously at Breokoffsky, suddenly narrows about two hundred versts lower down. A long, low spit of land juts out from the western bank into the river to approach the corresponding promontory of the Sopochnaya on the eastern side. On a clear day both points can be seen from Golchika, stretching across the mouth of the Yenesei like the claws of a giant crab. It took us about four hours to reach the long, low peninsula. I remember that Michael Petrovitch grumbled that with his dog sledge he would have been there and back again in the time. Nevertheless he was in high good humour, and laughed and joked all the way. He had dressed himself up for the expedition, and looked very fine in a bushy fur cap with ear flaps, which gave him a quaintly alert appearance, a black velvet coat and breeches, and gold watch-chain.

When we were still four or five versts from Och Marino we could see a little wooden hut at the end of the promontory. Here lived a Siberiak, Hachenkoff by name, who rented the fishing rights of the place from Antonoff, whose property they were; and beside it were pitched two native *chooms*. By one of the curious mirage effects so common on the Yenesei, the three dwellings seemed to stand in air several feet above the waterline. By and by, in the wide bay formed by the angle of the promontory, we met with a barricade of broken blocks of ice. At first they did not hinder our passage, for we could easily steer between them, but as we approached the point, they became so closely packed that it was impossible to force a way through them, especially as the whole mass was in surging motion. Just then, however, a canoe, with two Yuraks at the oars, and a Siberiak in the stern, put off from the shore and hailed us. By their directions we went round the pack and presently found an open passage. But even here it was necessary to go carefully, for the blocks, some of them as large as a billiard table, were all grinding against each other, and might easily have crushed the canoe had it been caught between them.

As soon as we landed, Michael Petrovitch introduced the Siberiak to us as his agent—" Vassilli Vassillievitch." The latter shook hands with us and invited us to his house, which was a smaller and meaner edition of those at Golchika. Deep drifts of snow were still piled around it, and these, with the clashing of the ice in the river, made the place seem more wintry than anything that we had yet seen. After passing through the dark entrance of storerooms and dog kennels that cluster against a Siberian house like a crop of barnacles upon a rock, we pushed open a low door and stepped into the kitchen, which in this case was also parlour, bedroom, and bakehouse. Although the sun was shining brightly outside, the room was so dark that at first I could not see very well what was in it. A slight, gentle-looking girl with a child in her arms came forward to greet us with shy hospitality, and made us sit down on the wooden settle behind the table. While she prepared the *samovar*, and Michael Petrovitch talked to her in his cheerful breezy way, I was able to look about me. Almost one-third of the room was taken up by the stove and great brick oven. On the top of the latter were piled a miscellaneous collection of household goods —loaves of sugar, flour-trenchers, and cooking-pots. In one corner stood a large four-poster bed, and in another were shelves, upon which the cheap coloured crockery was neatly arranged. The table was spotless, and the rough floor was likewise well swept and tidy. The place was not poverty stricken, in fact, it contained plenty of comfort, as comfort is reckoned in Northern Siberia, but I have seldom seen a room which even at first sight filled one with such a sense of oppression and distaste. Partly, no doubt, this discomfort may have been physical, for the atmosphere was not only hot but positively fetid. I do not think that those Siberian balagans are ventilated from one year's end to another. If you were to pull one of them down carefully, stick by stick, I verily believe that the atmosphere inside would be so thick and close that it would stand up by itself like a blancmange turned out of its mould! Chiefly, however, it was its inhabitants, who, so to speak, spread an *aura* of depression over the room. Vassilli Vassillievitch himself sat on a stool under the window and talked to Antonoff. He was a small, narrow-faced man, with bad teeth and a furtive manner, which was all the more conspicuous beside the open geniality of Michael Petrovitch. His hands were as restless as his eyes, and unless they were employed, as they constantly were, in rolling cigarettes, they twitched as they rested on his knee. It was easy to see that his nerves were all on edge, and not difficult to guess the reason why. The girl who was attending to the *samovar* by the stove was slight and pale, like a bleached plant. Her soft brown hair was arranged neatly, and her hands, which wore no wedding-ring, were slender and refined. She was unlike any of the balagan women that I had seen before. Her face was extraordinarily composed. Its expression was not exactly sad, but she seemed to have no vitality. At first sight she seemed to lack character, but afterwards I changed my opinion. The spirit was perhaps numbed, but nevertheless it was there. Strange to say, she had a voice which entirely belied the gentleness of her appearance. It was both loud and harsh, and when she raised it to speak to her husband, or to the little native girl who helped her, it sounded as if a dove were speaking with the voice of a crow.

Round her petticoats crept a whimpering baby of some eighteen months old. I have never seen such a heart-breaking baby. In the heat of the room it was clad only in a little chemise, under which its pitiably thin arms and legs appeared. Its tiny body had shrunk out of all proportion to its face, from which two terrible great eyes stared at us, as if demanding dumbly why the sins of its father should thus be visited upon its innocent head. Whenever its wailing became too insistent, its mother took it up and hushed it. Indeed, it never seemed contented out of her arms, and she seemed to have accustomed herself to do most of her work with one hand. We had brought some food with us, and when the *samovar* was bubbling, we set out our contributions beside those of our hostess, and all had tea. Meanwhile the room was gradually filling up with natives who had wandered in from their *chooms* to stare at the *Angliski*. The bed was taken up by an immense old lady with voluminous felt petticoats and a fat good-humoured smile which quite swallowed up her eyes. She told us with pride that she weighed seven pouds and had seventeen children. I think that most of the seventeen must have followed her into the kitchen, for by that time every nook and corner seemed to be filled up by male and female Yuraks of every age. Neither Hachenkoff nor his wife seemed to resent this intrusion into their already crowded kitchen, but this is typical of the Siberians. They are notoriously indulgent to the natives, and cases of cruelty to the inferior race are very rare. My anthropological companions were gleeful over such a collection of "specimens," and as Michael Petrovitch had business to talk over with Hachenkoff, I went outside to see what bird life the promontory harboured.

The river has built up the long peninsula of Och Marino in the same way as it has built up Golchika Island, by alternate layers of alluvial mud and driftwood. Two miles away to the west a range of low mud-hills showed where the tundra came down to the coast, but between them and the river lay a swamp, encumbered with rotting tree-trunks, which at the time of my visit was almost impassable with melting snow.

I can never forget that glorious arctic midnight.

There was one cloud in the east which the sun had chosen out from among its fellows to flush with pink, and beyond the ice barrier in the bay, the water caught up its reflection and repeated it and juggled with it and glorified it, until the river was like an opal in the shimmer of silver and rose. Closer at hand, over the ice the sunshine lay so golden and mellow that one quite forgot the chilliness of the air and thought of flowers and hay-fields. But although there were as yet no flowers beside the Yenesei, nothing could surpass the splendours of the ice as the light smote across the floes, discovering their grottos, bulwarks, and pinnacles of silver and malachite. Here and there a great block, melting after the day's sunshine, fell asunder with a crash into a gigantic shining star. Other slabs were fringed with a delicate tracery of rime, and more were so hewn by the ceaseless grinding to and fro that their blunted edges were white as marble with wonderful green veins. And the air was full of the strangest sound in the world. It was a peculiar hissing and rustling, not very loud, and yet as clear as a million mournful whispers. It was the noise of the melting of the ice, made by the smaller blocks, as, one by one, they split and dropped, tinkling, upon their fellows, and by the groaning of the larger pieces as the river forced them seawards before the advancing summer.

The only dark and ugly thing in all that glory of ice and sunshine was the little squat square house with its rubbish heaps and troop of prowling dogs; and I was glad to turn my back upon it and wander away over the marsh. There were two Yurak *chooms* close to the house, but they were both deserted, for the owners had all gone to Hachenkoff's house. It was not easy to walk over the swamp, for at every step one slipped knee-deep in water, and it was necessary to pick a way between the pools, along the narrow tracts of firmer ground which ran across the morass like causeways. Spring and summer come both together to the arctic; and although, as the ice bore witness, they had only just arrived, it was the heyday of the year, and the birds were making the most of it. Already, before the snow had melted, the swamp was parcelled out into various small-holdings; and as I went, the owners hovered round me a-tiptoe with that anxious expectancy which precedes the laying-time. Little stints flickered up from the sphagnum with a startled *drrrt*; grey phalaropes, with breasts like rubies, wheeled over the ice; Lapland buntings sought diligently for nesting material among the snowdrifts; and a flock of long-tailed ducks, in single file like a string of beads, paddled across a pool. Presently a troop of gulls began to clamour overhead, and while I was stalking them, five wild swans, in immature plumage—celibates for this season—crashed up from a small lake, and flew down the river with a mellow thunder of pinions. In the drier part of the swamp, a pair of Eastern golden plover were breeding. I lay down and watched them for a time, but, as I already knew to my cost, the plover is an exceedingly wary fowl, and it is generally futile to try to fool her (or him either) on the open tundra. She knows well enough that the supine neutral-tinted thing lying on the moss is neither a grass tussock nor a tree-trunk. And why the dickens is it pretending in that foolish way, keeping her off her eggs like this? she wails angrily from the vantage of a hillock a hundred yards away. Neither is it a bit of use to try and tire her out. The patient plover will settle down to a day-long vigil, sooner than return to her eggs if she thinks that all is not well. Consequently at the end of an hour I had done nothing more than locate the probable breeding-area. I tried to comfort myself with the quite vain reflection that probably the birds had not begun to lay yet, and then, as it was close upon two hours since we had landed, and Antonoff was anxious to start in good time for home, I turned back.

On the way, on a mound in the middle of the marsh, I came across a Yurak grave. The dead man must have been buried in the summer, for he lay under ground instead of in a wooden coffin. It is said in Holy Writ that a man brings nothing into the world and shall carry nothing out from thence, but evidently this is not the Yurak belief. A few pitiful possessions were lying round the grave—an old cooking-pot, a rotting sledge, and the bleached bones of his reindeer which had been slaughtered by the tomb. Surely it is a profound and poetical idea, this of the Yuraks, that even inanimate chattels, after they have long been in use, acquire a soul, which, after death, can follow that of their owner, and serve him once more in the spirit world. A little wooden scaffold was built over the grave, and from this hung a bell of cheap Russian workmanship. It tinkled softly as the wind swung it to and fro. It was placed there in order that the sound, ringing day and night, might scare away any evil spirits which lurked round the place. The relics of a forgotten life, the solitude, and the monotonous little tinkle of the bell, all made this primitive cemetery seem an eerie place, and I was glad to return to the house. Here I found my companions gathered outside the door, and learned on inquiry that Hachenkoff and Antonoff. having finished their business together, had both gone sound asleep! Here was a dilemma. We did not like to walk in and arouse them, for these were early days, and we did not wish to give offence. On the other hand, it was already after 2 a.m., and the red-throated divers in the marshes were loudly proclaiming a change in the weather.

While we were wondering what to do, the door opened, and Mrs. Hachenkoff (for so I must call her in default of a better name) came out to talk to us. It was then that we learned something of the tragedy of Och Marino. Vassilli Vassillievitch was the agent of Antonoff. That is to say that he was the latter's tenant for the fishing station, and was expected to pay his rent, etc., in fish. He was a good fisherman and trapper and might have done well, had it not been for drink. As it was, every kopeck that he could filch or earn was spent in vodka. Vassilli Vassillievitch came of a respectable family in Yenesiesk, and had gone through part of his university course in Petrograd. It was then that he had contracted the habit which now enslaved him. His family, thankful perhaps to get rid of their black sheep, had sent him down the Yenesei, and after a year or two he had drifted to lonely Och Marino.

But in his exile, with the fretful obstinacy that is the bane of such weak natures as his, he was constantly hankering to return to civilisation, to re-enter the schools and make a name for himself. Meanwhile during the long arctic night, he was slowly drowning his life in vodka, as surely as he had already drowned his youth.

The girl had originally come to him as his servant. Gradually they had drifted into closer intimacy. Their first child had died during the previous winter. This was the second one, and it was also very sickly. The strongest fibre of the girl's nature was her adoration of her good-for-nothing man. True, he did not work, but then why should he toil and moil at the fishing when she could labour for both of them? She was a poor, illiterate girl. He, on the contrary, could write and read, and had seen Petersburg and Moscow. She sympathised with him in his petulance, worked for him, trusted him. She even encouraged him in his drinking-bouts, because, as she humbly said, it must be so irksome for a man of his powers to be shut up with such an ignorant woman as herself. She hoped that he would not return to Russia, because, if he did so, she and the child would have to remain behind, but if it was best for him—— Meanwhile she kept the house clean and tidy and managed the fishing business, haunted always by the fear that the child, which was evidently her bit of Paradise, would slip away from her to join its brother in the little grave out on the tundra.

Before her story was finished, Vassilli Vassillievitch came out to tell us that Michael Petrovitch was awake, and we therefore went back to the kitchen to fetch our things. The baby was asleep, but we left a tin of condensed milk with the poor young mother, who seemed to look upon the English lettering on the label as a sort of talisman. At any rate we hoped that her faith in it might be of some comfort to her, even if it did not benefit the child. But in the usual leisurely Siberian fashion, these preparations, and the inevitable farewell cup of tea, all took up some time, and it was already five o'clock when we went to embark. Meanwhile the prognostications of the divers had been justified. An angry screen of clouds covered the eastern sky, and the surface of the water was ruffled by the wind. However, for the first two hours all went well, for we rowed slowly against the stream inside the barrier of ice. The water here was quite calm, but beyond we could see that the river was rising under the wind. By and by we came to the end of this ice breakwater, and were exposed to the full force of the wind, which came rollicking unchecked over two thousand miles of tundra. The river was now flecked with foam, while the choppy waves lashed against the ice and pounded the loose cakes together. The sound of their dissolution, which had lately been so hushed and sad, was now a continual crashing roar. However, Michael Petrovitch decided that it would be better to try and cross to the other shore at this point rather than higher up, where the river was wider. He himself was at the steering paddle, and Vassilli and Nill at the oars. It was soon clear that we should not have an easy passage. For every stroke we scarcely seemed to gain a foot of headway, and to make matters worse we were so low in the water that as we drew away from the shelter of the ice, the crests of the waves began to slop over the gunwale until the boat was half-full of water. The storm in itself was nothing, but Antonoff's boat was as wide and shallow as a saucer, and we began to be afraid, not that it would capsize, but that it would soon become water-logged. There was a wooden scoop in the stern, and for a couple of hours we took turns to bale out as quickly as possible. But no sooner was the boat empty than the least movement of her crew, or an extra large wave, would send another rush of water over the gunwale and set us to work again for our lives. At eleven o'clock we took stock of our position, and found that for all our labour we were scarcely half-way across the river. Everything in the boat was soaking wet, and it seemed as if each of the waves that went curling by must fill her altogether. It was then that Vassilli gave out. The man was not in condition for hard work in any case, especially after his three weeks of ease on the steamer. Antonoff was vexed with him for giving up, as he thought, so easily, and jeered at him by way of piquing him into taking up his oar again, but Vassilli was impervious to jibes.

"I am not accustomed to such work," he lamented. "My speciality is musical instruments!"

"I have an old mandoline at home," said Antonoff. "It is a pity that we did not bring it. Then you might have played a tune to us while we row."

Nill laughed loud at this sally, but Vassilli laid down his oar and announced despairingly that he was going to faint. A change could not be made without some difficulty, for the boat was pitching violently, and the least movement brought the water right up to the gunwale, but Michael Petrovitch presently went to the vacant oar, and Vassilli, with a sigh of relief, took up the steering paddle. I set to work with the scoop in the stern, while Mr. Hall baled out the bow with his boot, and, between us, we managed to keep the water down. But, blew it never so hard, nothing seemed to ruffle the good humour of Michael Petrovitch. No matter how much water came slapping over the side, whenever I looked at him I met a beaming smile and cheerful "*Horroshie!*" i.e. "First-rate!"—a smile which towards the end of our passage, what with the wet and the cold, I confess I found it difficult to answer equally gaily. He continually laughed and talked to Nill, and tried to make him forget his fatigue by telling him stories and recalling old adventures. And Nill, who evidently adored his master, grinned all over his ugly face and pulled at his oar like a hero.

But in spite of their efforts our progress was desperately slow. There was, I remember, a high mud-hill on the shore which we had just left. The snow lay upon its face in curious ridges, which recalled the rows of arches along a cathedral aisle. Subconsciously I made that cliff into a landmark by which to judge of our progress, and the detestable outline became, so to speak, photographed on my brain, so often did I look back at it, only to find that in spite of all our efforts we were slowly drifting backwards with the stream.

We had left Och Marino at five o'clock in the morning, and it was three o'clock in the afternoon before we were able finally to land on the farther shore. By that time the wind had gone down and a wan gleam of sunshine lighted the tundra. We reached an old balagan, deserted since the previous summer. It was half-full of water, but it was built in a warm-sheltered corner with plenty of driftwood near, and in our weather-beaten plight, it seemed like a haven of refuge. Here we made a fire, and were glad enough to dry our soaked clothes and have a meal, for we had had nothing to eat or drink since we left Och Marino in the early morning, and the men had been working hard all the time. We then rested in the sun for a couple of hours, and about six o'clock we started for Golchika.

The fickle Yenesei weather having given us a taste of its bitter mood, now veered round and smiled at us. It was a halcyon evening. To my thinking there is no place like the Yenesei for skies—or maybe it is that the country itself is so flat and bare that one appreciates the more the noble lines and curves of the clouds that lie above it. The sunshine draws up vapour from the basking river, and piles it along the horizon in huge cumulus masses. Then at once the east wind comes along and tears and ravels these up into plumes and banners of cirrus, which are blown across the sky and tinted red and golden in the evening. Along the northern horizon it is even possible to watch the actual birth of these clouds. Almost imperceptibly, they gathered like mist on the surface of the water and then, rising above their parent river, they floated away into the sunset like smoke rings blown from a gigantic pipe.

Large flocks of long-tailed ducks were resting close

inshore, and Michael Petrovitch shot a couple which flew close to the boat. We also saw a seal—"*Nyrpe*," as it is called on the Yenesei—which thrust its melancholy face out of the water about twenty yards from the boat. Antonoff fired at it, but his shot did not take effect. The Siberians say that seals are fond of red, and accordingly Nill was directed to stand up in the bows in the hope that if the seal rose again, the sight of him might lure it within shot. But I never quite understood whether it was the colour of Nill's shirt or of his beard which was supposed to be so attractive to the seal!

We reached Golchika at midnight in broad sunshine, and found Mrs. Antonoff beginning to wonder at our non-return. She had prepared a good supper for us, and, needless to say, we did full justice to her *pirogi*, eggs, and kaviare. And nobody knows the bliss of a warm, dry sleeping-bag unless they have previously spent forty-eight hours afoot, in a more or less soaked condition for the greater part of the time.

CHAPTER V.

People of Golchika — Protyvik — Antonoff and his household — The Prokopchuk family — Sylkin the Samoyede — His sayings — His religion — The natives at Golchika — Their manners and customs — The need for medical missions — The colonisation and future of Siberia.

FOR the next two months my life at Golchika was a double one. Much of my time, especially during the first few weeks, was passed out on the tundra or beside the river alone with the birds, but at the same time I was necessarily brought much into contact with the human inhabitants of the country. Golchika was a regular hotbed of gossip. Not a dog could bark, not a stone could be turned, but the neighbours knew all about it. This is more or less the case in small villages all the world over; but at Golchika, in proportion to the size of the place, we found it in an intensified degree. The social life was honeycombed with small feuds, small jealousies, and small intrigues; and before we had lived there for so very long, we found that willy-nilly we became caught in the snare ourselves.

There were only three houses in Golchika which were inhabited all the year round. The first belonged to Prokopchuk, who was the oldest resident in the place; the second was that of our friend, Michael Petrovitch; and in the third lived Mr. Hall's host,

Protyvik. The latter can be dismissed in a few words. His was the poorest of the houses. It was very damp, very dirty, and held nearly as many children as it held cockroaches, which is saying a good deal. Antonoff and Prokopchuk, however, both deserve further description.

Michael Petrovitch, and his wife likewise, came from Little Russia. He was by profession a railway engineer, and had a good post at Krasnoyarsk. Here, however, his socialistic ideas, and his efforts to educate the workmen under him, brought him under the suspicions of the authorities, and he was arrested. He spent some time in prison, and then considered himself fortunate to be exiled to Siberia. By some oversight he was sent back to the Yenesei valley, and at once set to work to make a home for his wife, who had remained with him all the time that he was in prison. He told us, smiling, how he went down the river with a number of goods for sale to the natives, and how he found that the stock-in-trade with which he had provided himself was useless, and that he was obliged to spend all his ready money in vodka in order to do any business at all. He and his wife were just beginning to make a new home for themselves, when there was an outbreak of brigandage at Yenesiesk. The criminals were really a number of exiles of the lower sort, idle and irresponsible youths for the most part, but the authorities believed that political agitation was at the bottom of it, and accordingly a number of exiles from Turukhansk were brought down to Yenesiesk for examination. It was wintertime, and these unfortunates were compelled to walk the whole distance—a thousand versts up the frozen river. Some died on the way: others arrived in a pitiable condition, and it is said that only a few of them were able to appear in court, for the rest were all in hospital after amputations for frostbite. Michael Petrovitch's great strength and vitality helped him to struggle through the terrible journey. But Madame Antonoff had remained behind at Turukhansk with the knowledge of the awful risk that her husband ran; and only a spirit as fine as hers could have come through such an ordeal and kept so much of its youth and brightness.

By and by, however, a friend in high places managed to obtain a pardon for Michael Petrovitch, and the couple went back to their native province. But they had grown out of touch with their old surroundings, and did not prosper there. In official eyes, the stigma of exile still clung to them. Besides, Siberia had taken hold of them. They came back, and brought Katrina's family with them into the new country. That was five years ago. Leaving his father-in-law to settle in Yenesiesk, Michael Petrovitch and his wife went down the river to remote Golchika, and set to work to build up a business there. The life suited them, for they were both young enough to enjoy carving out a future for themselves, and yet not so young but that they wanted a comfortable home to settle down in. In winter there were the traps to visit. In summer there was the fishing and the trade with the natives who came to buy and sell. In summer, too, Michael Petrovitch went to Krasnoyarsk to purchase the winter stores. In his absence Madame Antonoff not only looked after the house, but attended to the business and superintended the curing of the fish. She was a wonderful woman—Madame Antonoff—and her unfailing kindness to the four foreigners who came to her house is among the pleasantest of my Siberian recollections. She could steer a canoe as well as any man, and I well recollect meeting her in the marsh at the back of the house one day. She was wearing her husband's long boots, which were so much too large that she could scarcely drag one foot after another. In one hand she carried his gun, and in the other a duck which she had just shot; for, as she said in her housewifely way, Michael Petrovitch had eaten nothing but fish for so long that a duck would be a nice change. She very sensibly looked upon her kilted petticoats and huge boots quite as much of a matter of course as that she should pluck and cook the bird when she brought it in.

The longer we lived at Golchika, the more instances did we see of the goodness of heart of both Antonoff and his wife. For instance, her two orphaned sisters, girls of fifteen and sixteen, made their home there. Their father had died suddenly, leaving them penniless, and their brother-in-law had adopted them. Not only that, but he also entirely maintained their drunken brother who lived at Yenesiesk.

The two remaining members of the household were Nill, and Anastasia, his wife. Nill, we already knew after our excursion to Och Marino. Anastasia was likewise red haired, a dumpy little body with round eyes, who made the best *pirog* in Siberia. Nill and

Anastasia were both excellent people in their way, and devoted to their master and mistress, but they did not pull well in double harness. Perhaps Anastasia was a little inclined to be over strict with Nill's peccadilloes. At any rate there was sometimes a tiff in the kitchen, and Madame Antonoff had to make the peace.

Otherwise the little wooden house was the most cheerful in the world. To be sure, we only saw it in the summer-time, but even in winter, when, for days together, the inhabitants could not go outside, it was impossible to imagine it as otherwise than happy. In the kitchen Anastasia would look up from her baking to nod and smile "Good-day." The two pretty girls would greet us shyly, and hurry off to call their sister, who, however busy she might be, would always give us a welcome. Or else Michael Petrovitch himself, with his bluff, hearty manner, would come in. Outside, Nill whistled as he chopped firewood, and the lazy dogs crowded round the caller and flogged his legs with their bushy tails. Everybody in that house seemed cheerful and contented.

The house of Prokopchuk, on the other hand, was of a different type. It stood on the mainland on the left bank of the Golchika River, about a verst from that of Antonoff. In many respects it had a more favourable position, for the natives, when they came to trade, were able to walk straight in, instead of waiting for a ferry to the island, a fact of which old Prokopchuk—Gerasim Androvitch—took full advantage. We had lived for some time at Golchika before we understood the relations of the Prokopchuk household. Prokopchuk himself had been a *gendarme*. He was very proud of the fact, and liked to boast that he had formed one of the bodyguard of the present Czar, when, as Czarevitch, the latter visited Siberia. We never learned exactly why he left the police, but we suspected that he retired under a cloud, for he could not have been much past the prime of life when he exchanged the streets of Petrograd for the tundras of Golchika.

His wife lived down at Krasnoyarsk, in order, so it was said, to educate the younger children. Only two remained with their father—the huge son, Joseph, and a daughter, Marusia. Joseph, we had already seen on our arrival. Marusia Prokopchuk was a gentle, slatternly girl of nineteen or twenty. In face she was curiously like her father, but without the fire and humour which gave his countenance, dissolute though it was, its queer attraction. Her sweet voice and graceful carriage were her great charms. Her dark eyes were generally cast down, and her black hair was likewise hidden under the ugly drab shawl of the country. There was something almost Eastern in the beauty of Marusia, which even the darkness of the northern winter could scarcely bleach. The grandfather of Gerasim Androvitch came from the plains of Poland, and perhaps it was from this source, rather than from the more phlegmatic Siberian Russians, that Marusia derived her dark beauty, and her father his courtly manners and wit.

Mrs. Prokopchuk's representative at Golchika was her sister, Anastasia Ivanowna, the same who had rated Gerasim Androvitch for his conduct in the boat. She was a big, taciturn woman, with a square, determined face and a harsh voice. From the first she looked upon us with suspicion, and she evidently ruled the household with a rod of iron. Even Gerasim Androvitch was afraid of her; and as for Marusia, she was the slave of her aunt, and obeyed her in everything. In fact it was easy to see that the son and daughter of the house were nothing more than unpaid servants—and hard-working servants at that.

Although the Prokopchuks were at least as well off as the Antonoffs, their house was neither so well kept nor so comfortable, and the surrounding buildings were damp and dirty. The kitchen opened off the storeroom at the entrance. It was a small room, dark and most evil smelling. One corner was occupied by the bed belonging to the servant, Michael, and his wife and child. The other was filled up by the great oven and cooking stove. The rest of the furniture consisted of a bare table and a few kettles and stools. The remains of meals always stood upon the table, cockroaches swarmed unmolested among the food, and the bed was strewn with pieces of clothing. The bedroom, which also did duty as parlour, was more pretentious, but it was always in disorder. On the blue walls flamed cheap coloured prints of ladies dressed only in a nightdress and a wreath of roses. I once had the curiosity to count these works of art, and as there were nine of them, including one in which the same ladies were masquerading as guardian angels, I suppose this must have been the ideal of female loveliness of Gerasim Androvitch.

Below the house, on the river bank, stood a row of

storehouses and sheds. All around, partly covered by the kindly grass, the hillside was littered with all the ugly jettison of the household for the past seventeen years. None of the Siberiaks seemed to care at all about the outside appearance of their houses. Some, which were models of neatness indoors, stood literally in the middle of a rubbish heap of old boots, bones, rags, and broken crockery; and even the Antonoffs were no better than their neighbours in this respect. But it was not only the dirt and disorder which made the home of Prokopchuk a depressing place to visit. It was rather that there was something in the atmosphere of the house and of its inhabitants. Why this should have been it is difficult to say, for whenever we went there we were always received hospitably, even by Anastasia Ivanowna, while Gerasim Androvitch was geniality itself.

Gerasim Androvitch was the most striking personality in Golchika. Well over six feet in height, upright as a fir tree, and with a military-looking white moustache, he looked for all the world like a Field-Marshal. His manners were polished to the last degree, and his tact was unfailing. A greater contrast to Antonoff could scarcely be imagined. They stood at opposite poles. Antonoff's mien was open and hearty: he was short and thick set. Prokopchuk was tall and stately. Antonoff had been an exile: Prokopchuk had been a *gendarme*. Antonoff was as honest as the day: Prokopchuk—but more of that anon. Of the two, Prokopchuk had incomparably the finer presence. Antonoff's downright sincerity had won him the attention of the European workmen at Krasnoyarsk, but the natives at Golchika, although they could not but respect him, had not nearly such a high opinion of him as they had of Prokopchuk, who cheated them systematically. Indeed, they had a sort of awed admiration for the latter, which was difficult to understand unless one saw him in their company. Then one realised that his influence was partly physical. He towered above the little tundra men in stature, and instinctively perhaps they felt that he must dominate them intellectually. Therefore they gave him a homage and confidence that Antonoff, for all his jovial bonhomie, could never win from them.

The only time that Prokopchuk really lost his dignity was, as has already been related, on the occasion of our first introduction. Afterwards, even when in his cups, he always preserved his stately demeanour. If anything, perhaps his manners were a little more gracious, in measure as his gait became a little more uncertain, but otherwise he did not betray himself. One evening he came in to supper after he had obviously been drinking. He shook hands with charming politeness, seated himself with a deliberation which was if anything a little over elaborate, and then with engaging frankness asked us to excuse any eccentricities in his conduct. "For a man is not always responsible for his actions!"

However, drunkenness, on the Yenesei at any rate, is not looked upon as the disgrace which it is considered in England. Rather is it pitied as a sort of regrettable weakness, such as the tendency to sea-sickness would be elsewhere. There is a saying that, *It is an ill dog that bites a drunkard or a child*, and in this respect the Russian law is as lenient as the canine. In Siberia it is a punishable offence for a sober man to strike a drunkard, however great the provocation may be.

There are two aspects of inebriety—the humorous and the revolting. To anybody who wishes to make a study of the subject I should say, Go to the Yenesei. We had a practical illustration of them both, two or three days after the events related in the last chapter. The steamer of Mr. Kutcherenkoff, "the Alcohol King," arrived at noon, and by the evening there were only two sober men in Golchika. One was Michael Petrovitch, and the other was Kutcherenkoff himself. We were sitting in our room when our host brought in a young Siberiak, whom he introduced as Michael Prokopchuk, a nephew of Gerasim Androvitch of that ilk. Prokopchuk, with his wife and child, was just preparing to start on a fishing excursion down the river beyond Sopochnaya and suggested that I should go too. Of course the offer was a tempting one, for it would have given me the opportunity of seeing many places of ornithological interest; but like all such expeditions on the Yenesei there was not only the question of the outward journey to be considered, but also that of the return. In this case, I could have travelled northwards with the Prokopchuks; but in order to reach Golchika in time to catch the steamer back to the south, it would have been necessary to walk home, making thirty-mile stages from one balagan to another. This, combined with the difficulty of bringing home any specimens that I might have secured, made me refuse the offer, although Antonoff guaranteed that young Prokopchuk was a trustworthy guide. We were still weighing the pros and cons of the proposal, when Nill and one or two more ran in to fetch Antonoff. It appeared that the red-haired Protyvik, who had been celebrating the arrival of the " Alcohol King," had just insulted the wife of Michael Prokopchuk. The latter immediately rushed out, and fought Protyvik by the fishing station. When we went outside shortly afterwards, it seemed as if everybody in Golchika was raving. Along each horizon staggered figures, shouting and singing, and the balagans were as noisy as the *chooms*. Mr. Hall's late host was sitting in the swamp outside his door, blaspheming hideously, and struggling with some restraining friends who were nearly as drunk as himself. Around him all his womenfolk, who were also the worse of liquor, lamented hysterically. There were in our medicine chest some patent capsules, one of which was guaranteed to sober the most obstreperous drunkard or maniac, if it was broken under his nose. It seemed to be a good opportunity to test them, so Mr. Hall fetched a couple and, so to speak, stalked his raging host. Disgusting as the scene was, I could not help laughing, for the little capsule seemed such an inadequate weapon with which to quell the struggling Protyvik. But before the experiment could be tried, three stalwart friends seized the subject, and bore him away to recover his senses in bed. Meanwhile, his wife and several female acquaintances, who were in little better state, were standing near and screaming like bacchantes. Miss Czaplicka approached the most violent of them, who happened to be Protyvik's mother-in-law, and snapped the capsule in her face. The effect was instantaneous. The woman immediately dropped to the ground in convulsions. I really thought that, with the best of intentions, we had killed her, and so did her companions, who began to lament more loudly than ever. Miss Czaplicka, however, directed them to put her to bed, and by the following morning there was not much the matter with her. As we returned to the house, we met Mrs. Michael Prokopchuk herself, very intoxicated; and, saddest sight of all, on the doorstep, crawling on all fours like a beast, was her four-year-old child, quite bemused with vodka. The sight made me feel glad that I had refused to go down the river with the family.

Each time that a steamer arrived, Golchika was the scene of similar orgies, but it is only fair to say that it was never so bad as when Kutcherenkoff passed by. The fault lies not so much with the people, who indeed have such a desperate fight with the climate and conditions that it is hardly surprising that they should take their rare pleasures in excess. The blame should rather rest on those who, under the pretext of controlling it, actually encourage the traffic in alcohol. It is true that the Government have tried to make certain restrictions in the sale of drink on the Yenesei; but these laws are more honoured in the breach than in the observance, and are easily evaded.[1] For instance,

---

[1] The above was written before the recent action of the Russian Government with regard to the sale of alcohol.

technically it is illegal for a private person to carry more than a certain quantity of liquor north of Vorogovo. Kutcherenkoff overcame the difficulty by arranging that his cargo should be registered as part of the personal luggage of every one of his numerous crew! A year or two before, when the scandal could no longer be winked at, the authorities impounded his steamer. Unluckily they stopped him a few versts *south*, instead of north, of Vorogovo. Consequently when Kutcherenkoff issued a cross-summons for unlawful detention of his property, he not only won his case, but was able to claim compensation as well!

The natives drank as deeply as the Siberiaks, but however intoxicated they might be, they were never quarrelsome. The native settlement was on the left bank of the Golchika River. Only one family lived there all the year round. The rest came with the birds in the spring, and, with the birds, went south in the autumn. This was the family of Sylkin the Samoyede. Sylkin was one of the institutions of Golchika, and was by far the most Europeanised of the natives. He lived in a sort of patriarchal fashion with his numerous family in a small and exceedingly dirty balagan. Those who could not find room inside, overflowed into the *choom*, which stood beside it like a kind of annexe. Sylkin was a person of some importance among the other natives, and as he could speak, not only his own language and Russian, but also the Dolgan and Yurak tongues, he often acted as interpreter. He was a tall and not ill-looking man; but unfortunately, with the European language and ways, he had acquired a good

NATIVE CHILDREN.

SYLKIN AND HIS SON, NEROBI.

many of the European defects, and in many of our dealings with him we found that he had a good idea of feathering his own nest. Although, by his own showing, he was not much past forty, it pleased him to be thought elderly; and by way of keeping up the illusion, he always wore a pair of spectacles. When looking at a distant object, he made a great parade of adjusting and wiping these; but those who watched him closely might see that he peered out over the rims. Sylkin was quite a link with the past, for he could remember the famous Captain Wiggins, and had rowed Mr. H. L. Popham about the rivers, when, some years before, that distinguished ornithologist visited Golchika. Sylkin and I were good friends, and often felt the need of conversation. Therefore, knowing that my Russian was very limited, he generally accosted me as follows :

"*Riba horroshie; pagoda horroshie*"—then a pause, and, triumphantly, "*Pop-ham horroshie.*" Which being interpreted means, "Fish first-rate; weather first-rate; and Popham first-rate!" He was also accustomed to quote a trite maxim :

"*Malenki vino horroshie: mnogo vino nyet horroshie,*" meaning that a little drink is good, but that much drink is not good. Needless to say, he was fonder of preaching this doctrine than of practising it.

During the summer, three distinct races visit Golchika. The Samoyedes are the most northerly race. Their range extends from the Kamin Peninsula to North-East Cape, and southwards for about three hundred miles. The Yuraks are found between the

Taz and the Yenesei. Although quite distinct, they are allied to both the Ostiak and Samoyede races, and their language is said to have much in common with the Samoyede tongue. The third race is that of the Dolgans, who are of combined Ostiak and Tungus origin. Their principal territory lies from the south of the Samoyede country down to the Arctic Circle to the east of the Yenesei, and they are said to have linguistic affinities with the Yakut tribes of the Lena basin. These three races live side by side in harmony, and intermarry, but they are perfectly distinct, both in dress, language, and facial characteristics. They arrive at Golchika as soon as the ice breaks up on the river. Half of the family pitch their *choom* there for the fishing season, and the rest go back to the tundra to find pasturage for the reindeer. In the autumn, they come down to the Yenesei to fetch their friends, and the whole family travels south to the edge of the *taigà*, where they spend the winter. A few of the natives fished for their own profit, but by far the greater number worked either for Prokopchuk or Antonoff. They hired a boat from one or other of the merchants, and each evening brought their catch to the sorting station and received payment for it.

At the time of our visit, there were only half the usual number of *chooms* at Golchika. Instead of twenty or more, there were only ten pitched on the river-bank. We wondered a good deal at this, and happened one day to mention it to Madame Antonoff. Whereupon she gave us the following reason for the scarcity of their numbers; and the story is such an illustration of the intrigues by which business is carried on by the Lower Yenesei, that I cannot resist quoting her story. She told us that on account of her health, she herself had spent the previous winter at Tomsk; and that during her absence, her old father, with her two young sisters, had lived at Golchika. In the course of the winter, the old man died of heart-disease; and as Prokopchuk and Anastasia Ivanowna were just at that time starting for Dudinka, whither they went each year on business, Michael Petrovitch wrote a letter to his wife telling her of her loss, and gave it to Anastasia to deliver. But at Dudinka, the couple met most of the natives who were accustomed to spend the summer at Golchika. Thereupon they carefully spread the report that the death in Antonoff's family had been due to measles, and that the house was consequently infected.

The natives have great fear of measles, which are almost as fatal to them as smallpox is to Europeans; and such was their alarm, that more than half of them would not settle at Golchika during the following summer. Their absence made no difference to Prokopchuk, who had several agencies at different places along the river, and who, if he could not trade at one point, did better business at another; but it was a serious blow to Antonoff. On his return, Prokopchuk, having the monopoly of the trade, soon sold out of goods, and then had the cool impudence to offer to buy more from Michael Petrovitch. Antonoff, quite unwitting of the wrong that had been done him, not only agreed to do so, but as a mark of neighbourly feeling allowed him to purchase them at wholesale rates. Meanwhile another merchant in a smaller way of business fell ill of pneumonia. Whereupon Prokopchuk gave out that this was another case of measles. The terrified natives immediately boycotted the unfortunate man, with the result that he was ruined. Unable to sell his goods, and in urgent need of cash, he begged Prokopchuk to take over his stores at a reduced price, and needless to say, Gerasim Androvitch was only too pleased to do so. The first that the Antonoff family heard of this piece of treachery was when Madame Antonoff herself passed through Dudinka and learned of her father's death; but it was not until she reached home that she and her husband realised the cruel trick that had been played upon them.

This story shows something of the difficulties under which the Yenesei merchant works, owing to the lack of communication with the south. Michael Petrovitch in particular used to lament grievously about the impossibility of learning the rise and fall of prices in Krasnoyarsk. This inconvenience hampered Prokopchuk less because he was able to travel up the river in winter, and learned what Dudinka could tell him of the outside world, but he also used to look forward to the time when wireless telegraphy would link remote Golchika with the south. The telegraph wire now extends as far as Turukhansk, and it should not in the future prove such a difficult business to supplement it with a wireless station having a transmission area of a thousand versts.

Although the natives are gradually coming more and

more under the influence of the Europeans, it will be a long time before they are finally submerged. In the summer they come in contact with the Russians at the fishing stations, but in winter, when they go into the tundra, they slide back again into their primitive life, away from vodka, and away from the hundred other ills that are the curse of the white man wherever he goes. The natives are the wards of the Empire, and on the whole the Government fulfils its trust towards them. They are judged by their own people, and in so far as they do not come into collision with the Russian settlers, they are allowed to obey their own laws. If one Samoyede injures another, he is judged by his prince. If he injures a European, the case is heard by the native prince and a Russian official together; but for the most part the northern races are peaceable and good tempered, and difficulties seldom arise. The grand mistake is that the aborigines are taxed, not individually, but by their clans or tribes. This system directly discourages family life, and destroys the social relations, which, as with so many other primitive nations, have until now filled almost the part of religion to the natives of the Yenesei. The tribes tend to break up and wander off by themselves, in order to escape the tax which would be levied on them if they were proved to belong to their clan. Thus the old customs and ties are put aside, and as their compulsory admittance into the Orthodox Greek Church is at present the merest farce, it will not be long before they have no religion at all, either in the form of practical ethics or else in that of faith and rite. At present, the majority of those who live round the settlements have undergone baptism, some of them several times over, in order to gain the bonus that the Government pays at each christening. A few years ago a couple of Samoyedes came to Golchika from the tundra, and asked the pope to marry them, and baptize their children. This was done, Michael Petrovitch standing sponsor, and they received the gratuity. The following year, the same people appeared again. Antonoff was away from home, but they saw Prokopchuk, and went through the ceremony over again, and received new Russian names. On the third year they tried the trick once more, but unfortunately for themselves, they were recognised, and the fraud was discovered. But what else can be expected from a people who, although technically baptized Christians, yet have no instruction whatever in Christian doctrines, and who say openly that they prefer the Russian god to their own because *He demands no sacrifice and therefore His is a cheap religion.* A sickness or misfortune drives them back to the gods of their fathers; and several times when there was illness in the *chooms*, we heard the dull rumble of drums which showed that the Shammaness or priestess was conducting the ancient rites for the exorcism of the evil spirit.

Sylkin was wont to relate a naïve tale which throws some light on his attitude to his accredited religion. One of his sons was taken dangerously ill. There happened to be a doctor staying in Golchika at the time, and he visited the child. Medicine was prescribed ("Only such a little drop of medicine in much water, and he so ill!"). Sylkin waited for a week, and still the child was no better. Then, said Sylkin, he lost patience. He solemnly collected all his ikons, and carrying them up to the roof of the house, he spread them out to the weather with ignominy, to show his contempt for the Russians and their beliefs. Then he returned to the gods of his own people. Alas for the moral—the boy recovered!

The honesty of the natives on the Yenesei is a striking contrast to the thievishness of the Siberiaks. Sledges loaded with winter furs, *chooms* unguarded by lock or key, are left out for weeks on the tundra, and no one dreams of pilfering. If a native picks up anything that he thinks belongs to you, he will not rest until he has returned it. This honesty is by no means caused by lack of intelligence. The intellect of the native is not a whit inferior to that of the European. As I write I have before me models of sledges, fox traps, etc., carved out of driftwood, and considering the rudeness of their tools, the neatness and ingenuity of the work is wonderful. Another point which must strike anyone who comes in contact with them is their good manners. If a Samoyede eats or drinks in your house, he never puts down his cup without crossing the room in the gracious Russian fashion to shake hands, and say thank you for the meal. If cigarettes or sweets are handed round, there is never any snatching or jealousy. Nobody thinks of meddling with a stranger's property, no matter how curious he may be concerning it.

Men and women are more or less on an equal footing in the *choom*. A woman is even permitted to hold the office of *Shamman* or medicine-man. Some of the Samoyedes have several wives, but those who are christened generally have but one. Women are wedded, not for their beauty, but for their skill at work, and their absence of nerves! Love does not often enter into the transaction. The amount of roubles and reindeer that the parents of the young couple can supply, seems to be the determining factor in Samoyede matchmaking. Nevertheless the men are fond of their wives, and a widower will not remarry for four or five years after the death of his wife.

Contact with the Russians has taught the natives the full value of money, but it must all be in the form of silver rouble or half-rouble pieces. It is difficult to persuade them to barter in kind. If they bring furs for sale, they like to see the price in cash, even if immediately afterwards they exchange it for provisions and felt. We often used to see small parties at Prokopchuk's store. They trotted up on their little sledges, and leaving the reindeer to graze outside the door, filed into the kitchen. I have watched an elderly and economical German lady buying a chicken; I have sat by and listened to the attempts of one of the canniest horse-dealers in Co. Cork to sell a doubtful horse to a brother coper of equal experience; and I am well acquainted with the romances by which English house agents beguile their clients; but these were all brief and plain transactions compared to the dealings of Prokopchuk with his native customers. If a party of Samoyedes went to the house in the forenoon, it was certain that they would not depart before the night, for time counts for little in those regions of eternal daylight.

After the wheels of barter had been oiled by many cups of tea and *vino*, and the sale of their foxskins placed on more or less of a business footing, both parties went down to the store, and the huckstering began all over again. We were never present at the latter part of these mysterious negotiations — Gerasim Androvitch never permitted anyone to hear how he clinched the final bargain, but after a longer or a shorter time, according as there was much or little *vino* in the house, the natives were seen returning to their sledges, dragging after them bundles containing felt, knives, kettles, and *souhari*. *Souhari* are square chunks of coarse bread, dried in the oven until they are as hard and crisp as biscuit. Prepared thus, bread will keep for a long time, and both Prokopchuk and Antonoff had large supplies in their stores. The natives had a very shrewd idea of the value of things. English goods, however cheap, were greatly prized, and considered to be much better than those of Russian manufacture. Sylkin, for example, never tired of relating how once many years before he had gone on board Captain Wiggin's steamer, and had been given a cup of "*Angliski Koffe*," *i.e.* English coffee. He seemed to think that the name conferred upon the drink some virtue which was absent from coffee brewed in Siberia. The Samoyedes fully appreciated good work. When I first went to Golchika, I wore a pair of Cording's fishing boots for wading in the marshes. These boots won universal admiration, and as soon as they had shaken hands, our callers used to examine my feet curiously, and feel the texture of the leggings. "*Voda nyet?*" they inquired, and when assured that the boots were thoroughly waterproof, there would be an approving chorus of "*Horroshie.*"

It would not be a bad thing if everybody, no matter who they may be, were compelled, as part of their education, to spend a month in a *choom* on the tundra. They would then learn the true value and real uses of their possessions. The first thing that strikes one who returns after a few days spent among the natives, is the enormous number of useless and cumbersome chattels which we have gathered round us as the price of our civilisation. It is a real relief to meet people who wear gloves, not for appearance sake, but to keep their hands warm; who use saucers under their cups, not as a matter of custom, but because the tea must be cooled before it is drunk; who, when they yoke up a draught animal, do not weigh it down with a ridiculous paraphernalia of blinkers and pad, but reduce all harness to the essential minimum of a collar and traces. But although they have few possessions, these are dearly prized. When it takes you a week of labour to fashion a pipe stem and bowl from driftwood and hammered iron, is it to be wondered that you value it greatly and set the price at fifteen roubles—the price of a reindeer? When your knife blade is made from an old Russian file, ground and sharpened by many hours of polishing on a flint stone, and when the wooden haft has been turned, not by some factory process, but by your own brown hand, no wonder that you are loath to sell it. The needs of a native are very few and elemental. The tundra gives him reindeer hides and foxskins for clothing. The river brings him wood for his fire and for his sledges. For six roubles, less than the price of a foxskin, he can buy enough felt to make himself a thick warm *sakoöy*. In the old days he made his own crude pottery, but now that he can sell his fish and his skins he can afford to buy Russian kettles and crockery. But even so he has not lost the instincts of the days when he himself must fashion his goods with much labour ; and although they are now more cheaply come by, he is careful of them and never wasteful.

The wealth of most of the Samoyedes is in reindeer. One young man had succeeded to so many herds from father and uncle, that his deer, grazing on the tundra, covered an area of six versts. No one else could graze their herds where this man had camped, and as it was impossible to count them all, six men on sledges used to drive round and round the pasture, and where the tracks showed that some of the deer had strayed away, they used to follow and round them up again.

Most of the diseases of these poor people are due either to dirt or to evil living. The inhabitants of the balagans are in these respects as badly off as those of the *chooms*. Immorality is fearfully common among the Siberiaks, and consequently syphilis is a scourge which attacks both races alike. I saw many bonny intelligent native children, but I saw scarcely a single Siberian baby that looked as if it could grow up to manhood. It was quite pathetic to see the faith and gratitude with which both Siberiaks and natives brought their sick to Miss Czaplicka, who had some knowledge of medicine, and doled out simple remedies from the medicine-chest to them. Much of the illness was preventable—wounds which had become septic through want of care, neglected ophthalmic affections, and, especially among the natives, bronchial coughs and phthisis. Sometimes the hut was turned into a regular dispensary as patient after patient arrived for a poultice or fresh boracic dressing; and as each such invasion meant a general scouring, not only of the utensils, but also of the floor of the room, with Condy's fluid, we found that an amateur dispensary entailed a good deal of work. Three or four years previously the Government became aware of the condition of things, and sent a mission to Golchika, including two doctors and some nurses. One of the latter was that Madame Nerotova, whom we had met as a merchant's agent on the *Oryol*. The mission stayed at Prokopchuk's house and spent the days very agreeably in drinking and card playing with Gerasim Androvitch, while the people were uncared for as before. Some disinterested person informed the authorities of the scandal, but the only result was to make the Government withdraw the subsidy, so that now the people of Golchika have no medical service at all—not even a bad one.

What is really required are a few devoted men, like our own medical missionaries, who would minister to the souls and bodies of Siberiaks and natives alike—baptize, marry, heal the sick, and teach the people the simple rules of hygiene. Such a medical mission ought not to be difficult to establish. The first steamer reaches Golchika, at the beginning of July; the last leaves at the end of August. For two months such missionaries travelling on the river between Pustoy and Sopochnaya would find an untilled field which would abundantly repay their work. A great deal of what is apparently loose morality among the Siberiaks is due, not to the vicious tendencies of the people themselves, but to the conditions of the country. It is often impossible for a man and a woman to marry, because they cannot find anyone to perform the rite. There was a little dilapidated church on the island at Golchika, but service was held there only once a year, when the pope came down the river from Dudinka for the purpose. His visit just coincided with the fishing season, and consequently very few of the balagan dwellers of the district could spare the time to travel on foot or by boat for forty or fifty versts to attend. In winter the people cannot, in summer they will not go to church. As the result, the inhabitants of the Lower Yenesei live in deeper heathendom than even the poor natives around them, who at least are bound by their own tribal code of laws. They live beyond the pale, with nobody to care for either their bodies or their souls.

Nevertheless, degraded and brutal as so many of these balagan people appeared, I must confess that, except from a purely academic point of view, I found them more interesting than the natives with whom my anthropological companions used sometimes to contrast them to their disparagement. After all, it is they who must take part in the future development of Siberia—a part which the aborigines will never be able to play.

The resources of Siberia are immense both in and under the soil, and as yet not a twentieth part of them is developed. There are plenty of coal mines that have never been worked. The people say, "When we have burned up all the wood, then we will dig out the coal." There are hundreds of miles of valuable timber. There are thousands of miles of pasturage. There are minerals of many kinds which have never been prospected. The navigable rivers are the mightiest in the world: nowhere is there any natural bar to a great railroad system. The Russian Government realises the importance of developing the northern territory. For instance, the young men of the Lower Ob, Yenesei, and Lena are not called upon for military service, but are encouraged to push forward the colonisation of the land. Nevertheless, the European stock of a country where the climate is so severe as in arctic Siberia, would die out at the third generation if it were not constantly recruited from the south. And naturally the new-comers who settle in those outposts of Asia are not the best of their race. For the most part they are broken men, criminals, and ne'er-do-wells, who have drifted thither in spite of themselves. Of course the political exiles are often of another class; but an exile, even of the highest type, when removed to lower surroundings and cut off from most of the incentives that urge a man to rise, is more apt to sink to the level of his environment than to improve the tone of his neighbours. Colonisation by deported labour has been tried successfully in some parts of the world, but the colonists must be freed locally, and given a fair chance to start afresh. This unfortunately is not the case in Siberia, where the exiles are constantly hampered by official restrictions and espionage. Consequently those who are undergoing a life sentence seldom have the spirit or the opportunity to carve out more than a meagre livelihood for themselves; while those whose banishment is temporary have no interest in the land, and hasten to return to Europe when their time has expired. There are few who, like Michael Petrovitch, return to the place of their exile.

Therefore it is not upon those who are her citizens by compulsion that Siberia must depend, but rather upon free immigration from the west. And so far this immigration has been slow. In the course of three centuries perhaps only three millions of Russians have emigrated to Siberia, and these have not always been of the type most suitable for colonisation. But during the last ten years, the number of settlers has increased by leaps and bounds. Between 1902 and 1912 three millions of colonists entered Siberia, and the population of such towns as Yenesiesk and Tomsk has almost doubled. During the five years between 1909 and 1913, 75,850 square miles of new land has been parcelled out for colonisation, and about two million souls have settled there. During the same time about 6300 miles of roads have been constructed. Figures such as these bring home the extent of this development. It is not merely a new country which is growing up year by year, it is half a continent, and that the richest continent in the world. *Plantations are among ancient, primitive, and heroical works.* If Russia never did anything more than colonise Siberia, still she would have amply justified herself as a nation.

There is a strong party in the country who look forward to the day when Siberia shall receive her autonomy, if not her independence. Whether this can ever be in a land whose local needs and conditions differ so profoundly remains to be seen. Siberia is as yet like a giant in infancy, nursed by Russia. And Russia herself, the youngest of the nations, is only just coming into her own. She is still a country of enormous possibilities, of the crudest paradoxes. With the most autocratic government, hers is the most democratic society in the world : with a church whose function has dwindled into the effete repetition of ritual, religion is the very fibre of her people. Apart from a strong vein of Tatar blood, the Siberiaks are the siftings of the Russians—even cruder, even less aware of their own potential greatness. Nevertheless, if we believe that nothing can finally check the onward progress of man, then their development, though slow, is certain. Some day the dream of such idealists as Michael Petrovitch may be fulfilled, and a free United States of Siberia extend from Chelyavinsk eastward to Vladivostock.

CHAPTER VI.

The birds of Golchika—Seebohm—Popham—The effect of the season—The curlew-sandpiper — The grey phalarope — The red-necked phalarope—The little stint—The Temminck's stint.

ALTHOUGH Golchika is such a small and remote place, we have three more or less exact lists of the birds that breed there in the summer. To these my own notes may make a fourth. The first is that of Seebohm in 1877. Owing to various accidents he did not reach Golchika until 17th July, by which time, of course, the birds were hatched out, and he only spent six days in the place. The most notable species that he mentions are the little stint, the Eastern golden plover, and the rock ptarmigan.

The next account is that of Mr. Popham in 1895.[1] Mr. Popham reached Golchika on 7th July, nearly a fortnight earlier than Seebohm. He records the little stint, grey phalarope, rock ptarmigan, bar-tailed godwit, pomatorhine skua, grey plover, and Eastern golden plover. The third account is also that of Mr. Popham in 1897.[2] He reached Golchika on 29th June, and three days later proceeded down the river as far as the Krestovskiy Islands, where he was lucky enough to

---

[1] *Ibis*, 1897, vol. iii.
[2] *Ibis*, 1898, vol. iv.

take the first authentic eggs of the curlew-sandpiper. On 11th July, "having given up all hope of the ice allowing us even to see Kuzkin Island," he returned to Golchika. The birds of that neighbourhood mentioned on this expedition are Eastern golden plover, little stint, and the grey plover, although of the last species he writes: "I certainly saw far fewer birds on the marshes where they were breeding in 1895."

I reached Golchika on 29th June, and spent two months there. During that time I observed the Eastern golden plover, little stint, grey plover, grey phalarope, curlew-sandpiper, bar-tailed godwit, and rock ptarmigan.

It is evident that there is great discrepancy, not only between these four lists, but even between the two lists given by Mr. Popham in 1895 and 1897. I think that it is very doubtful whether, if four censuses were taken of the birds in a district in England, there would be the same amount of variation. For instance, on his second visit, although he was aware of their occurrence and was doubtless looking out for them, Mr. Popham does not record the grey phalarope, rock ptarmigan, nor bar-tailed godwit, and he observes a decrease in the numbers of the grey plover. But the most remarkable list is that of Seebohm, who made two or three excursions into the marshes and over the tundra. On the 18th he records: "I shot a couple of female little stints, the first I had seen in the valley of the Yenesei," and on the 19th: "On the hills I shot a male little stint." We are left to infer that these three specimens

A SUMMER ON THE YENESEI

were the only ones seen at Golchika; and yet, in 1895, Mr. Popham records the species as numerous, and in 1914 I found it common both by the river and out on the tundra. It is true that Seebohm visited Golchika late in the season, but by 20th July, although the eggs were hatched, the birds must have been feeding their young, and must have been in evidence for some time after that date.

The only explanation is that the bird population of those high latitudes is a very variable one, and depends upon the climatic conditions to a far greater extent than in the south. The yearly cycle of the tundra is very remarkable. For nine months of the year the whole land lies under four feet of snow, and nothing moves over the lonely white plain. Then in June, the river bursts its ice, and for three weeks or a month the whole country rings from end to end with the tinkle of running water. It seems as if a great pulse drove warm blood through the body of the frozen, stifled land, when hundreds of little transitory brooks flow down from the tundra to join the great flood that old Yenesei pours out to the north. Now, although the ice breaks up with a fair amount of uniformity between, let us say, for example, latitudes 62° and 72°, yet the snow in the country round does not disappear by any means with the same concurrence. As we ourselves saw, the banks at Platina might be nearly free from snow, while the coasts of Golchika were white.

The birds migrate down the river, the bulk of them, as Seebohm has recorded, probably arriving at the Arctic Circle about the second week in June. Thence they press northwards in the wake of the thaw, wherever they can find sufficient uncovered ground to afford them food and drink. Sometimes, in their passion to reach their breeding-grounds, they overshoot the edge of the icy zone, and, landing in a country where an arctic winter still prevails, they are obliged to return southwards again—if they are able—and attend in due course the advance of spring. If the season, for some cause or other, is a late one, this bird host—this "aery caravan"—is held up at the edge of the receding ice cap and delayed, sometimes for days together. This sometimes happens during migration in temperate climates, but there the birds soon pass on, for the snow seldom lies so deeply that no feeding-grounds are uncovered. But on the Yenesei a bird may reach a certain spot and summer there quite comfortably, while a hundred miles farther north the country may not support bird life at all. While she lingers there, the physical need to breed may overtake her before the winter has retreated sufficiently to allow her to reach her usual haunts, and compels her to make her nest and rear her brood where she can. Probably this is the reason why I found the curlew-sandpiper not uncommon near Golchika, while Messrs. Popham and Seebohm did not see it there at all. I have no information whether it was an early or a late season when these observers visited the Yenesei, but the summer of 1914 was both a cold and a late one. The ice broke up, and there were signs that it would be an early spring, but before the snow melted, the weather changed, and the east wind brought up blizzards from the Taimyr. The

A SUMMER ON THE YENESEI

birds, who had hurried northwards at the first promise of spring, were trapped and bound to make a living as best they could, while they waited to proceed on their journey to the river's mouth. The passions of the season caught them unawares, with the double result that the Golchika tundra was more than usually populous that year, and a certain amateur ornithologist was more than usually fortunate.

This, of course, is nothing but a theory, but there is some evidence that tends to confirm it. The Samoyedes from the north reported that the lakes on the Taimyr never thawed, and that snow was lying on the tundra all the summer. When I first reached Golchika, grey phalaropes were common on the island for three or four days. I shot several hen birds and found that they were about to lay. Then the wind changed, and with the warm spell most of the phalaropes disappeared. Undoubtedly they had migrated farther north. But if the cold weather had continued for another three or four days, there is no doubt but that they would have bred in the marshes. As it was, a few were caught, for I was lucky enough to find five nests and take a young one in down, whereas the other three expeditions had recorded only one nest—in 1895. And next year there may not be a single bird to be seen!

The great prize of my bird's-nesting at Golchika was a nest of the curlew-sandpiper. This bird is especially interesting to ornithologists, because, although well known throughout Europe and Asia on migration, its breeding-grounds remained a mystery for so many years. The naturalist, Severtzoff, even suggested that it must nest on the tops of the Pamir Mountains! The first nest ever found was that taken by Mr. H. L. Popham at the river's mouth in 1897, and as the bird had not hitherto been recorded from Golchika, I did not expect to find it so far south. However, on 6th July, as I was returning from a long round over the tundra that lay in the northern angle of the Yenesei and Golchika Rivers, all at once I saw a little rufous curlew, which was standing on a tussock about twenty yards away, watching me quietly. When I stopped she flew away, but soon alighted again and looked at me. Full of excitement, but still rather sceptical as to the likelihood of finding eggs, I lay down and watched her, but at the end of an hour and a half I could come to no conclusion, for the bird only strolled about and preened herself nonchalantly. I was not even certain of her sex, and her solitude and her quiet behaviour made me doubt whether, after all, she might not be a non-breeding bird. Nevertheless, I marked the place and turned homewards, meaning to come back next day. On the way I saw two more curlew-sandpipers on a high slope of the tundra, but they were very wild and would not permit a near approach.

On the morrow I turned out early and tramped over eight swampy miles of tundra. The second pair of sandpipers were not to be seen, but the first bird was still pottering round the same spot. To-day she was a little more demonstrative, and flew about uneasily. Once she uttered a sharp, anxious note: *wick-wick-wick*, two or three times repeated. By this time I was convinced that the nest was close at hand, but it was difficult to locate it; for although the bird could dodge me successfully enough behind tussocks of moss only six inches high, my person unfortunately was too bulky for these, the only available hiding-places. The ground was on a very gradual slope. On the right hand and on the left were two small tarns, still covered with blue ice. In the distance grazed some herds of reindeer, and once a Samoyede sledge glided swiftly over a ridge. Heavy drifts of snow still lay in the sheltered hollows, and the sleet showers that came slapping over the tundra made me glad to wrap myself up in my Burberry coat.

The bird had whirled away round the tarn at my approach, so I hid myself as well as I could behind a tussock, and settled down to wait for her return. Twenty minutes passed—half an hour. "It's time she was coming back," thought I, and turned my head carefully to reconnoitre. And lo and behold, not thirty yards behind, the sandpiper stood and studied me contemptuously! She had been watching all the time. "What a fool!" doubtless would have been her comment if she could have spoken. It is no use to try and gull the waders: up to a certain point I believe that they can almost see you *think*!

I retired abashed to another hiding-place about fifty yards farther up the slope. The bird at once showed her appreciation of this move by flying towards the spot where I had first seen her. She was so small that it was very difficult to mark her as she tripped between the tussocks. When I thought that she must be settled on her eggs, I jumped up quickly. She took wing at once, but when I went to the place whence she had risen, there was no sign of the nest. This happened twice, but as she returned to the same spot each time, I knew that the treasure was there all right, and that patience would win it. The great difficulty in marking down nests on the tundra is the absence of all landmarks. You settle exactly in your own mind where the place is, and then note the position by means of some hillock or grass tuft on the skyline. This mark looks enormous through the field-glasses, and you think that it will be impossible to mistake it. When you look for it with the naked eye you are not quite so sure: it may take a minute or two to pick it up again. Then you stand up, and away goes your bird—and your landmark likewise, faded from the skyline, back into the tundra. I marked the bird down by a dodge that I used when looking for grey plovers' eggs under similar circumstances, and which is described elsewhere; but each time that I flushed her, she seemed to jump up from a different place. She was so little and so nimble that she could run over the moss for some yards before she was seen. The next time I gave her ample time to settle down, and lay still in the wet, sucking lumps of sugar until I nearly fell asleep. Then all at once a Buffon's skua came overhead, flying low in the squally wind. I snatched my gun and shot him as he flew by, and as he fell I saw the sandpiper spring up from a spot where I had marked her once before. I left the skua and ran up to the place. The bird began to call again, and drooped a wing to decoy me away. Half a minute's search and there was the nest at my feet. It exactly

A SUMMER ON THE YENESEI

answered to Mr. Popham's description—a little depression in the moss, of an apple's diameter, and deeper than the nests of most of the waders. The four eggs, greenish in ground colour, were much blotched with umber at the larger end, like those of a snipe. The nest was so narrow and so deep that, as they lay, they were tilted almost vertically, with their apexes pointing downwards, and the blunt mottled ends uppermost, flush with the surrounding brown tundra. In measurement they average $35\cdot1 \times 25\cdot1$ millimetres. Compared with those taken by Mr. Popham, my eggs are less distinctly marked, and the blotches are more blurred and confluent..

The discovery of this nest so close to Golchika encouraged me to search the country further, and although I found no more eggs, I was fortunate enough to secure specimens of the young in down, as will be told in a future chapter, and also had the opportunity of observing the bird's behaviour throughout the summer.

As the result of these observations, I came to the conclusion that this nest was not in a very typical position. Judging by other breeding-grounds that I located later on, I should say that characteristic curlew-sandpiper ground was the slope of the dry, open tundra, especially where the reindeer moss was more or less broken up by tufts of grass, and where the bird could have an uninterrupted view of the surrounding country.

Mr. Popham shot the female at the nest, and it is significant that all my skins are those of hen birds. As far as I know I did not see a cock bird while I was on the Yenesei. While I was watching the nest, the male did not come near, and later on there was no evidence that both birds take charge of the young, as is the case with the stints and other of the waders. However, it is difficult to speak dogmatically, for the following reason. As soon as the young were hatched, which was about the third week in July, the curlew-sandpipers came down from the uplands of the tundra into the marshes, and while the chicks were still in down they united into small parties. This tendency to flock together during the breeding season was a remarkable and suggestive feature of the bird life of the tundra. It also made it very difficult to take a census of the number of pairs breeding in a certain district. Until the middle of July the birds seemed scarce, for they were scattered over a wide area, and their behaviour at the nest was so quiet that it was possible to walk across the nesting-grounds and not notice them at all. All this was altered when several broods met in the marshes, for the old birds then became very demonstrative, and the species seemed to be twice as abundant as before. There is no doubt that the young were brought to these places, and were not hatched there. On 15th July I carefully quartered one small bog while looking for little stints' nests, and there was not a sandpiper to be seen. A week later two birds appeared, and, judging by their behaviour, they evidently had young ones close at hand, though whether they were both females or a cock and hen I cannot say. Afterwards I repeatedly met little parties like this in the swampy parts of the tundra. When their haunts were invaded the old birds would dash wildly round the intruder with their white undercoverts flashing. Mr. Popham says of the bird's call: "At one time I thought I heard it make a sound like a dunlin, but as I afterwards saw dunlins close by I was probably mistaken."[1] The alarm cry which I constantly heard was a shrill triple note: *wick-wick-wick*, repeated two or three times, and uttered when the bird was both at rest and on the wing. The curlew-sandpiper was not as bold as the dunlin when the breeding-ground was approached; and when the young were hatched the parents became very wild and circled rapidly over the tundra just out of gunshot. At the beginning of August, I secured a bird of the year in a big swamp swarming with little stints and golden plover. It is a wise provision of nature that these young waders should sprout their flight quills before they are many hours out of the egg. They fledge with incredible rapidity, and once they can fly it is very difficult to approach within shot of them. I stalked one bird which was following its parent, but each time that I came within range, up she would jump, call her youngster to follow her, and escort him to another part of the marsh. It was difficult to follow the movements of the bird, owing to the swarms of mosquitoes, but at last I thought that I had marked him down, and fired. But when I went to pick up the specimen, I found to my disgust that I had "shot at a pigeon and killed a crow," for it was not a sandpiper at all, but a young dunlin. However, later

[1] *Ibis*, 1898, vol. iv.

on I obtained a young bird in the buff-breasted plumage of the first autumn. The nestlings have a black bill and legs and chestnut down which is almost indistinguishable from that of the little stint and dunlin, but there is a rufous tinge on the breast which is recognisable even at this early stage. How curious it is—this red breeding plumage of so many of these arctic wading birds! We find it also in the knot, sanderling, bar-tailed godwit, and phalarope; and to prove that it has its origin far down the stem of the race, we see the same tint in the russet plumage of the ruffs of the year, and in the bib of the mature little stint.

As soon as the young curlew-sandpipers are strong upon the wing, they and their parents disappear. The stints and the golden plover linger on until the end of August, but the sandpipers vanish early in the month. The tundra is the sadder for their going. You may walk for miles and not see a bird, except a plover or two or a moulting bunting in the whortles.

The most charming birds were the grey phalaropes. I saw them first of all on 1st July, when a little party, both males and females, were feeding together in the frozen marshes. With their brilliant chestnut plumage, they looked more like passerine birds from some tropical region than waders on the northern ice. You may only speak of the male and female phalaropes by convention. You should, to be exact, say the female and the male, for in this species the lady is entirely the managing partner. She woos the mate of her choice shamelessly, and later allows him to incubate the eggs and take charge of the young. We wonder what called for such a revolution in the order of the sexes, and what the goal of such natural experiments may be.

Classificatory systems have sandwiched the phalaropes between the plovers on the one hand and the snipes on the other, but when seen swimming the birds sit high in the water like little sea-gulls, and the only limcoline things about them are their grey mantles picked out with buff. When they run, as they love to do, over the spongy sphagnum, their gait has the quaint, perky dignity of the moorhen.

I found the first nest which contained fresh eggs on 8th July, on the island at Golchika. It was within fifty yards of a ramshackle balagan which had just been taken over by some fisherfolk; and it was lucky that I found it when I did, or else the people, or more probably their dogs, would certainly have done so. The cock bird drew my attention to the place by flying round anxiously while he uttered his *drrrt-drrrt*. This note is like that of the red-necked phalarope, but is shriller and quite recognisable where the two species breed side by side. I sat down and watched him for twenty minutes, and at the end of the time he ran on to the nest, which was hidden in the grass like that of a redshank.

On the following day I flushed a cock bird from four eggs on the other side of the island. This nest was in a much drier situation; nevertheless, the eggs lay upon a good platform of dry grass, for the bird's instinct taught him to raise them as high as possible above the wet ground. I resolved to photograph this phalarope at the nest, so I returned to the house and fetched my camera and small green hiding-tent. It was not an easy matter to pitch the latter, for the wind always raves over that flat country, and even after it had been weighted with timber it flapped so threateningly that I did not expect much success. But the bird was most accommodating, and in about ten minutes' time he slipped quietly on to his eggs. I gave him time to settle down comfortably, and then released the shutter. He flounced off the nest, but more with surprise than with fright, and in a quarter of an hour he returned, completely reassured. After that our friendship ripened rapidly, and the sound of the camera disturbed him not in the least. Twice I left my hiding-place in order to readjust the lens. Each time the phalarope ran off the eggs to a little hillock twenty yards away and watched me until I had re-entered the tent, and then he returned at once. In spite of his gay plumage, the bird was curiously inconspicuous. On the eggs he fluffed out his red breast, which—a neat adaptation of means to ends—in deference to his swimming powers, unlike that of the other waders, was feathered closely and thickly like that of a duck. But when he left the nest he seemed to shrink to half his former size, and his buff and black shoulder bands, and his long blade-like secondary feathers, harmonised exactly with the long grass around him. I sat by the nest for the greater part of the day, but all that time the hen bird did not come near the eggs. Towards evening I wanted to leave the tent, and in order to drive him from the nest without scaring him unduly, I threw some small pieces of moss at him. This had the desired effect, but as he strolled doubtfully away, a second piece fell into the nest. Without hesitation the plucky little bird, disregarding the strange upheavals of the tent, ran back and tried to clear the precious eggs. I photographed him for the last time as he stood over them, piping his solicitude lest they should take hurt. I have seldom seen a bird that I liked so well—so beautiful, so innocent, and so occupied. There is something very touching in a cock bird's care for his eggs. The hen is proverbially attached to the nest, and it seems only natural that she should be so, but her mate's pride and devotion is pretty to see.

I obtained another male phalarope and a newly hatched chick on 16th July, but the young ones fledge incredibly quickly, and by the beginning of August there was not a bird to be seen in the marshes. The grey phalaropes are the first migrants to leave Golchika in the summer.

The red-necked phalaropes were much more common than the last-named species, and they were also more sociable. They began to nest about the same time as the grey phalaropes, but they lingered much later in the summer, and I obtained young birds in the plumage of the year until the end of August. Our British phalaropes are so tame in the breeding season that they may almost be caught in a butterfly-net, but the Siberian birds were rather wild, especially when they had young ones in the neighbourhood. When a red-necked phalarope was feeding in shallow water she would begin to pirouette round quickly on her own axis, and at the same time snatch up small particles from the surface. After watching this performance several times, I came to the conclusion that the water was just too deep to allow the bird to reach the mud at the bottom. Therefore, by the circular movement of her body, she created an eddy which sucked the floating matter to the surface, just as by stirring a teacup with a spoon it is possible to draw the tea leaves to the top.

Golchika is a great stronghold of the little stint. The morning after our arrival at the island I saw at least a dozen of these pigmy dunlins feeding round the house in company with a few Temminck's stints. The latter were fractious, waspish little things, who chased away any other bird which trespassed too close to their own particular puddles; but the little stints were much too busy to squabble. Each was guzzling away as if his life depended upon it. And so it did, and not only his own life, but the life of the race also, for the summer was short, and eggs must be laid and hatched, and chicks reared into strong-flighted birds all in the space of eight weeks. Most small birds, especially the waders, have an intensely solemn demeanour. Perhaps it is their long beaks, reminiscent of patriarchal beards, that gives them such a ludicrously staid expression. The little stint is the most serious of them all, and exceeds both the dunlin and the snipe in gravity. His deportment would be becoming in an archdeacon.

I found the first nest on 3rd July beside a little lake. The bird rose quietly and alighted again at a little distance. I had watched stints behaving like this for the past four days, and had searched in vain for eggs, but this time the bird rather overdid the business. She, or rather he, drooped a wing and that gave the show away at once. I sat down to wait, and in two minutes the bird had cuddled down upon his eggs again. After that I found many nests, both out on the tundra, and also in the riverside marshes, in company with reeves and phalaropes.

The bird shown in the illustration was photographed on Golchika Island itself. I went to the place armed with a large reflex camera, racked out to its fullest extent. It seemed rather like taking out a siege gun to shoot rabbits, but the bird was so small that I feared that she would not appear upon the plate at all unless a lens of long focus was used. But this turned out to be quite unnecessary. The chief difficulty was to get sufficiently far away from the sitter (it was *she* this time), who tripped round my feet, not afraid, but just a little nervous lest I should accidentally crush her eggs. When I touched the nest, she sprang up almost as if she would have flown at me, and then toddled sideways with wings trailing distractedly and puffed-out feathers. The tameness of the little stint at the nest is quite uncanny. It seems as if the life of the race that she fosters has power for a season to raise the bird above such commonplace matters as food and fear, and fills her with a sort of ecstasy of maternity. Later on, when the eggs are chipping, this passion to brood rises to such a pitch that the bird will actually suffer herself to be taken in the hand rather than leave her nest. I use the words he and she indiscriminately when writing of the stints, for both sexes share the duties of incubation, although most of the birds that I obtained at the nest were males. When the chicks are two or three days old, both parents unite to care for them, and become very noisy and rather wild when the place is approached. One morning I watched a cock stint whose nest held three moist chicks. One by one he collected the broken eggshells and flew with them to a spot some fifty yards away. This habit is general among birds whose young are helpless in the nest, but baby stints run almost as soon as they are hatched, and it scarcely seemed worth the parents' trouble to carry off the egg-shells.

Even before the chicks are fledged, the gregarious instinct asserts itself, and the family party unites with another family party until quite a large flock is formed. These flocks linger on the sandy flats until the end of August, when all the birds disappear before the easterly gales as if they were swept away with a broom. Sometimes the stints mix with the dunlins that also haunt such places, and it is very comic to see the two species, like pocket and quarto editions of the same work, feeding side by side.

The Temminck's stints were also common at Golchika, but they were to be found only along the river-banks. For this reason they breed a week later than *Erolia minuta*, for the shores of the river are flooded at the end of June, and the birds must wait until the water has subsided before they can begin to lay. But one or two pairs nest early, and one of the first clutches of eggs that I found at Golchika was that of a Temminck's stint on a grave-mound in the little

A SUMMER ON THE YENESEI 137

cemetery beside the Antonoffs' house. Even where the two species bred side by side there was never any difficulty in distinguishing the nests. That of the little stint, as a rule, was lined with dry willow leaves, while that of the Temminck's stint was finished with grass-bents. The eggs too are quite distinctive, although I took two clutches of little stints' eggs which approached to the type of *Erolia temminckii*.

When we came to Golchika the Temminck's stints were courting. It was a very pretty performance. The bird (he or she—the stints make no distinction of sex) took wing suddenly, and spun away down the river bank with a high shrilling call: *Trrrrrr*. Sometimes it sank down, tired out by the spring ecstasy, but more often it circled round slowly, head to wind, and hovered for a while with rapidly vibrating wings and throat. When a number of birds thus hung poised in the air the effect was very charming. It seemed as if they were so much in love with one another, and with the day, that a sudden rapture lifted them above the common earth and impelled them to take wing. At such times they were fearless of man, but later on, when the eggs were laid, they became rather shy.

On 16th July I pitched my hiding-tent beside a nest with three eggs among some scrub willows. It was impossible to disguise the tent in any way, for there was no material at hand to cover it. I was obliged to enter it in all its nakedness, and hope that the green cover would not offend the eye of the lady stint. However, a three hours' wait among the mosquitoes was quite fruitless. The bird flew wildly round the tent, but never once returned to her eggs, and in the end I gave it up as a bad job. I was a good deal hampered also by a drunken native, who staggered through the marsh with a vodka bottle, begging all the world to join him in his cups. That is the worst of vodka. It must have some of the properties of the mediæval love philter, judging by the kind of universal affection and philanthropy that it seems to inspire in its victims!

On the following morning I called on our next-door neighbours, and pressed into my service little Nicolai Protyvik, the youngest but three of the large family of that ilk. Of course I could not explain to the small boy why I wanted him, but with the delightful obligingness of his race, he followed me at once. In fact, the only difficulty was to restrain all the rest of the household from coming too, so eager were they to find out what my business might be.

The photographer always has a bad moment when approaching a marked nest. Will the bird have forsaken it, and are his preparations made in vain? In this case the eggs were hot, showing that the bird had only just left them. Doubtless she was watching us from somewhere close at hand. I crept inside the tent with the camera and bade Nicolai go home at once. If he did, I promised him sweets—*konfetie*—in the evening. But Nicolai's face fell, and he hung about dissatisfied. What was the matter—didn't he like sweets? No use to give him kopecks, for at Golchika there was nowhere to spend them. With a beseeching smile and expressive gesture, he said: " *Koureet—*

A SUMMER ON THE YENESEI

koureet!" A thorough little Siberian, he wanted, not sugar, but cigarettes!

Before he was out of sight the bird was back at the nest, for this trick of sending an ally away from the tent is one which seldom fails to deceive even the wariest of fowl. But the Temminck's stint was unusually shy, and at each exposure the click of the shutter drove her away with a flash of small dagger-grey wings. Then followed a wearisome time of waiting, while she flew round and round the tent and tried to find out what the sound-maker inside might be. She never flew directly on to her eggs, but always alighted a little distance off and ran up in little zigzag rushes between the willows. Her small grey body and jerky movements made her seem more like a mouse than a bird. Here again I am taking the bird's sex for granted, and yet, as I did not secure this stint, I have no idea whether it was a cock or a hen. This case illustrates pretty well the limitations of photography as a handmaid to ornithology. Enthusiasts sometimes claim that the camera has revolutionised the field-study of birds, and this is so to a certain extent; but what can be said for the scientific value of a record which does not even prove the sex of the original! Bird photographers are too apt to take it for granted that the bird at the nest is necessarily the female, and each year a number of pictures are published, definitely titled as to sex, without any more proof than that the observer "judged by its behaviour that the bird was the female." If such workers could be persuaded to use the gun in connection with the camera for a season, it would perhaps shake their confidence in their own judgment in this matter.

I obtained both male and female Temminck's stints at the nest, but whether the sexes incubate in turns, or whether one bird takes over the whole business, I cannot say. The chicks are much greyer in colour than those of the little stint, which, except for their size, resemble young dunlins. At the end of July, baby stints swarmed everywhere. The Antonoffs' dogs spent most of their leisure in rambling round the island and gobbling up all that they could find. When hard pressed I have seen these fledglings take to the water and swim as cleverly as phalaropes.

For an expedition of this kind the choice of a camera is not an easy matter, for it is impossible to carry a number of bulky appliances about with you, and therefore any instrument chosen must be able to do the work of two or three. It is particularly difficult for the ornithologist, for bird photography requires a specialised apparatus. There is only one kind of camera that will fulfil all requirements, and that is a reflex. The objections to the reflex type are its weight and its costliness, and also it is not very suitable for taking nest pictures. But for the rest, the advantage of focusing up to the moment of exposure far outweighs the drawbacks, especially when the sitter is likely to be anything so restless as a bird. All the ornithological, and most of the other illustrations used in this book were taken with a "Birdland" reflex camera, built for me by Mr. Armytage Sanders of London. It is expressly intended for bird photography; and as far as

I know it is the only reflex of quarter-plate size that can be used with a lens of fourteen-inch focal length. I found the latter arrangement of inestimable use during my Siberian trip: in fact, in very many cases it was indispensable.

CHAPTER VII.

The Eastern golden plover—The bar-tailed godwit—The distribution of birds at Golchika—The dotterel—Some other birds—The Siberian herring-gull—The long-tailed duck—The king-eider—The wild swan—The black-throated diver—The red-throated diver—The white-fronted goose—The red-breasted goose—The migration of geese—Scarcity of birds of prey—The blue fox—Some smaller birds—The Lapland bunting—The red-throated pipit— he autumn migration—Young blue-throats.

ONE of the commonest birds on the tundra was the Eastern golden plover, or "Tilyoko," as the Samoyedes called it. One of the birds met you half a verst from the nest and whistled his mate off her eggs. They then both escorted you to their boundaries, and there you were, so to speak, handed over to the next couple for espionage. This happened over and over again, until for miles your progress was accompanied by a chorus of plaintive pipes—*klee-ee-kee*—from that of the bird who was running before you within gunshot, to those on the distant ridges of the tundra, who could only be seen through binoculars.

I found the first nest on 4th July. It contained four slightly incubated eggs, and was made of broken lichen haulms on the side of a long grassy slope. Both Seebohm and Mr. Popham found the European golden plover (*Charadrius apricarius*) on the Yenesei. Mr. Popham says that where they breed side by side on

Eastern Golden Plover (Charadrius d. fulvus).

Lapland Bunting (Calcarius l. lapponicus) immature plumage.

Little Stint ♀ (Erolia minuta.)

the tundra it is possible to distinguish the two species by their calls; and he shot a bird with parti-coloured axillaries which has been pronounced to be intermediate between the eastern and western forms, but as far as I know, I never met with anything but *Charadrius fulvus* at Golchika.

The eggs hatch out about 20th July, and as in the case of the curlew-sandpiper, as soon as the chicks are old enough to run over the tundra, the parents take them into the swamps, where, as they fledge, flocks are gradually formed. On 1st August I explored a piece of marshy land which lay about twenty versts from Golchika. In a patch of ground of not more than a quarter of a mile square, I counted no fewer than five pairs of golden plover, the same number of curlew-sandpipers, and many little stints. The latter for the most part kept aloof and flocked only with their own kind, but the sandpipers and plovers associated freely. Little anxious parties made up of two or three of both species swooped wildly over the marsh; and I frequently observed on this, as on other occasions, that no sooner did a plover alight on a tussock than a sandpiper pitched beside her. The two stood side by side, crying, for a minute or two, and then dashed off together to another perch. The bond between two species so distinct was very interesting and even remarkable. The *wick-wick-wick* of the curlew-sandpipers put all the plover on the *qui vive* at once, just as the melancholy *klee-ee* or *kee-a-ko* of the plover sent the sandpipers buzzing all over the breeding-grounds in hysterical " wisps."

This tendency to flock before the young were fledged is easily explained. Sociability is one of the principal laws of animal life. It is abnormal to find a solitary species, and where such a one occurs it can generally be explained, as in the case of some birds of prey, by a peculiar mode of feeding. But more often it is due to the change produced in the animal world by the rapid increase of mankind. It is worthy of note that there are species living quite an isolated life in densely inhabited regions, while the same species or their nearest cogeners are gregarious in uninhabited countries.[1]

To some extent this is the case with the golden plover. In our own country breeding-grounds are becoming scarce. You must walk very many miles in England to meet with a dozen pairs of nesting plover, and thus the birds scattered over the moors have no incentive to congregate until the autumn, when their numbers are recruited by migrants from the north. But on the tundra, where the birds are plentiful and live under primitive conditions, their natural inclination towards social life is very marked, and the same applies to the curlew-sandpiper.

I used to wonder what brought the birds down from the grassy hillsides where they nested into the sphagnum marshes, and I came to the conclusion that it must be the need of the young broods for water. There is no doubt that it was the marsh that attracted them. In August a number even came down to the banks of the Golchika River, a mile or more from the

[1] Kropotkin, *Mutual Aid among Animals*, p. 20

nearest breeding-place. I shot a young bird there in the spotted ochre plumage of the first autumn. He still wore a little coronal of down among his new frontal feathers. The golden plover do not leave Golchika until the end of August, at which time I saw flocks of twenty or thirty birds flying up the Yenesei.

The bar-tailed godwit was the last of the six rare waders of Golchika, and it was the only one, alas! whose nest I did not find. It was very scarce in the district. I saw only two pairs altogether. The Samoyedes called this bird "Tufek." They said that she arrived very early in the spring, and ran round the frozen pools, tapping the ice with her long bill and crying impatiently for the thaw. Like most of the bird-lore of country people all the world over, this fancy probably has a germ of truth in it. The godwits breed on the highest parts of the tundra, which are the first places to be freed from snow; and I should think that they lay their eggs very early, for birds that I saw on 12th July evidently had young ones close at hand. The alarm note has been syllabled as *lou-ey-lou-ey-lou-ey*. To me it sounds exactly like the *clapper-clapper* made by sharpening a scythe on a whetstone.

There were three distinct types of country round Golchika, and in a short time one learned to know just what birds to expect in each. First there were the river banks and the neighbouring swamps. Stints, phalaropes, reeves, and dunlin were the representative species in such places. Then there were the dry, stony hills that divided the tundra from the marsh. Here you might expect to find the shore-lark—a quarrelsome dandy with a canary and puce gorget—a wheatear or two, and scores of ringed plovers. Lastly, on the tundra itself, there were golden plover, Lapland buntings, curlew-sandpipers, and the dotterel. The latter, although of less interest than most of the waders of the neighbourhood, charmed me as much as any of them. She is such a gentle, innocent little bird, and both her tameness and her trim, sober-hued plumage are so engaging. I found several nests, and also two or three pallid, fluffy babies, who already wore the first suggestions of the tangerine-coloured vests that would be theirs by and by. Later, the dotterels gathered into little family parties, or "trips" as the old English fowlers called them, but all through June coveys of unmated birds haunted the tops of the hills. Sometimes, as you stumbled over the rough, mossy ground, you would hear a little tinkle of notes, like falling drops of sound, and half a dozen grass tussocks (so it seemed) sprang into a flock of timid, throbbing birds, who skimmed away over the tundra and pitched into invisibility again a little farther on.

I was once lying behind a hillock, watching an old dotterel with three young ones, who were already strong upon the wing. Presently a rough-legged buzzard circled overhead. I think that he was really on the look out for lemmings, not for dotterel, but the mother bird took it for granted that he had designs upon her brood. With a soft *chirrr*, the three fledglings took wing, for they were well able to take care of themselves; but the plucky little mother (who, like many human mothers, could not understand that her babies had outgrown the need of her protection) held her ground, and began to curtsey sideways, and cry softly, shamming a broken wing with pretty art. At first she and the buzzard were at cross-purposes. He had not even seen her brood, and if he had, he knew that it was waste of time to chivy birds so strong upon the wing. If she had known enough to lie still while his sinister shadow wheeled around her, all would have been well. As it was, her flutterings tempted him, and he stooped at her viciously. I could not see such an ending to her show of maternal devotion, and so, exchanging my field-glasses for the gun, I pumped 2 oz. of dust-shot into the hawk. Of course, at that range, it scarcely ruffled his stout breastplate of feathers, but the report made him sheer off, and gave the gallant little plover time to escape.

Another bold parent was the willow-grouse. At the end of July I found a brood in a little valley much beloved by red-throated pipits and mosquitoes. After a hot chase I captured three of the youngsters, and imprisoned them in the camera case. As soon as the mother heard them *cheeping*, she ran up with the greatest solicitude, and I was able to photograph her over and over again as she stood within ten feet of me. The cock bird also showed much concern, but dared not venture so close as his mate. From the photograph it will be seen, in these high latitudes, the willow-grouse never lose the white winter plumage entirely.

It is interesting to find that even the British Islands are not so far south of the arctic avifauna but that five-sixths of all the species I observed north of latitude 70° are on the British lists. Of these, twelve species breed regularly in this country, and most of the others are frequent on passage. Some of them are so well known in their European haunts that I shall mention them only in passing. Such were the reeves and dunlins who nested in the long grass in the marshes, and a single common snipe who flew round the island, bleating his lonely love-lyrics all day long. There were also some arctic terns who nested in a vociferous colony close to the river. The terns on the Yenesei had decadent tastes. In this country they are the cleanest and most skilful of fishermen, seizing only live prey in clear water. But at Golchika they were the veriest little scavengers, and hawked all day round the packing stations in search of fish entrails and any refuse that might be thrown into the water. Here they were helped by the gulls, hundreds of which gathered round Golchika in August. These were all the Siberian herring-gull (*Larus fuscus anteluis*), as our ornithologists are pleased to call it, or the Siberian lesser black-back, as nature seems to have designed it to be called. It differs from our *Larus fuscus* in its slightly larger size and paler mantle. Mr. Popham informs me that when he visited Golchika, he found a considerable colony of these gulls. No such colony exists now, and although once or twice I found a few pairs breeding at Och Marino and Sloika, I never obtained any eggs. The birds seen round Golchika were nearly all in the plumage of the second or third year, and of nine that were brought to me by Sylkin, eight were females.

The only duck that was common at Golchika was the long-tailed duck. These birds were common on the

A SUMMER ON THE YENESEI

lakes, and flocks of unmated birds were seen on the Yenesei until the middle of July, when they went into the tundra to moult. I often heard their fine, harsh clamour, or watched them preening themselves on the blue ice-floes, as I crossed the swamps by the light of the midnight sun. He who named the long-tailed duck *Harelda glacialis* knew not only what was due to science, but also what was picturesque in nomenclature. So it is with the golden-eye—*Clangula glaucion*, and the petrel—*Oceanites oceanicus*. The actual meaning of the names may be nothing to the ordinary man, but they please the ear, just as the National Anthem, or the "Marche Funébre" played on the organ, may by their stateliness and dignity impress a man who properly has no soul for music. Even if we did not understand Latin, we could not call the little dipper *Colymbus glacialis*, just as *vice versa* we could not recognise the great northern diver merely as *Cinclus aquaticus*. He who gave the red-necked phalarope its trivial name had not such a fine idea of the value of sounds as the ornithologist who first called it *Phalaropus hyperboreus*. In one case the specific name falls flatly on the ear—it is equally well suited to a new variety of chicken; but the other rolls off the tongue grandly enough, with a certain sonorousness befitting a being whose life is spent in battling with wind and wave in desolate and solitary places.

I never saw the king-eider at Golchika, but at the beginning of July, Prokopchuk brought in a couple—a splendid drake and a duck. Prokopchuk had a story, though whether of his own invention or that of the natives, I do not know, that the "ga-ga," as he called it, is in some sense a bird of distinction; and that if a bird of prey harries it in the nesting season, the ducks of other species will unite to drive the foe away. It is curious how we human folk thus allow legend and sentiment to gather round certain birds. Sometimes it is by association, as round our own redbreast and barn-swallow; sometimes it is by their utility, as round the eider-ducks of Iceland; sometimes, as in the case of the "ga-ga," we can trace it to none of these things.

No bird has gathered such a wealth of myth around its life-story as the swan. From the tragedy of the children of Lir to the coming of Lohengrin, its legends are so many and so beautiful that it was scarcely surprising to find the same sentiment on the Yenesei. The wild swan does not nest at Golchika, although it is found at the Sopochnaya, and the natives there hold it in high esteem. Indeed, they invest it with the same qualities with which the people of the south used to endow the pelican. The swan is their personification of maternity. The goose, they say, is a bad mother. When the young foxes go into the tundra to steal her eggs, she will fly screaming away; but the swan will face the robbers, and kill anyone who touches her nest. She will be slain herself, rather than desert her brood.

The divers were the latest birds to breed at Golchika, for they were obliged to wait until the ice on the lakes thawed, and this did not happen until after the snow melted. I took fresh eggs on 12th July. Both the red- and black-throated species were found, but my experience agrees with that of Mr. Popham, as against that of

Seebohm, that the former was much the commoner of the two. The white-billed diver (*Gavia adamsi*), which breeds on the eastern tundras, visits the Yenesei occasionally during the spring migration.

I had met with the black-throated diver in Scotland, but there I never heard more of its language than an uncouth shriek. But, on the Yenesei, I constantly heard a beautiful modulated whistle, two or three times repeated, as wild and as far reaching as the call of some wading bird. In fact it seemed such an incongruous sound to proceed from the " ga-garra's " grotesque body that, although I frequently suspected the blackthroat, I never really solved the mystery of its authorship until one day when lying watching duck beside a lake in the tundra, a pair of divers flew towards me, unsuspecting, and pitched in the water about two hundred yards away. They began to play about the tarn, chasing each other, diving beneath the surface, and swimming side by side along the shore. Frequently, with rigid necks and tilted bills, they uttered this weird, melancholy whistle, which was audible for a mile or more. I think it must be the love-song of their kind.

There was a small pool behind Sylkin's house, and here a pair of red-throated divers hatched out two young ones. Sylkin's boys caught one of the chicks the same evening, and brought him to me. He was a hideous little monster, whose scaly, sprawling limbs and goggle eyes bore the saurian stamp that in his parents was discreetly veiled with feathers. I had photographed this diver in the Outer Hebrides during the previous summer, and wanted a picture of the downy youngster to complete the series. As the light was failing, I had to put off the sitting until the morrow, and went to bed with the foundling snuggled for warmth inside my nightgown. At first he was a most uncomfortable bedfellow, poor little wretch, and cried unceasingly until he had warmed his cold webbed toes against me, and then he nestled down quietly enough.

In the morning I tried to photograph him, but he was a most troublesome sitter. Professor Newton [1] cites the case of a young dabchick, which could not have been more than twelve hours old, which crawled across a table from side to side, " dragging itself forward by means of its wings quite as much as propelling itself by its legs." My diver easily capped this feat. With legs and wings, he moved himself in rapid jerks, and crossed a strip of mud thirty feet wide at a pace that gave me all I could do to catch him. Whenever he was placed in the water, he invariably swam ashore and crawled into the grass. I am inclined to think that in very early days divers are able, not only to progress on land, but also make good use of that power. Otherwise it is not easy to explain how it was that at Golchika they were found so often upon small pools and streams at a distance from where they were hatched, and how they reached the river before their wings were fledged.

The twin of my chick was reared safely. From the first he was slightly bigger than his brother. It is usual for one of a diver's brood to be larger than the other, but I do not know whether the difference in size is due to sex. He had all the care and solicitude that by

[1] *Ibis*, 1889, p. 577.

A SUMMER ON THE YENESEI

rights he should have shared; and all day long his devoted parents flew backwards and forwards between the pool and the sea with fish to satisfy his growing appetite. When you visited the place, you might see the anxious couple swimming to and fro with their bills raised in that attitude of supercilious haughtiness that is characteristic of these birds. After them paddled the awkward squab, with *his* infant bill tilted also, in absurd travesty of their gesture. He always seemed more at ease when they took wing and left him to shift for himself. Then you could only tell that he was nervous because every now and then he pretended to drink. This little habit is typical of the adult diver when uneasy, and it was interesting to notice it in so young a bird.

The divers laid their eggs so late, and the incubation period was so long, that this chick, like many more, was still in down by the middle of August, and I used to wonder however he would acquire sufficient wing-power to carry him hundreds of miles to the south before the snow came. On 25th August he reached the river. He was still quite unable to fly, and unless his parents carried him, he must have crawled across half a mile of sphagnum and driftwood, for there was no outlet to the pool where he was hatched. He screamed terribly, just like a child who fears a ducking, and tried to clamber on to the back of his mother, who dodged him each time by diving down and popping up again a yard or two away. Three or four more old divers came to look on at the youngster's initiation into the home of his order, and between them they kept up a hideous chorus of shrieks until nightfall. But after dusk the little one must have mustered enough courage to swim downstream; for, with his parents in attendance, he passed the hut during the night, and by morning he was swimming safely where nothing could hurt him, out on the broad turgid breast of the Yenesei.

The commonest goose at Golchika was the white-fronted goose (*Anser albifrons*). Seebohm mentions the lesser white-fronted goose (*A. finmarchus*), but I saw none of the latter species. The natives once brought in a bean-goose that they had killed in moult on the tundra, and another day they brought a pair of red-breasted geese (*Branta ruficollis*), the only ones that I saw on the Yenesei.

The march past of the geese began on 14th July, and continued for a week. During this time the birds migrated by day in twos and threes, in dozens, and in battalions a hundred strong, to their moulting haunts in the tundra. They gag-gaggled sedately to one another as they flew, and each squad rigidly followed the course of the Golchika River. Thus for four or five weeks they loiter beside the inland lakes, as helpless as nestlings, waiting for their flight quills to grow. Then, during the latter part of September, they return in leisurely troops, young and old in brand-new plumage, to spend a couple of halcyon weeks on the flats of Breokoffsky.

When Mr. Popham took the eggs of the red-breasted goose in 1895, he records that in each case the nest was built at the foot of a cliff occupied by a peregrine falcon or a rough-legged buzzard, " possibly for protection

A SUMMER ON THE YENESEI

from foxes." Prokopchuk, who took some interest in birds, recognised this as a habit of the white-fronted geese that bred near Golchika. He compared them to the wild reindeer, who, in the summer-time, will bring forth their young safely by the lairs of the wolves who may hunt them to death later on. Possibly it was the same wish for protection that led the bar-tailed godwits mentioned by Mr. Popham[1] to nest in the breeding-ground of a pair of Buffon's skuas.

It is impossible both to eat your cake and have it at the same time, and the cold season that brought the curlew-sandpiper and the grey phalarope to the southern limits of their range, cut down the supply of lemmings, and, with the lemmings, the numbers of the birds of prey. Falcons and buzzards were scarce, and I saw the snowy owl only three times altogether. Skuas, both long-tailed and arctic, were seldom seen, but early in July I picked up two or three of the former species dead in the tundra. Probably they had been poisoned by the baits laid down for foxes.

The failure of the lemmings probably affected the numbers of foxes, and this directly touched the people of Golchika, for much of their income is derived from furs. From what I could learn, there were three kinds of fox traps in use at Golchika. The first was a large wooden contrivance on the dead-fall principle, by which the victim was crushed by the fall of a baulk of timber. The second, used by the Siberiaks, was an iron gin, like an English rat trap, but with fangless jaws. The third, I never saw at work, but a model was made by Sylkin's

[1] *Ibis*, 1897, vol. iii.

son, Nerobi. It works by means of a strong spring, which, when released by the raising of the bait, allows a stout block of wood studded with long iron pins to crash down and impale the animal. When the Samoyedes go fox-catching, they track their quarry to his lair. They then scrape away the snow with a long-handled bone instrument, shaped something like the "back scratchers" that our ancestors used in a less polite age, and set a trap at the entrance of the hole. They say that thus the fox will not suspect human interference, as he would do if he smelt the taint of hands on the snow. Sometimes they smash the ice at the edge of a pool, and set a trap at the place where the animal will come to drink. A few years ago a mammoth was found close to Golchika, and all through the winter the natives fed their dogs and baited their traps with frozen meat that was many times older than history.

In 1914, white foxskins cost thirty roubles apiece for picked pelts. That was considered cheap. The previous year the price was forty roubles (£4). That was for winter skins. White fox is sometimes sold in the summer, when it is grey in colour, and it is then known as "crossed fox," because of the dark markings on the shoulders. Real blue foxskins now fetch a hundred roubles or more apiece. Not so very many years ago they could be bought for five or ten roubles each, but that was in the golden days of the fur trade, before the poor native knew the value of his goods in the Western markets. Nowadays it is almost as cheap to buy furs in Yenesiesk as to buy them in the *chooms*.

At the end of August, some Dolgans came to

BLUE FOX.

Prokopchuk and sold him a blue fox cub, a couple of months old. He passed it on to us, and for a week it lived in a kennel outside our hut. It was a beautiful thing, blue-grey from the tips of its furry ears to its little tag of a brush. Even its eyes, set wide apart in its droll, innocent face, were tinted to match its coat. The *koursa*, as the Samoyedes called him, never really became tame, although he showed more anger than fear when handled, but he was an exacting charge, and was apt to rouse his guardians at all hours with his screams for condensed milk. He constantly mistook Jest for one of his relations (now, alas, a flaccid pelt hung up in Prokopchuk's store), and pursued her with hideous squalls of affection, much to that respectable animal's disgust. If he was given a piece of fish, he hastened to bury it, growling very imposingly as he did so. He would then find it again a few minutes later, and congratulate himself upon his achievement. And so on, *da capo* until the delights of discovery had staled. Poor little fellow! It would have been impossible to bring him all the way to England, and so when we left Golchika, we gave him to Anastasia Ivanowna, who had a notable gift for taming wild animals, and I trust that he throve under her care.

The fox cub has tempted me from the paths of ornithology, but there are few birds left on my list to chronicle, except the little finches and their like. A few pairs of snow-buntings lived among the bleached driftwood by the waterside, and one or two white wagtails bred in the roofs of the balagans. A pair of mealy redpolls haunted the island for some time: I shot one which turned out to be a non-breeding male of *Linota linaria*. Wheatears and shorelarks were fairly common on the dry hills on the tundra. The latter were among the earliest birds to breed, and on 20th July I shot a male in the pretty spotted plumage of the first summer. The Lapland bunting was most abundant. When I first arrived at Golchika, the males were still in song, and their brief, cheery music, uttered as they soared aloft and then dropped down into the willows, often gave a touch of liveliness to the dreariest scenes. They had also a little long-drawn call which was so high pitched that it seemed to have a kind of ventriloquial property. More than once I scanned the skyline for a distant golden plover, only to find that I had been deceived by a bunting almost at my feet. I found many nests of this bird upon the tundra, but my efforts to photograph the parents feeding their young were a complete failure. I hid the tent carefully, and sat with the camera focussed upon a half-fledged brood for the greater part of two days, and was not able to expose a single plate. The old buntings frequently adopted the waders' trick of shamming a broken wing in order to draw an enemy from the nest. Later on, one became heartily weary of the little monotonous double note, with which, as by the strokes of a tiny gong, they announced a trespass on their breeding-grounds. In August, the old birds went up to the higher tundra to moult, while the young broods gathered into flocks and visited the neighbourhood of the balagans as confidingly as sparrows, which, in the dun and brown plumage of their immaturity, at a first glance they resemble.

At Golchika, where all birds began to nest on the same date, all eggs of the same species hatched out on the same day. Thus you had Little Stint Day, when every marsh and streamside buzzed with little stints; Lapland Bunting Day, when the tundra was full of Lapland buntings, and so on. Red-throated Pipit Day came last of all, for these were the latest of all the birds to breed. They waited for the mosquitoes. The red-throated pipit was the only bird on the tundra that was a songster. He was of the blood royal of the skylark, and it was fine to watch his glorious parachute from the upper air to the accompaniment of a rain of melody. Like the skylarks, these pipits were very quarrelsome. Each pair occupied a certain patch of ground—generally a shallow glen where a stream trickled down from the tundra—and guarded it jealously. I have seen a bird chase away a pair of ruffs of four times his own size, and they constantly bickered with the shorelarks when the latter strayed down from the hilltops.

The red-throated pipits fed their young for some time after they left the nest. I have a note that I saw a female with a bill full of mosquitoes on 7th August, long after all other birds except the geese and divers were able to shift for themselves. It seemed as if they fed their fledglings almost up to the day of the return migration, for about 15th August they all disappeared, together with the mosquitoes.

It was not easy to obtain information about the birds from the natives, partly owing to my ignorance of the language, and partly because they themselves divided all birds into two classes: those that could be eaten, and those that could not. They were sapient concerning the first division, which included ducks and geese; but they took little interest in the second, which comprised most other birds. The following names were given to me by an old Samoyede who recognised the skins in my collection. I am indebted to Miss Czaplicka for the proper English spelling of the native sounds.

Willow-Grouse	Abba
Pintail Duck	Nyavoie
Goose	Dgiotu
Golden Plover	Tilyokko
Godwit	Tufek
Seagull	Tannykka
King-Eider	Tulloni

Golchika was the most difficult place in the world from which to make observations on bird-migration. This was partly owing to the enormous extent of the country, but more so because it was so far north that the different species that passed on their way up the river were no guide to the region whence they came. On the English coasts, a rush of greater wheatears means a migration from Iceland, and the appearance of bramblings and bluethroats spells movement in Scandinavia. But in most cases, Golchika itself was an Ultima Thule of winged things; and the visitors from the north were so often represented on its own breeding list that it was impossible to say whether they were passengers from higher latitudes or no.

I observed only two species which did not also nest at Golchika. The first was a hirundine bird, which, on 14th July—a cold, wet evening—was observed hawking backwards and forwards over a lake on the tundra. I

A SUMMER ON THE YENESEI

shot at it twice as it swung past me, and missed it both times. *What's hit's history: what's missed's mystery.* The identity of the stranger will never be known for certain, but from its white rump, from its size, which was greater than that of our common swift, and from its dull underparts, I believe that the bird was the Siberian swift (*Cypselus pacificus*), a native of Eastern Asia, which ranges as far north as Kamchatka. At any rate, a hirundine of any species is an interesting record from the Yenesei tundras.

The next movement among non-breeding species was noticeable on 12th August, when, for two or three days, numerous little parties of turnstones passed the island.

The departure of the breeding birds is more difficult to chronicle. The following dates are only approximate, but they may give some idea of the disappearance of species after species as the summer declined :

Grey Phalarope	Departed August 5th.
Curlew-Sandpiper	,, August 15th.
Shore-Lark	,, August 10th.
Red-throated Pipit	,, August 15th.
Arctic Tern	,, August 18th.
Red-necked Phalarope	,, August 18th.
White Wagtail	,, August 20th.
Little Stint	,, (Most of the birds) before August 25th.
Temminck's Stint	,, (Most of the birds) before August 25th.
Dunlin	,, About August 25th.
Ruff	,, August 25th.
Lapland Bunting	,, August 25th.
Snow-Bunting	,, August 25th.
Wheatear	,, August 20th.
Golden Plover	,, September 2nd.
Grey Plover	,, August 25th.
Ringed Plover	,, September 2nd.

Prokopchuk declared that the snowy owl and the willow-grouse sometimes lingered until October.

One of the most interesting little facts connected with the autumn migration at the river's mouth was the appearance of a number of young bluethroats of the year during the first week in August, and they haunted the river banks and balagans until the end of the month. Mr. Popham[1] also mentions that he saw young birds at Golchika in August. As far as I know, the bluethroat does not breed north of Pustoy, which is a hundred miles higher up the river. It seems as if with this species there was a tendency among the young birds of the year to perform a wholly meaningless migration to the north. The fact would not perhaps be worth remarking if there was not some slight evidence that the young of some other species travel northwards during the few weeks that pass between their flight from the nest and the time that they must join in the great autumnal migration to the south. What can be the purpose of such wanderings when neither weather nor hunger press the birds to move? Is it possible that the call of the north, which has been answered so many, many times in the life of the race, can meet with a response thus early in the life of the individual bird? I wonder if it is so.

[1] *Ibis*, 1897, vol. iii.

CHAPTER VIII.

First days at Golchika—The coming of the steamers—Our hut—The commissariat—A home-made sundial—The *Lena*—Disturbance in the Prokopchuk family—"The Alcohol King"—Mosquitoes—Native fishermen—The people of the balagan—An unwilling ferryman—The spell of Golchika.

FOR the first fortnight of our stay at Golchika we lived, as I have already mentioned, in the bakehouse of the Antonoffs. During that time the place was more or less in a buzz of excitement, owing to the coming of the steamers from Yenesiesk, which brought the first news of the outer world which had reached the river's mouth since the previous September. A day or two after the *Oryol* had returned, the *Yenesei*, belonging to Mr. Kutcherenkoff, came in; and, on 4th July, the Government steamer *Turukhansk* appeared. With each of these ships, summer visitors arrived at Golchika. Kutcherenkoff brought two men to work in his fish-packing station. One was a young Siberiak from Yenesiesk, Micha by name, and the other was a Jew, a political exile of the lower sort, called Cherniavinski. His sentence was for ten years, of which he had already served eight in the service of Kutcherenkoff. His crime was that he had belonged to some proscribed society; but his enforced stay in Siberia had taken away his taste for politics, for he was wont to declare that when he had served his time he would never again meddle with politics. Cherniavinski was the only soul, with the exception of our own party, with whom I could talk in any language except Russian. He often ferried me across the river when I went on shooting excursions, and we found that we understood each other fairly well if he spoke in Yiddish and I replied in German. These two men had been sent to Golchika by Kutcherenkoff, ostensibly to help with the fishing, but actually to keep watch over the dealings of Prokopchuk, their nominal superior. As Kutcherenkoff's packing station was on the island beside that of Antonoff, Cherniavinski and his companion lived in one of the little balagans close to the waterside.

The *Turukhansk* also brought as passengers two workmen for Antonoff. These were Alexis Petrovitch, a tall, long-bearded Lett, and his handsome son Vassilli. With the addition of all these newcomers, Golchika became quite a populous place, especially when the Samoyedes began to come in from the tundra. The native settlement, which on our first arrival consisted only of Sylkin's hut and two or three *chooms*, increased until by the middle of July there were seven or eight families encamped beside the river bank; and the neighbouring tundra was dotted with herds of grazing reindeer. Much of the marsh was already free from snow, and the rivers, which until now had overflowed their banks, subsided until long stretches of sand lay bare on each side of the mouths of the Golchika.

But meanwhile it behoved us to look about for a

A Dolgan Cap.

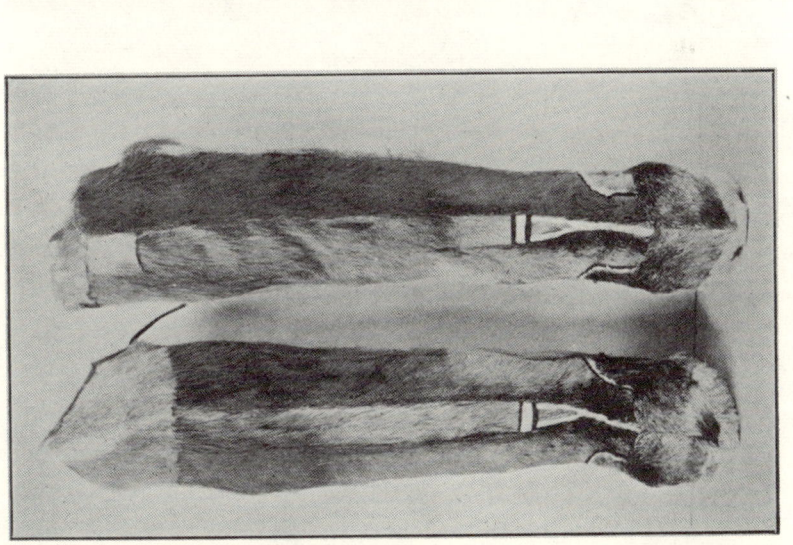

Yurak Boots.

A SUMMER ON THE YENESEI

new lodging, for, kind and hospitable as the Antonoffs were, we could not occupy their bakehouse indefinitely. Michael Petrovitch himself was to go to Krasnoyarsk in the *Turukhansk* to sell his furs, and during his absence, the house was to be rebuilt and enlarged. It is true that we had brought a tent with us, but Golchika is the worst place in the world for camping, and its flat, boggy shores, under their covering of snow, looked most uninviting. At this juncture, however, Prokopchuk came forward with a proposal. On the mainland, half-way between his house and the mouth of the river, stood a disused bathhouse, which at one time had belonged to his workmen. With a little alteration it was turned into a capital hut, and a few days later we moved into it.

The hut stood on the mainland, about half a verst up the left arm of the Golchika River. From the door you could see everything that went on in every corner of the settlement. If you turned to the left, and looked down the river and over to the island, you could see the Antonoffs' house, with the two fishing stations in front of it; and, were you curious enough to take field-glasses, you could see Anastasia hanging up her washing to dry, and Nura and Tania gossiping with Vassilli, the handsome young Lett. If you turned to the east you looked up the Golchika River and saw the low hills which bordered the tundra; and nearer at hand, just where the river disappeared behind a curve a quarter of a mile away, was the low grey homestead of Prokopchuk. If you looked straight in front, you saw the shallow Golchika River and the island, and beyond them, on the opposite mainland, the *chooms* of the native settlement, which stuck up like a row of tiny pyramids. And if this was not far enough, you might climb on to the roof and look beyond the island and beyond the *chooms*, right away to where of an evening the sun went down to the wide horizon of the Yenesei.

Our hut stood close to the water's edge. Like all the balagans of the country, it was built of driftwood with a turfed roof, and as the chinks were all stopped with moss, it was as warm and cosy as only a wooden house can be. There were two rooms in the hut, each with a door which opened on to the river bank. The right-hand one, which was taken by Miss Czaplicka, Miss Curtis, and myself, was a little the larger of the two. The smaller room belonged to Mr. Hall and Vassilli.

The wooden settles of the bathhouse had been left in place, and when sheepskins and sleeping-bags were spread upon them, they made luxurious bedsteads. Each room had a stove. The Russian stove is a notable institution—an iron box on four short legs. It becomes hot in five minutes, and in half an hour the room is warm. We used to do most of our cooking over these stoves—such at least as could not be done outside over an open fire. Our balagan was a sumptuous one, in that each room had a good window. Along our sill Miss Curtis insisted upon arranging a box of matches, a bottle of Worcester sauce, and a piece of soap, because she said that it made the place look like a shop. That it certainly did, and confirmed the people of Golchika in their belief that, in spite of

A SUMMER ON THE YENESEI

our denials, we were really merchants, who had chosen disguise as a subtle kind of advertisement.

When we had put up a few pegs and shelves the hut began to look quite homelike. Gerasim Androvitch, who, I think, was as pleased with the place as if he had been going to live there himself, lent us a small table, besides which we had brought another with us, and also some campstools. Needless to say, there was not a great deal of space for the possessions of three people in a room twelve feet by fifteen, and therefore during the daytime many things were piled up on the bunks. Miss Czaplicka's bed contained notebooks and calipers, and above it gradually appeared a fine assortment of native implements—knives, pipes, and pieces of reindeer harness—hung upon the wall. Miss Curtis was fortunate in that her "stock in trade" consisted of brushes and sketching books which would pack away flat; but my corner was the most crowded of all, and whenever I was not occupying it myself there was not a square inch which was not strewn with a collection of birds' skins, photographic apparatus, and specimen boxes.

Although the Golchika flowed within twenty yards of the door, it was too bitter and muddy to drink, and all the water had to be fetched from a little stream which ran down from the tundra, about a furlong away. Wood was to be had for the gathering, for at Golchika the river banks for miles are littered with the timber which the spring floods bring down from the forests. Most of the driftwood is willow and poplar, thoroughly seasoned by the water, and the inhabitants use nothing else, either for building or burning.

On 4th July, when the *Turukhansk* returned to the south, we said good-bye to Michael Petrovitch, and we did so with all the more regret that it was uncertain whether we should meet him again before we started for England. When Michael Petrovitch went to Krasnoyarsk, he wore his town clothes. Instead of the characteristic fur cap, black velvet coat, and *sapakgi*,[1] which he wore at Golchika, he cropped his hair and put on a bow tie, cheap yellow boots, and a bowler hat which was many sizes too small for him. He fancied himself immensely in these clothes, and was quite hurt that we should prefer his former suit.

After the *Turukhansk* had sailed away beyond the misty, quivering horizon, Golchika settled down seriously for the fishing season. Work went on, day and night alike—in fact, there is no night in Golchika during the summer. Everybody ate and slept when it pleased him, but the usual hour for going to bed was 3 a.m., and consequently, as a rule, nobody stirred before midday. These hours were most inconvenient to a photographer, for although the sun was shining for every hour out of the twenty-four, yet when he was low on the horizon the quality of the light was not nearly so good as when he was higher in the sky, but that was the time when most of the pictures had to be made. The people seemed to come out like rabbits when the best of the day was over, and worked until the following morning. There was no standard

[1] Long boots.

clock in Golchika. Of course our watches had been set right when we left the *Oryol*, but in a week or two they began to vary. One gained five minutes, another lost ten, and so on. One morning we visited the Antonoffs at an hour which we supposed to be eleven o'clock, but which they declared to be only eight. In proof of this they showed us a home-made sundial, devised by Alexis Petrovitch, the Lettish workman. It consisted of a nail driven into a block of wood, and the noontide shadow had been checked by the compass. Accordingly we all readjusted our watches, and for several days tried to live by the new ruling. But we soon discovered that something was wrong, for the sun, instead of reaching the zenith at noon, arrived there at ten o'clock. We therefore went to look at the sundial again, and found that when Alexis had placed the compass beside the indicator, the magnetism of the latter had deflected the needle. When a *wooden* peg was substituted for the iron one, the reading was quite different.

On 18th July, Kutcherenkoff, who had been trading at the Sopochnaya, called at Golchika on his way southwards. He had been very kind to us, and it was mainly to him that we owed our comfortable quarters in the hut, for his letter of recommendation had made a great impression in our favour on Prokopchuk. I had been working on the island all day, and on my way home I called upon him in his steamer, which was moored beside the fishing station. He invited me to take *tchai* in his cabin, and we mutually praised the weather, but that was as far as our conversation could go. He knew no English and I knew no Russian, so that we could only look dumbly at each other and laugh apologetically at ourselves. Then, luckily, my host had an inspiration and called his boatswain into the cabin. This man was a Greek, who spoke both French and Russian, and who, consequently, could interpret for us. After that we got on splendidly, for what I said in French the Greek repeated in Russian to Mr. Kutcherenkoff, and *vice versa*. The merchant was very entertaining, for he had travelled up and down the river for many years, and as the Yenesei, in spite of its size, is like a village street—a street seventeen hundred miles long!—where everybody knows everything about everybody else's business, he had many curious tales to relate. He himself, although one of the richest merchants on the Yenesei, was the grandson of a criminal of peasant extraction, a fact of which he made no secret. One of the feats of his younger days is still celebrated on the Yenesei. Many years before, he and seven other men towed a load of a thousand pouds up the river from Potapooskoye to Yenesiesk. It took them a month to walk the distance, and they wore no boots for the journey—" it was not worth while," as he said with a smile. He had known Captain Wiggins well, and also Schwanenburg, the Courlander, who was associated with the efforts of Wiggins to open up the commerce of the Yenesei. He told me that Schwanenburg spent all his spare time in shooting small birds (*malenki pteetza*) and never laid his gun aside, even when at meals. He constantly left the cabin and ran ashore to shoot some bird whose note he had heard through the porthole. These reminiscences interested me very much, for Schwanenburg collected many specimens for Seebohm, and it is probable that many of the skins now in the National Museum were originally obtained by him. Captain Wiggins is still a name to conjure by on the Lower Yenesei. People even now relate how he made the journey to Krasnoyarsk in the winter-time by horse sledges. Not a hundred yards from our hut there was an interesting relic of one of this daring man's ventures. In 1889 a cargo of animal bones was sent to Golchika for shipment to Europe through the Kara Sea. The barge that carried them went ashore in the Golchika River, and the remains of her hulk, under a heap of bleached bones, can still be seen on the bank. It is pleasant to find that those Englishmen, such as Captain Wiggins and Messrs. Seebohm and Popham, who have visited the Yenesei country, have left behind them a name which is still remembered for their honourable and honest dealing. It is to be hoped that those traders of other nationalities, on whom the mantle of Wiggins has fallen, and whom the ignorant natives and Siberiaks therefore still call *Angliski*, will do nothing to destroy this favourable impression.

After the departure of the *Yenesei*, we began to look forward to the arrival of the Government steamer, the *Lena*, which, with her barge, had left Krasnoyarsk on 20th June and was due to reach Golchika on the 10th of the following month. We looked especially to this vessel to bring our mails—the first that we had received since we left home at the end of May. Therefore, when the steamer arrived, ten days overdue, and there was no post-bag for us, we were all very disappointed.

The coming of the *Lena* was made the occasion for an orgy, both in the *chooms* and in the balagans, and as the revellers were sometimes wont to make a descent upon our hut, we were glad when, in the evening, Madame Antonoff invited us to go to her house for supper. Owing to the building operations, one side of the kitchen had been pulled down, and the fireplace had been taken out. An English "general" would have given a month's notice if she had been asked to cook a meal for about twenty people under such circumstances, but Anastasia stolidly baked her *pirog* and prepared the *samovar* over a makeshift stove in the bedroom. Several of the *Lena's* passengers were in the parlour. Among them was a Polish lady, the wife of a political exile at Turukhansk. Her husband, who, though but thirty-nine years old, had already spent more than sixteen years of his life either in prison or in exile, had been sent to the Yenesei for three years. His sentence would expire in the following spring, and they were both looking forward eagerly to their release from the mosquitoes and monotony of Monastir. This lady very kindly undertook to post our letters for us in Turukhansk, and at her invitation we went aboard the steamer for an hour. The *Lena* compared very unfavourably with the *Oryol* as far as passenger accommodation was concerned, for the cabins were both cramped and dingy. She was, however, the fastest boat on the river, and although the people along the riverside complained bitterly about the conduct of the officials, who would sometimes deposit goods a hundred versts from their destination rather than trouble themselves to put in shore for a second time, she carried most of the Yenesei fish cargoes.

The arrival of the *Lena* caused a great stir in the Prokopchuk household, due to the unexpected appearance of a younger Miss Prokopchuk. This girl was evidently of stronger stuff than poor subdued Marusia, for during the previous summer she had told her father roundly that she would no longer stay at home to see her aunt usurp the place of her mother, and had gone to Krasnoyarsk to educate herself. Now she had come to Golchika for a month to pay a farewell visit before travelling to Europe. She was evidently the favourite child of Gerasim Androvitch — perhaps in his case absence made the heart grow fonder. We surmised that she read him a lecture on the way in which he was consoling himself during his "grass-widowhood," and told him that unless her aunt was sent away immediately she would not remain in the house for a day. It had been arranged that Anastasia Ivanowna should go to Krasnoyarsk in the *Lena*, in order to buy the winter stores. She, however, dreaded lest her strong-minded young niece would destroy her own influence over Gerasim Androvitch; and at the last minute she declined to start unless the girl accompanied her. On the evening before the steamer returned, we went to pay a farewell call. We found Gerasim Androvitch in a more or less inebriated condition, while the rest of the household wore that air of gloomy preoccupation which generally means that the guest has intruded into a family dispute. We were invited into the bedroom, and the demeanour of the whole company was so portentous that the state meal which followed was as imposing as a sacramental rite. Anastasia in particular neither spoke nor ate, but only glowered at us from the end of the table.

Scarcely had we left the house than Marusia ran after us, crying hysterically. Her aunt had just attempted her own life by drinking a bottleful of strong essence of vinegar. The patient was lying outside the door, evidently in great pain. The women of the household, who were all weeping loudly, made no attempt to help her. Old Prokopchuk was hovering round with a glass of raw cognac, which, if he had been allowed to administer it, would probably have killed the sufferer outright, for her mouth was terribly burned with the acid. Rather dim recollections of the instructions received some years previously during a course of lectures on "First Aid to the Injured," counselled the administration of an emetic, and the directions in the medical chest prescribed mustard, magnesia, or baking-soda and water for the purpose. None of these things could be found in the house, however. Then someone remembered that in emergencies plaster from the wall, powdered and mixed with water, was a good substitute. We immediately turned to the walls, but, alas! these had been painted bright blue, and we dare not administer such a fearful and unknown dye on the top of a dose of acid. In the end Miss Czaplicka had the happy inspiration of condensed milk! The woman was very ill for some hours, but towards morning she took a turn for the better. Probably she had judged the dose of poison very accurately, and by giving him a good fright, hoped to reinstate herself in the affections of Gerasim Androvitch. The jealous differences of aunt and niece were finally settled by the arrangement that they should both go down to Krasnoyarsk together; and therefore Gerasim was left alone for the summer, with nobody but Marusia to look after him. At first he was very forlorn, and having nobody to talk to at home, he used to make evening calls at our hut. He frequently walked in with a courtly greeting just about supper-time, and sat there, making agreeable conversation, while the meal was prepared. There was no false shame about Gerasim Androvitch. He was above the convention, so common in our society, of making a pretence of taking leave in order that he might be pressed to stay. He accepted his invitation and his welcome as a matter of course. His son, on the other hand, came very seldom. When he did so, he would neither talk nor eat. The most that anyone could draw out of him was a sedate: "*Nyet spessibo.*" Often he sat in silence for an hour after the meal was finished, because he was too bashful to get up and say good-bye. Generally he was too busy to call. All day long, he and little Michael, the servant, worked on the river-bank, piling up great stacks of firewood for the winter, or else in building new sheds to house the stores that Anastasia Ivanowna would bring back from Krasnoyarsk; and every evening they went over to the island to receive the fish that the boats brought for Kutcherenkoff.

It would be too tedious if I were to tell of our doings every day during our stay at Golchika, for although really full of incident to ourselves, the details of our life would make but humdrum reading. Immediately after breakfast my companions set out to sketch or visit the natives on the other side of the river, and I went for a long ramble over the tundra with gun or camera. We were usually out all day, and only met in the evening. Vassilli was cook, but his culinary efforts, although they were all right as far as they went, required some supervision. We had brought flour with us, but as we found that we could buy excellent bread both from Madame Antonoff and the Prokopchuks, we had no need to use it, which was fortunate, for Vassilli's attempts to bake on one of the wood stoves would not have been very appetising. As the summer went on, fish could almost be had for the asking. In Golchika, indeed, it is a point of etiquette that if a stranger asks for fish you shall *give*, not sell, it to him. The principal fish caught was the omul, a kind of white-fleshed sea trout. It made excellent eating and yielded a very good red caviare. There was also the nyelma, or white salmon. It was larger than the omul, and, I thought, very nasty, for its flesh was pale and flabby, like the flesh of what fishermen call a "spent" fish. Vassilli and I sometimes provided ducks for the pot. We had been warned that the flesh of these Yenesei duck was rank and fishy, but all those that we ate were excellent. Even the flesh of the king-eider, although a little tough, was quite palatable. The eggs of the long-tailed duck, however, had a distinctly fishy flavour. I found a nest with a newly laid clutch, and we scrambled them for supper over a spirit-lamp. The result was excellent, and the fishy taste was really an improvement to the dish. Sometimes we bought a little reindeer meat from Prokopchuk, but, on the whole, the venison was tough and nasty. However, it made a change from perpetual fish and tinned food. It is wonderful how the people in those bitter climates manage to live without either fresh or preserved fruit and vegetables. Potatoes and lemons are both very expensive, owing to the cost of freight down the river, and are only seen on the tables of the better-to-do settlers. It is no wonder that scurvy is very common in Northern Siberia.

The *Lena* and the mosquitoes arrived at Golchika almost on the same day. We had heard so much of these pests, and had brought such a defensive paraphernalia of veils and gloves that we were agreeably surprised to find that things were not nearly as bad as we expected. The mosquito season lasted only for a month, and although they were very tiresome during hot weather, yet for days together, if the wind was cool, we saw nothing of them. I generally took a veil on my excursions into the tundra, but owing to the discomfort of it, and the difficulty of watching a bird through the meshes, I seldom wore it. Luckily the bite of the arctic mosquitoes was not nearly so virulent as that of these insects in the south. The Siberiaks and natives did not seem to mind the nuisance. I have seen a Samoyede go calmly about his business while half a dozen of the brutes straddled their bloodthirsty proboscis into his neck. It is only fair, however, to say that it was an unusually cold season, and this may have accounted for the moderation of their attacks.

A good deal of misconception prevails in England about the climate of Siberia, and if I had been guided by my friends, I should have gone out equipped as for arctic exploration. Of course, in winter the cold is severe, and in June and September it is often very chilly, but during July and August the weather is generally fair, and although never so warm as, for example, a Scottish summer, yet there is plenty of sunshine. A northerly or easterly wind is generally cold, but in winter the Golchikans say that the southerly gales are the most severe. All the inhabitants had something to say of the *pourga*. Sylkin, in particular, was full of tales of this terrible blizzard of the tundra. One night he and another man were returning from Veronsova, a fishing station some four or five versts south of Golchika. On the way they were overtaken by the storm, and utterly lost their bearings. After wandering about the tundra for some time, Sylkin stumbled into a Samoyede cemetery, and realised that instead of reaching Golchika, they were now about three versts higher up the river. He scraped a hole in the snow, and shouted to his companion to do likewise. The storm lasted until the following day, and when Sylkin rose from his lair, he found himself alone. The other had not heard the call, and had wandered on into the blizzard alone. His body was never found. Michael Petrovitch had a yet more terrible experience. He was out alone in his sledge when the *pourga* overtook him. He and his dogs were entombed in a drift, and lay there for six days. Two of the team died, but the rest were able to drag the sledge back to Golchika when the storm had passed.

August the 2nd was kept as a high holiday. It was the Feast of the Blessed Ilia—a saint who seemed to be a kind of Siberian St. Swithin, and exercised a good or baneful influence over the weather, according as his votaries did, or did not, observe his festival. Vassilli believed firmly in the power of the saint, and told the tale of a priest of Achinsk who urged his parishioners to gather in their harvest on the holiday. This displeased St. Ilia so much that he sent down storms and lightning upon their crops and destroyed them all. The Golchikans certainly did not tempt his wrath by working. Instead, they all became gloriously drunk. All day jovial parties reeled along the river bank, and besought their neighbours to join them in their revelry, for the native is a generous fellow, and asks for nothing better than to share his bottle of *vino* with his friends. We, however, kept our door discreetly closed against such boon companions, and allowed Vassilli, who was an expert diplomat, to persuade them that we were not at home—as indeed we were not, in the conventional sense of the phrase.

However, something must have annoyed the saint, for although the morning was very fine, the sky clouded over threateningly towards night. This was disappointing, for on 2nd August, at midnight, the sun dips for a minute or two below the horizon, and we wished to see him set for the first time for two months.

On the following day I went for a long walk down the shore of the Yenesei. The ostensible reason for the excursion was to look for the nesting-grounds of the Buffon's skua, but it was typical of many such rambles that I took over the tundra and along the rivers in August when the first rush of ornithological work was over, and there was time to explore parts of the surrounding country which had previously been overlooked.

I left home early in the morning, and crossed the river to the native settlement. This, however, was deserted, for all the inhabitants were out fishing. Golchika Island lay at the point of a long, swampy peninsula, which formed one side of a vast bay. The shores of this peninsula were low and sandy, and cumbered with driftwood. For more than a furlong from the beach the water of the bay was scarcely knee-deep, and along the shallows the boats of the natives were moored for the day's fishing. They were clumsy, flat-bottomed craft, hired for the season from the Siberiaks. They were rowed by three short, broad-bladed oars, two on one side and one on the other, and they were steered, not by a tiller, but with a paddle. It requires no little skill to steer a heavy Yenesei boat against the wind, and the novice's first attempts generally result in a wonderful and ignominious succession of curves backwards and forwards across the river. When they go a-fishing, the Samoyedes beach the boat upon some sandbank, and one or two members of the family are landed with one end of the net. The rest then row out for a couple of hundred yards, gradually lowering the net as they go, and presently return to the shore, bringing the other end with them. Then the whole family unites to pull the net in. Sometimes it is so heavy with omul that one is reminded of the old pictures of the Miraculous Draught of Fishes. At others it is almost empty. But, whether the catch be good or bad, the natives are always gay and full of chatter. They accept fair or ill weather as it comes, alike without either gratitude or grumbling, and if you ask them whether it will be fine or wet in the morning, they answer stolidly, "How can we tell? We are not acquainted with God!" The fishing at Golchika has been growing worse for the last eight years. The record season's catch was 15,000 pouds, but in the year of which I write scarcely 2000 pouds were exported, though at Breokoffsky Ostrov, two hundred versts to the south, one net alone landed 700 pouds of omul. Each boat chooses its own pitch and works there all day. In between the hauls, the natives sit on the sand and smoke or make tea.

When I came up, a number of Siberian herring-gulls were flying round the boats, and presently I shot one bird, which fell wounded into the water. The oldest and dirtiest of the natives gave a roar, and pushed off his boat. I tumbled into the bows and took the oars, and away we went in pursuit, while all the rest of the family ran up and down the shore in high amusement. The gull led us a fine chase into the river, and by the time that we had retrieved it, both my Samoyede and I were exceedingly hot. Just then a second boat came along, manned by a regular kindergarten, the eldest of whom could not have been more than twelve years old. They promptly began to race us to the shore, yelling with glee and splashing all over the place. The natives thoroughly entered into the joke, and scooped away with the paddle while I tugged at the oars, but the kindergarten were already past-masters of oarsmanship, and beat us squarely by half a length to everybody's delight. Afterwards I distributed cigarettes to everybody who was over ten years old, and we parted the best of friends.

After leaving the natives, I went along the shores of the great bay, which were as firm and hard to walk upon as a rolled gravel path. It was a treat to walk along easily at a brisk pace instead of stumbling over the sphagnum and tussocks inland. The tundra itself was terribly heavy to walk upon, and what with the frequent stoppages to identify some bird, I do not think that we ever averaged more than two miles an hour when crossing it. At the end of the day, one was apt to suffer from a complaint whose nature will be sufficiently indicated by its name — I christened it *tundra legs*!

About twelve miles from Golchika, where a stream ran down the beach, stood the small turf-roofed balagan of Kuria. The sand was strewn with fishing nets spread out to dry, and a couple of boats lay off the shore. Four pretty Siberian girls, who were salting fish, looked up much surprised at my approach. I asked them to give me some boiling water to make *tchai*,

A Native Fisherman.

Natives Fishing by the Yenesei.

whereupon they not only fetched tea, but in the hospitable custom of the country brought out a fine fish. In return I invited them to taste an *angliski riba, i.e.* English fish, and loud was their laughter when I produced a tin of skipper sardines. They told me that their names were Maria, Olga, Elena, and Katrina. They were what are known as *townsmen* on the Yenesei—that is, they came down the river for the summer and fished for themselves, not for either Antonoff or Prokopchuk as the Golchika people did. The latter looked down upon the townsmen as upon an inferior class. This family had come from Turukhansk in the barge of the *Oryol*, and had camped at lonely Kuria. Their flour sacks and fish barrels were stacked beside the stream, and the rest of their worldly goods were contained in two gaudy Russian coffers. For six weeks they fished night and day, hoping to earn enough to live upon for all the rest of the year, and at the end of August they would travel south again. They were all fine-looking girls, tanned by the sun. None of them had ever seen a doctor, and none of them could either read or write. All the summer through they never saw a stranger's face unless they went over to Golchika, but there was little enough time for that. Day and night they worked at the fishing, hauling on the nets or packing their catch into barrels. Each ate when she was hungry, and slept when she was sleepy, without any regard for time. And behind the balagan, the water ran down from the melting snowdrifts with a little musical *drip-drip*, like a clock whose perpetual ticking marked the flight of the short, sweet northern summer. The life of these balagan people was hard and monotonous enough. Nature had provided them with only two things in abundance, wood and water, both of which lay outside their doors. Nevertheless they seemed very happy and contented, and we had quite an enjoyable picnic on the shore, until presently two men landed from the boat and joined us. Neither of them seemed quite to have recovered from the feast of the previous day, especially one, a hot-coloured red-haired young man with a most unprepossessing cast of countenance, and I liked him still less from what I understood of his sly winks to his neighbour and his remarks to the girls. He was very inquisitive, and began to play with my gun, asking if it was for sale. I replied no, but he still seemed so reluctant to give it up that I feared he wanted to keep it altogether.

I therefore told him that it was a *horroshie angliski rouschye*—a splendid English gun (English being the equivalent of the treble X hall-mark in Siberia)—and under the pretext of showing him how the ejector worked, I persuaded him to give it up to me, and slipped in a couple of cartridges. After this he did not meddle with the gun any more, but instead tried to beg first my binoculars and secondly my gold watch. I took refuge in the ever-useful, "I do not understand Russian," which always parried inconvenient questions, and in order to distract his attention, suggested that the party should be photographed. This proposal met with great approval, and the whole family ran into the balagan, whence they presently returned dressed in their finest clothes—the women in holiday kerchiefs and the men in their long boots and canvas weather-coats. The red-haired man became more officious than ever, and pushed them all into their places while he gave them his views on photography. It is a curious thing that, all the world over, a man who is speaking about his own job never patronises his audience. It is only when he talks some kind of "shop" in which he is only an amateur that he is prone to condescend. If my rapacious friend had been asked to explain the difference between omul and nyelma, or some other (to him) equally ridiculous question about fishing, he would have replied simply enough. As it was, he gave himself great airs, as he explained the camera to the rest of the party, and lectured them pragmatically upon their behaviour. He was the only one who could write, and after the sitting, he laboriously traced some hieroglyphics in my pocket-book, to which address a print was to be sent from England.

After saying farewell to the balaganers, I went for a long ornithological ramble over the tundra, the results of which are chronicled elsewhere, and towards evening, returned to Golchika. Most of the natives were still away, and for some time I looked in vain for someone to ferry me over the river. Presently a Yurak put off in a tiny canoe, and when I hailed him, he very obligingly turned back and took me in as passenger. However, instead of turning down the river to the hut, which was about a furlong away, he paddled across to the island, and said that he was going to the Antonoffs' house. I asked him again to take me to the other side, whereupon he explained volubly that if I would disembark here, and walk across the island with him, that one of the men at the fishing station would ferry me over the other arm of the river. I sat where I was and repeated that I did not understand Russian, and wanted to go to Prokopchuk's. My Charon expostulated and gesticulated for another five minutes. Then, finding me still immovable, he scratched his head ruefully, and his perplexity was so comic that I could not help laughing, although it seemed too bad to trouble the poor man. While he was standing thus, a woman came out of one of the *chooms*, and asked what he was doing. He evidently replied that he did not know what to do with this mad *Angliski*. His better half gave him some tart advice, acting upon which he tried to pull the canoe up the beach with me inside it. However, it was too heavy, and as he could not leave the little boat in the water, he was forced to make the best of a bad job. Shrugging his shoulders resignedly, but quite good-temperedly, he embarked again, and paddled round the island to the hut, where a glass of *vino* made amends for his trouble in going out of his way.

Golchika was seen at its best late on those August evenings, when the sun, just dipping to the northern horizon, spread the glamour of sunset and afterglow over the tundra. The low, flat marshes lay in the profound stillness of dew-fall, and along the riverbank, the little *chooms*, and their attendant stacks of driftwood, were ranged darkly against the sunset. Even the voices of the birds were hushed, except when far away up the valley a diver whistled to its brood, or a flight of waders passed overhead. A holy peace seemed to brood over the whole vast land from Yenesei to the Taimyr.

Then just as the calm was deepest, the tired Samoyedes rowed home from the day's fishing. Their subdued voices broke the silence, just as the passing of the boats dappled the surface of the river with ripples. Sometimes they sang—a low, monotonous chant with a little catch in it—music at its baldest—harmony as crude as the lip-lap of the lazy water under the boat, or the footfall of the reindeer on the tundra moss. Crude, mystic, and melancholy, their song sounded the day's "Last Post," and the night breeze, bearing it over the tundra, found an echo there.

CHAPTER IX.

Bird's-nesting on the Golchika—A morning call—Grey phalarope—Dunlin—A Dolgan—Red-throated divers—Pintail duck—Richardson's skua—Peregrine falcon—Sylkin's perplexity—Willow-grouse—*Vino*—A fish hunt—White-fronted geese—Grey plovers—A narrow escape—A bird pirate—Plovers' eggs.

ABOUT fifteen versts from Golchika, up the valley of the Golchika River, was a marsh containing a number of small lakes. Sylkin said that several years before, Mr. H. L. Popham had found the nest of the *chorna chika*—either the long-tailed or pomatorhine skua—there. He gave such a glowing account of the ducks and geese which bred along the river-bank that I arranged to go there with him, accompanied by Vassilli, as soon as the floods caused by the melting of the snow should have subsided sufficiently. This was not until 11th July. Sylkin had promised to call for us at 9 a.m. At five o'clock, however, we were aroused by a very inebriated Yurak who beat upon the door, crying out to his "sister" to give him some medicine for his headache! Vassilli, whose manner with the natives was perfect, being a blend of patronage and camaraderie, went out, and after some difficulty persuaded the sufferer to go away and sleep off his carouse at home.

In the usual happy-go-lucky native way, Sylkin

did not arrive until noon. His canoe was just big enough to hold three people, two guns, and a kettle, and it needed some care to stow away my camera, but in the end I was glad that I had taken the latter.

We rowed past the house of Prokopchuk, and round the point beyond which lay the open tundra. Vassilli and I soon landed on the left bank, and leaving Sylkin to pull the canoe against the stream, which here ran swiftly, we tramped over the bog. The marsh was still half submerged, and in the drier parts it was overgrown with dwarf willows which had not yet broken into bloom. These willows were full of Temminck's stints, but the latter are very late breeding birds, and we found only one nest, which contained fresh eggs. Presently, Vassilli flushed a male grey phalarope from a clutch of four eggs. Like all the nests of these species found at Golchika, the situation was so wet that the bird must literally have been sitting in the water. Reeves were very common, but we did not stop to hunt for their nests in the coarse herbage, for I was anxious to press on to the breeding-grounds of the geese. In the rough tussocky grass, we flushed a Lapland bunting from five eggs, and Vassilli shot a long-tailed duck. Dunlin were so common that their husky *pchurr* was heard everywhere, but the Siberian dunlin seems not to use that shrill, trilling call that is so characteristic of the bird's British nesting-grounds. We did not beat this bog very exhaustively, for it was within easy reach of Golchika, and might therefore be worked another day. When we reached the bend of the river, we waited until Sylkin came up in his canoe, and made him ferry us over to the right bank. This was even marshier than the other side, and at each step we sank above our knees into the sphagnum. Red and black-throated divers were swimming on the brimming pools, and Siberian river gulls were certainly breeding in the vicinity, although we could not find the nests. I shot another grey phalarope here—a female this time. The nests of this species are not easy to find, for the phalaropes do not advertise their whereabouts as do the plover and stints. The sitting bird slips quietly away through the herbage, or else flits round and round the intruder like a great moth, uttering its shrill *drrrt-drrrt* note at intervals. About a furlong from the river-bank, where the flat marsh gave place to a row of low hills, there was a *choom*, and the surrounding tundra was dotted with herds of grazing reindeer. Presently we heard a whoop, and one of the natives dashed up on a sledge. He was a Dolgan, as his handsome embroidered bonnet testified, and he was evidently very eager to find out who we were. The native, however, like most other primitive people, has naturally good manners, and will not directly question a newcomer. To be a stranger on the Yenesei is a passport to considerate treatment and courtesy. It is an unwritten law that a stranger shall not pay for his fish. It is given to him freely. This is very different from the custom of an English village, where, too often, the cry is, "Here's a stranger—let's rook him!"

So this Dolgan only grinned at us in friendly wise, until Vassilli told him that Sylkin was near by; and then he shook up his rein with a shout and dashed away like the wind to find his old friend. For every native on the tundra knows every other, from Dudinka to Dickson, and from the Pyasina to the Ob, and recognises them by face and name whether they belong to his own *orda* or not.

A little farther on, where the marshes were still flooded, a pair of red-throated divers screamed anxiously. I waded out for a hundred yards through the sedge, and found the nest. When first built, the birds must have been able to swim right up to it, but the water had subsided, and now they were obliged to drag themselves for twelve or fifteen feet over the sphagnum, which was scored by their breasts as though by the coulter of a plough. I was splashing my way back through the swamp, when Vassilli whistled to warn me that a *chorna chika*—a Richardson's skua—was stooping at a bird in the willow scrub, about a hundred yards away. We both ran to the spot, and found that the prey was a pintail duck. At first I thought that the bird was a female with a nest, for it only flopped helplessly over the grass, as if willing to draw us from the place; but after it was secured it turned out to be a drake in the middle of the moult, and quite an interesting specimen, partly in breeding, and partly in the so-called eclipse plumage. Most of the primary wing feathers had been shed, and the bird was quite unable to fly. The skua sheered off at my approach, and I could not have a shot at it. It belonged to the light-breasted form of the species, as did all the other Richardson's skuas that I saw on the Yenesei. It is probably the Eastern form of the race. Meanwhile Vassilli went on to the higher tundra, and flushed a peregrine falcon from an eyrie at the top of a steep, grassy mound. The nest contained three eggs, which all were hopelessly addled, and were so discoloured by lying in the nest that it seemed as if the bird must have incubated them for weeks. Vassilli tried to shoot her as she swooped overhead, but she was too quick for him, and kept out of shot, though her cries pursued us a long way up the river. Half a mile farther on, we picked up Sylkin and the kettle. There was no fuel except the green willow twigs around, but Vassilli, who, like a true Siberiak, could make a fire out of nothing, produced a slip of wood from the bottom of the canoe, and soon made a blaze which looked cheerful enough, for the evening was dull and grey, and the wind was uncommonly cold. Before us, the river, broken up by shoals and sandspits, meandered away into the tundra; and on each side, the wide, flat plain stretched on, so it seemed, into infinity. A curious restlessness always seized me when I watched that immense horizon. Not to speak of its own mysterious lure, a whole ornithological wonderland lay behind it; but the tundra is one of the most inaccessible of hunting-grounds in the world, and it will be many years before the wonderful bird life that must exist in the secret river valleys and mountains of the Taimyr is thoroughly investigated.

Sylkin roused me from a brown study by a question

which had evidently been perplexing him all day. Were there geese in England? If so, why did I come up the Golchika to look for their eggs? If not, what sort of a country could it be? I therefore gave him a succinct discourse on the migration of birds, which is probably the shortest lecture that has ever been delivered on the subject. Translated from the original pidgin-Russ, it ran something as follows:

In summer—weather warm—geese plenty to eat—eggs and little geese at Golchika.

In winter—weather very cold—ice on river—geese go to England to eat.

A promising piece of marsh lay in front of the mound where we were resting, and this time Sylkin went bird's-nesting also. He beat Vassilli hollow at the work. This was partly because Vassilli cared nothing for either eggs or birds unless he could turn them into either an omelette or a stew afterwards. Presently he put up a willow-grouse. The bird feigned a broken wing, and Vassilli, falling into the trap, instead of shooting her at once, followed her as she dodged through the whortle bushes. When she had decoyed him for a certain distance, she sprang up out of shot, and boomed away unhurt, while Sylkin roared with laughter at Vassilli's sheepish face. The bird had been sitting upon eleven hard-set eggs. The nest was exactly like that of a partridge, being a mere hollow scratched in the ground. While I went back to the canoe to fetch my camera, Vassilli tried to revenge himself on the grouse for having fooled him, but she was wise, and did not return. Meanwhile Sylkin had found a little stint's nest and snared the female upon the eggs by means of a string noose. I found another clutch shortly afterwards, and presently flushed a red-necked phalarope from a nest with three eggs. Lapland buntings were very common in the coarse, tussocky ground where the marshes abutted on to the mudhills, and we took two nests, in each case with half-fledged young. Some arctic terns were breeding in a deep marsh on our right hand, but we did not look for their nests. Every half-verst or so, a wide, muddy stream flowed sluggishly into the river, and we were obliged to wait for Sylkin and his ferry boat. He was having hard work, for the wind and the current were both dead against him. Earlier in the evening the sky had been full of sleet showers, but these gradually cleared away, and by midnight the sun blazed out from the fringe of the cloud rack. The light was so rich and golden that it looked, even if it did not feel, warm, but the birds, following their usual custom, were all at roost; and for three hours we saw very few of them, except when a drowsy Temminck's stint fluttered out of the willows. Vassilli and I beat systematically round a large lake; and presently he put up a cock willow-grouse, which only flew for a short distance and then perched on a hillock.

After his last mistake, Vassilli was burning to avenge himself upon all the grouse tribe, so he stalked the bird elaborately, and shot it. A long-tailed skua flew past us. These bold, bad marauders fly up and down the river night and day without resting, like spirits of evil. About 1.30 a.m. we returned to the river-bank to pick up Sylkin. The accounts of my excursions

WILLOW GROUSE ♀ (LAGOPUS ALBUS).

EGGS OF GREY PLOVER (SQUATAROLA SQUATAROLA).

EGGS OF CURLEW-SANDPIPER (EROLIA FERRUGINEA).

from Golchika seem so often to be merely the records of meals that I am almost ashamed to say that here we had some more food, six hours after the last. The only excuse is that tramping over a swamp in the crisp air of a Siberian night whets the appetite more thoroughly than anything else that I know of. Vassilli and I had bread and cheese; to Sylkin, who, as a Samoyede, was immune from ptomaine poisoning, we gave some ham which had been condemned by our commissariat department at the hut. Sylkin, however, seemed to enjoy his highly flavoured ration, to which was added a tot of *vino* to keep the cold out. *Vino* on the Yenesei is the popular name for prepared vodka. Vodka itself is nearly pure alcohol, and the natives cannot afford to drink it in its raw state. Therefore they dilute it with water, and in order to preserve the burning flavour, they doctor it with vinegar, pepper, or anything else that will give it a sting. We used even to mix our brew of *vino* with curry powder and Worcester sauce. The hotter it was, the more the natives liked it, and even the women can gulp down a draught that would blister the throat of a European. Sylkin tossed off the decoction approvingly, and quoted as a grace his favourite maxim that a little drink was good.

On the opposite bank of the river stood a large sledge. Vassilli and Sylkin discussed it for some time, and then the former explained in graphic pantomime that it belonged to the gods of the natives, to whom they prayed. In some of the *chooms* there is a sledge set apart for sacred purposes, and occasionally a white foxskin is hung up outside the tent as a shammanistic offering; but whether this was really a kind of wayside sacrifice to the spirits of the flood and fell, I cannot say.

Close to where we sat, a large pool discharged its water into the river by an outlet which descended the bank in three cascades. Presently Vassilli discovered that three fair-sized fish were lurking in the stream, and he and Sylkin began a hunt, with the idea of driving the fish into the shallows, where they might be shot. They both became wildly excited and thoroughly wet, while their shouts must assuredly have scared away any birds that may have been roosting in the neighbourhood. They would have continued their sport until the sun was high, had I not called them away at last.

Half a mile farther on, a pair of white-fronted geese crashed up from some willow bushes. The goose had been covering five hard-set eggs, and the gander was standing beside her. Mr. Popham also remarks that in this species, contrary to the usual custom of the duck and goose tribe, the male bird visits the nest with the female. I shot the goose, and as she fell, I heard a delighted cry of "*Horroshie myaso*"[1] from my henchman, who was panting up the hill behind. He wavered for a minute, custom warring with his desire to pick up the bird. Then custom conquered, and out came the inevitable pocket-book.

"*Pa Russki, myaso; pa Angliski*——?"

"Oh—goose!" said I.

The goose eggs were photographed *in situ*, a process that both Sylkin and Vassilli thought a mere waste of time; and considering that the makers of exposure

[1] Good meat.

calculators do not reckon that their customers may want to make pictures at 1 a.m., the attempt was not unsuccessful. The nest was a small depression on a high ridge of tundra, lined with down, but it was more like a duck's nest than that of a goose, for the down was arranged neatly round the eggs instead of littering the surrounding grass.

While I was packing up the eggs, a pair of plover began to pipe close by. To my surprise and delight, the binoculars clearly made them out to be grey plover —the first that I had seen on the Yenesei. They were undoubtedly breeding in the neighbourhood, but to find the nest was more easily said than done on that bald expanse of tundra. Clearly the only way was to watch the bird on to the eggs, but in order to do this, it was necessary to get rid of my two companions, whose only idea of birds'-nesting was to wander aimlessly about until they either noticed the eggs or accidentally trod upon them. An ignorance of Russian was a disability under these circumstances, but Sylkin quickly grasped what was required of him, and went off. It was more difficult to dispose of Vassilli, but at last I thought that I had done so by bidding him go away for an hour to shoot geese.

As soon as he was out of sight, I took covert under the river-bank. When the coast was clear, the plovers quickly recovered from their alarm, and ventured back into the neighbourhood. My hopes were rising proportionately, when all at once they both took wing and flew screaming up the hill. Judge of my feelings, when into the field of my binoculars walked Vassilli, with a levelled gun, whose report threatened to sound the knell, both of the plover and of the chance of finding the nest. Luckily the shot did not take effect, for it was Vassilli's rule never to fire unless the bird was at least a hundred yards away; and before he could reload, I said what I thought so loudly that both he and the plovers fled over the hill. After such a shock to her nerves it seemed hopeless to expect the bird to return for some time, even if she ventured back at all; so, whistling to Sylkin, I walked on up the river to the lakes.

The actual river-bank here was of sand, overgrown with close, springy grass and golden moss. The whole appearance of the place was so much like that of a typical English warren that one quite expected to see rabbits popping in and out of their burrows. On the other side of the sandbank lay a tract of deep green marsh studded with small meres, and beyond the marsh, the ground sloped gradually up to the higher tundra. It all seemed so homely and so fertile that it was difficult to believe that we were really in the heart of the wilderness. It would not have been surprising to see a large country house built on the hill, with lawns sloping down to the river and golf links beyond. One felt that one had often walked in such places before. As it was, though there were slots of reindeer in the moss, the place was profoundly solitary except for the birds. Half a dozen geese rose gag-gaggling from the waterside, and I took another nest of four eggs. Divers of both kinds were plentiful, and bred together on the same pools. Sylkin found two more nests, one of the red- and the other of the black-throated species. The little stint was scarce and the Temminck's stint was not seen, but I saw a turnstone, the first that I observed on the Yenesei. I took another clutch of grey phalarope's eggs, and then went inland to look for the king-eider, which, although I did not put much faith in the report that it bred so far south of the seacoast, Sylkin declared bred there. Presently two long-tailed skuas flew overhead. A red-necked phalarope was flying over the marsh, and immediately one of these harpies made a most unprovoked attack upon it. Double and dodge as she would, the victim could not escape, for the skua, who, with his long rectrices for a rudder, well knew all the tricks of wingcraft, followed every zigzag ascent and dive like a pursuing thunderbolt, and fairly hunted down the poor little bird. This chase seemed to be undertaken purely out of wanton mischief. Most birds seldom attack another unless they need it for food, or see that it trespasses upon their breeding-ground, but the skuas will harry anything that comes in their way, just for the sport, and for the pleasure of hearing the poor thing scream. They are almost as diabolically cruel as our own hooded crows.

By far the most interesting birds in this marsh were two more pairs of grey plovers. I lay down for some time to watch them, but there was so little covert that this was no easy matter. They were wilder than the first pair, and evidently had young somewhere in the marsh, but it proved impossible to mark them down. I should have liked to explore farther up the valley, but the water there was too shallow for the boat, and as I had now spent twenty-two hours afoot, most of the time in tramping over heavy marsh, I did not feel physically capable of walking another verst. The men, too, were getting tired and hungry, and began to look longingly behind them. We therefore turned back down the river, but when we reached the place where we had first seen the grey plover, there were the two birds still flying round the spot. This was more than I could stand, so I explained in elaborate pantomime to Vassilli and Sylkin that I was going ashore again to find the nest. They both looked rather sulky, and then went off to a neighbouring creek to eat bread and cheese, while I lay down under the bank of the river.

With two observers who worked together, that nest could have been located in half an hour. As it was, it took four times that length of time to find it. The tundra sloped upwards from the waterside, and it was not difficult to keep the birds under observation, but between the river-bank and the bottom of this slope there was a deep hollow filled with snow. Consequently, when the plover was marked down to a given spot, instead of walking straight up to the eggs, as can sometimes be done, I was obliged to take my eye off the place while crossing this gully, and found myself hopelessly at a loss when I reached the other side. At length I tried a dodge which afterwards proved very useful when looking for the nests of other waders on the tundra. A scrap of paper is pegged down (with the ever-useful hairpin) where it is roughly calculated that the nest may be. The observer then hides up until the bird returns, and then by flushing her for a second time, he can judge the position of the eggs from the paper. Sometimes, as in this case, it is necessary to try the trick for a third or even for a fourth time, always moving the marks, and thus narrowing down the area of search. The male bird nearly caused me to fail at the outset, for he found out my hiding-place, and stood for an hour on a sandbank, piping out to his mate that there was a great big brute of a human being lying in wait under the river-bank, and mind she didn't go near the eggs until it had gone away O! However, in about two hours' time, I was able to flush the bird and walk right up to the eggs. The latter were lying on a ridge about two hundred yards from my hiding-place in a little hollow in the reindeer-moss. I was too cold and stiff to fetch the camera stand from the boat, so I disarticulated my gun, and using the barrels as a rest for the camera, made a couple of exposures upon the eggs. Presently Vassilli came up, and in order to make the identification complete, I told him to shoot the bird. He stalked one, which from its fine plumage I took to be the male, but which afterwards proved to be the female. In the colour of the eggs, and also in the language, the grey plover seems to stand half-way between the golden plover and the lapwing, but it is a lumpier, less elegant-looking bird than either of the smaller species. The note that I heard over and over again that morning in tantalising monotony was a threefold one, *pee-a-weep*, as if a lapwing were calling with the pipe of a golden plover. Seebohm gives the alarm note as a monosyllabic *köp*, or a double *kl-eep*, but the note that I heard on the Golchika was distinctly three syllabled. When the nest is approached, the bird has a way of dashing violently down from a height, and then whizzing aside, which is very reminiscent of the lapwing's aerial antics over our English water meadows. At other times the flight, although rapid, seems heavier and less graceful than that of the golden plover, but this may be only the effect of the bird's more solid build, and conspicuous colouring. On the wing, indeed, the grey plover, with its violent rushing flight and pied plumage, frequently reminded me of a domestic pigeon.

After this success, we turned homewards. We were all very cold by this time, and as I watched my followers refreshing themselves with a drink of the Worcester-sauce-and-alcohol beverage, I almost envied them, for at least the mixture must have felt hot inside. As it was, we had no wood to make a fire, and even if we had, we could not have made tea, because as all other receptacles, including the camera case, had been filled with our previous prizes, the plover's eggs were packed away in the kettle!

So ended an interesting and not unprofitable night's work. The only fly in the ointment was that the clutches of both geese and plover were so far incubated that in the case of the latter at any rate it was not possible to blow them properly. This, however, is one of those drawbacks that must be reckoned with in working in a place like Golchika where the season is so short, and the difficulties of reaching

A SUMMER ON THE YENESEI

the birds' breeding haunts during the spring thaw are so great. At least the memory of that quiet river under the midnight sun, and the calling of the birds on the surrounding tundra, is one that for me will never fade.

CHAPTER X.

The charm of the tundra—The reindeer sledges—"Into the tundra"—A wet drive—The sense of locality—A difficult passage—The *choom*—A wet night—The Dolgan family—Sunshine on the tundra—Photographing the Eastern golden plover—A goose hunt—Good-bye to the tundra.

To us, whose maps are speckled all over with the names of hills and rivers and townships, there is something arresting in the blankness of the map of Northern Siberia. Here and there a hair streak of river wanders up into the Arctic Ocean: the rest is emptiness. And actually when you visit those parts your first impression is the same—of great rivers pressing to the north, fed as they go by nameless lesser rivers; and around and beyond them, a grey and wind-swept waste, unbroken either by valley or bluff, stretching away into the lonely distance. In the country of the Yenesei, the natives themselves have no name for the vast land that lies on either side of the river. When they enter it, they say simply that they are going "into the tundra."

For those who live beside it, the tundra has a weird kind of fascination. Its vastness, its loneliness, its hopelessness grip you. At first, when you explore it, you think that you are the first human being who has ever walked there, and feel as solitary as Robinson Crusoe on his desert island. But in a day or two, you realise that, on the contrary, the tundra is a place with many highways, and a deal of trafficking. Sometimes, as you trudge across a sphagnum bog, and believe yourself to be all alone except for the golden plover, you hear a long, low *ai-aie*, and over the ridge comes a little sledge, drawn by reindeer and guided by one of the little tundra men. It skims smoothly over the moss, and disappears swiftly and silently from view. Presently you realise that where you are standing is not really a solitary place at all. It is part of a country, which is as exhaustively mapped and charted as any in the world. And each day, as you look at its shrouded, quivering horizon, you want to thrust it back farther from the limit of your knowledge, and long to learn a portion, however meagre, of its secrets.

Unfortunately, however, travelling in the tundra is difficult during the summer. The only possible way of crossing it is by sledge; and in the hot weather, the natives are unwilling to work their deer, for the animals are then moulting their coats and are liable to be galled by the harness. Most of the herds are taken far out into the tundra for pasturage, and only now and then does a team visit the banks of the river. Therefore, for nearly three weeks after our arrival at Golchika, I could only explore the surrounding country on foot; and, wandering on from one rolling ridge to another, gaze impotently at the mysterious distance and vainly long to reach it.

Then at last a chance came. It may be remembered that on our excursion up the Golchika, Vassilli and I had seen some Dolgans. These men were three brothers, and during the summer, Prokopchuk employed them as his shepherds to take his reindeer out into the tundra. A few days after the events related in the last chapter, two of the brothers came to buy food at Golchika, and Prokopchuk arranged that we should accompany them back to their *choom*, which was pitched at a place called Sloika, about forty versts east of Golchika. They were to start on the following day, and of course we gladly consented to go back with them.

A reindeer sledge is not a very roomy conveyance. All luggage has to be cut down to the minimum, and therefore, besides a gun and a camera, my personal baggage for the trip consisted of a pair of dry socks to sleep in. We strapped our sheepskins down upon the sledges, and the rest of the space was given up to the kettle, cooking-pot, and food. Each traveller had a sledge to himself, and these sledges, each drawn by four deer, were tied one behind the other to the sledges of the Dolgans. Vassilli, the eldest of the two brothers, led the procession, and after a few false starts we moved off at a smart trot.

As the punt is on the river, so is the reindeer sledge on the tundra. You may do what you will with it—turn it this way and that, let it slide down an eight-foot drop, ride in it up a slope of forty-five degrees, or drive it full tilt at a four-foot dyke, and it will never overturn, but glide easily and safely from one bank to the other. Before we had gone half a verst, we had a practical illustration of this, for just where we were to leave the flat bank of the river to turn up into the tundra, there was a brook of running water. Even in a hunting country, it would have ranked as a fence, and the other sledges turned aside to ford it. Vassilli Sotnikoff, however, drove straight at it with my sledge following him. His deer took the channel in their stride, and the sledge lumbered safely after them. But one of my team, slipping in the boggy ground, leaped short, and down plunged the sledge into the stream on to the top of the hindermost deer. As I clutched at my seat with both hands, I had a vision of struggling bodies straining gallantly at the traces. Then, with a splash, the sledge was jerked up the opposite bank, with me, exceedingly wet, still clinging on behind.

A soaking more or less made little difference, however, for as we turned aside from the river-bank, and trotted up the steep incline which led to the higher tundra, the rain came down thick and fast, wrapping all the landscape in a veil of mist. Before us, stretching, so it seemed, into infinity, lay the old sled track, along which generations of Samoyedes had travelled "into the tundra." For a couple of miles after leaving the river, this track was quite plain, but presently it grew fainter and fainter, and finally disappeared altogether. To right and left the country lay as flat as a plate, and— to the inexperienced eye—almost as featureless. There was not a hill by which to take bearings, no sun by which to set a course. Here and there the ground was broken into gullies down which poured turgid streams, and in the angles of the slopes, besmirched snow-drifts still lingered. More often our way lay over broad, flat moss-hags, broken and here there by a low mound, from which a snowy owl or buzzard flapped majestically at our approach. Vassilli, however, never hesitated, and drove unerringly ahead. Every five or six versts he stopped to give his deer a breather, and we stood up to shake the water from our knees and stamp our cold feet back to warmth again. Then, as soon as the reindeer had snatched a mouthful of moss, and Vassilli himself had lighted his long brass-bound pipe, he pulled the teams into position, and away he went once more. As a rule, however, there were several false starts. The deer were harnessed by a trace which was fastened round the neck, and then passed under the near fore-leg, and as long as the sledge was moving all was well; but as soon as the traces slackened, the hind legs of one or other of the deer usually became entangled in the harness, and there was nothing for it but to stop the sledges and put the matter right. This happened so often that I could not help being secretly both amused and exasperated by the stolid patience of the natives, who were conservative enough to prefer the delay and inconvenience of the frequent halts to release the deer, to devising some more effective system of harness.

The pace of the deer was a steady seven-mile jog-trot, and they scarcely dropped into a walk even for a piece of ground as rough as a Scottish moor, or a swamp where the water spurted high on either side of the runners. Sometimes we raced down a slope so steep that the sledge slid down upon their haunches, or else rattled and bumped through the bed of a brawling stream. It says much for the stability of the sledges that during that thirty-mile drive only one of them was overturned, and that was mine. My team, following their leaders too closely, cut a corner as we slid into the bed of a torrent. The right-hand runner caught a protruding stone, and the sledge turned completely over, tumbling me and my gun and cooking-pot into the water. At this mishap the Dolgan brothers laughed like schoolboys as they picked up the overturned sledge and released the struggling deer from the traces.

But no matter how thick the mist, nor how winding our way, Vassilli never hesitated, but chose his path as confidently as a Londoner who walks from the Marble Arch to Piccadilly. As an example of his absolute knowledge of the country: we were crossing a wide sphagnum swamp, when he presently turned aside to a little knoll, which, to the untutored eye, was exactly like hundreds of others on the desolate plain. Here he jumped off the sledge and picked up a small object. It was a tobacco-pouch which had been forgotten during a halt on the previous journey, and for which he had now returned. That a native should have a general sense of direction highly developed is not so remarkable, for it is a faculty which in a greater or less degree is shared even by civilised man; but that he can remember one spot amid hundreds, all so similar, and identify it again, is sufficiently wonderful. Several times we noticed this *instinct* for locality, if one may call it so. A party of Samoyedes once came to buy from Prokopchuk. They had travelled from what the Golchikans call "the other tundra," *i.e.* from the country which lies hundreds of versts to the eastward, in the basin of the river Lena. Their leader, an elderly man who could speak scarcely any Russian, remarked naively that he had not visited the Yenesei tundra since he was a boy, and had half forgotten the way to Golchika! On another occasion we were at the *chooms* one evening, when we saw half a dozen Samoyede boys and girls just starting for the tundra. Their people were herding reindeer about a hundred and thirty versts away, and they were going out to join them. Both boys and girls were riding astride the deer, and behind them, on a sledge, they carried a little tea and *soushki* for the journey, and also a canoe in case they came to a river. They were all in high spirits, and neither they nor the crowd who had collected to watch them start seemed to think it at all unusual that a party of children, none of whom were more than fifteen years of age, should thus set out alone on a two days' journey into the wilderness.

Towards six o'clock in the evening, we descended a long gradual slope from the higher tundra into a river valley. It was raining harder than ever, and the bitter east wind seemed to drive the rain through waterproof and jacket alike, and chilled us all to the bone. We thought gratefully of the comparative shelter and warmth of the *choom*, which now lay not far ahead. However, it turned out that we were not to reach it as easily as we expected. The river, though shallow enough, was wide, and the wind, blowing with the current, drove long white tongues of foam down the channel. Vassilli shook his head as he dismounted from the sledge and drew a little bark canoe from under the overhanging bank. He first tried the ford with Miss Czaplicka, the lightest of our party, behind him in the boat.

"Sit still, or death!" was his dramatic and rather disquieting command in broken Russian to his passenger as he cautiously pushed off his little craft. But it was soon evident that it would be hopeless to try and cross at this point. The current was so strong that even Vassilli, with all his skill with the paddle, could do no more than keep the canoe's head to the wind, and so prevent it from drifting broadside on and overturning in the rough water. He was soon obliged to give up the attempt and return to the bank.

It would have been impossible to find a more forlorn-looking party in the whole of Asia. Although it was only six o'clock, and, according to the calendar, still the season of perpetual day, the sky was so lowering that a grey twilight seemed to brood over the wet tundra. Out of the misty mud-hills to the east, the nameless river flowed, no man knew whence, and disappeared among the mud-hills to the west, no man knew whither. Little lonely streams, whose sources were visited only by the tundra foxes and the wild-fowl, ran down to meet it. We seemed to be the only living things in a land where there was no colour, nor any sound at all except the swish of the wind over the lichens; and as I looked around I had the fantastic idea that here was a world in the making. It seemed, as if in obedience to the enunciation of some great law, the waters of a new chaos had rolled sullenly back and let the land in all its nakedness appear for the first time. I seemed to see earth in its beginnings, as I stood with my back to the wind, wriggling my toes in my wet boots to make sure that they had not been frozen off altogether, and watching the raindrops drip from the flanks of the patient deer, while Vassilli and his brother Nicolai debated as to what to do next.

Suddenly a shout was heard, and Maxim, the youngest of the three brothers, appeared on the opposite bank. By his directions, we went to another ford, a couple of hundred yards up the river. Here, although the channel was wider, it was less deep, and the current was less rapid. Moreover, there was a sandbank in midstream where we might break the passage. Everything was unloaded from the sledges, and, one by one, Vassilli ferried us across to the sandbank. Then our goods were brought over also, and although we had cut all baggage down to the minimum, it needed several journeys, for it would have been disastrous to overload the canoe. At length only Nicolai was left behind. He led the deer, team by team, down the bank, and drove them into the river. After the first couple had entered the water, the rest followed them readily enough, and then Vassilli paddled over for the last time to fetch his brother. Meanwhile, a tragedy occurred, for, during his absence, the last team landed on a muddy spit, which was almost as unstable as a quicksand. Before the deer could be driven on to firmer ground the treacherous surface melted beneath them, and they sank down over their hocks. With some trouble three of the deer were dragged ashore, but the fourth could not rise, and when we hauled it out, we found that in its struggles the poor brute had broken its hind leg grievously. There was no help for it. Vassilli cut it out of the harness lest it should hinder the others, and we were obliged to leave it behind on the sandbank, for any delay might have resulted in the same accident befalling all the rest of the team. The second channel was much easier to cross. In fact, it was not necessary to use the canoe, and we made the passage safely by kneeling on the sledges, while the deer waded up to their bellies in the water. After relashing our goods upon the sledges, we made ready to go on to the *choom*, which was now only a verst ahead; but Maxim went back to bring in the wounded deer, which was hobbling painfully to the ford. Animal suffering is always painful to see, and although we knew that in this case it was accidental and could not have been avoided, nevertheless, the suffering of the beautiful innocent thing saddened us all very much. I must confess, however, that the behaviour of that reindeer, although it did not reduce my regret, considerably modified my views as to the depth of animal suffering; for no sooner had it limped ashore painfully on three legs, than it put down its head and began to graze as placidly as if its leg were not dangling merely by the sinews!

Ten minutes later we reached the *choom*, which stood upon a little knoll in a sheltered valley. A clear stream bubbled past the door, and all around the slopes of the valley were dotted with grazing reindeer. Not so very long before, I should have thought that the little tent, hidden away in the heart of the tundra, was the very acme of dreariness and solitude. But two months of travel in Northern Siberia overset many preconceived notions, and now, on the contrary, we welcomed the small brown dome. In our wet and hungry plight it seemed like a haven of refuge—almost homelike; and we pushed aside the door flap and crept inside gladly. A bright fire was burning in the middle of the floor, and beside the fire sat old Maria Sotnikoff, the mother of our three guides. Although she sat cross-legged upon a heap of hides, and all her household goods would have packed easily into the old wooden coffer beside her; and although her *choom* was suddenly called upon to house just twice as many people as it was designed to hold, no gentlewoman in civilised lands could have received her unexpected guests with more courtesy and composure than did Madame Sotnikoff. She graciously shook hands with each of us in turn, and although she understood little Russian, and was too deaf to hear our greetings, she smiled at us kindly, and pointed out our quarters for the night—the guest-chamber, so to speak—which was that half of the *choom* which lay to the left of the doorway. Meanwhile, the three brothers, who had waited behind to unharness the deer, came in, and we all gathered round the fire for supper. But first of all Maria took her sons' wet outer garments and hung them up to dry. Later, as we waited for the kettle to boil, I watched our hostess across the hearth, and I could not help admiring the methodical way in which she set her primitive house in order. I have not often seen greater neatness and precision in far more pretentious rooms in Europe. First of all she took the little squat table that is found in most of the *chooms* along the Yenesei, and dusted it carefully. On this she set three pink cups and saucers of cheap Russian crockery. In my ignorance, before visiting the Yenesei I had believed that saucers

REINDEER GRAZING.

were among the most easily dispensable of the innumerable superfluous chattels with which our civilisation is cumbered. But in the *choom* the saucer is as important as the cup, for the tea is poured out into it before it is drunk. Indeed, we found that the natives actually despised our saucerless mugs, and regarded ours as an ill-appointed tea-table. When the kettle boiled, the meal began. There were three courses—tea and *soushki*, reindeer meat, and fish. The men were too hungry to talk much, and what they did say related chiefly to the loss of the deer. As the price of a good draught reindeer may be anything from fifteen to fifty roubles, they were much troubled at the accident. After supper the beds were brought out, and each of the brothers, taking off his outer garments, crept into a warm reindeer-hide sleeping-bag. I noticed that although their hands and faces were so dark, the skin of these Dolgans' arms and chests was as white as the skin of a European. The Dolgans, however, are a cleanly race: I have seen Yuraks and Samoyedes who were so dirty that it seemed as if their skin must long ago have renounced its proper function.

All through the night the wind and rain yelled over the tundra. A *choom* is a marvellously weather-proof dwelling. Like all things which have evolved slowly from the practical experiments of hundreds of generations, it is the simplest and most effective adaptation of means to ends; but, at the same time, even a *choom* has its limitations, and long before morning the pitiless rain had beaten an entrance and was dripping dismally on to the hearth. It was too cold to sleep in the wet sheepskins, and for the greater part of the night we lay awake, listening to the rustle and grunting of the reindeer as they grazed outside.

Our hosts were early astir, and the first to awake was the hard-working little mother, for she must make the fire. Now a fire in the northern tundra, you must know, is not a lavish heap of wood and coal, sprawled all over the hearth to squander or replenish carelessly, whenever and however you please, as it may be in the south. In the tundra, fuel is of peculiar preciousness —all wood must be carried from the banks of the Yenesei, which may be scores of versts away, for the only timber found upon the spot is that of the little green willow scrub. Hence, when a fire is laid for kindling, each chip and twig is placed after a careful plan, and when it is lighted, the pile is watched jealously and raked together scientifically from time to time, in order that the kettle may boil with the maximum of speed and the minimum of fuel. Before the tea was made, the three sons awoke and washed in turn. Each took a mouthful of water from the scoop in the bucket by the door, and let it trickle from his mouth over his hands. We, who had not been educated up to this rather feline but decidedly practical means of obtaining warm water, contented ourselves with a splash in the icy stream outside. These ablutions over, the Dolgans had a good breakfast of fish, while we ate the European fare that we had brought with us, and which, I am bound to say, did not look nearly so good as theirs did!

The Sotnikoffs were in better circumstances than many of the natives in those parts. Each spring they came to the north with their reindeer, and during the short arctic summer, they wandered over the tundra from one pasturage to another. When autumn came, however, they packed up their goods on the sledges, and travelled southwards for four or five hundred miles to the border of the great Siberian forests. Here they had another *choom*. Were they not afraid to leave it unprotected all through the summer, lest someone should steal it, we asked? They shouted with laughter at our simplicity. "Who would touch it?" they asked, scornful of the very idea, for they knew the scrupulous honesty of their own race.

No doubt this migration was well enough for the three young men; but it seemed little short of marvellous that the little, fragile old woman, who could scarcely hobble fifty yards from the *choom* door, should travel thus on an open sledge through the first snows of a Siberian winter. Maria, however, seemed to regard the journey with as much equanimity as a London housewife regards the annual holiday trip to Margate. Vassilli, the eldest of the brothers, was a middle-sized man with a little hair on his face. His cast of countenance was the least amiable of the three; and we heard later that, although of marriageable age, he remained a bachelor willy-nilly because all the girls of his people were afraid of his temper! Nicolai, on the other hand, had a round face with such a joyous, comical expression that it was not possible to look at him without smiling in sympathy. Maxim, the Benjamin of the family, was a small edition of Nicolai. All three were as merry as schoolboys, and had the simple ready humour of children. Nicolai, wishing to light his pipe, opened the match-box, only to find it empty. His discomfiture drew shouts of laughter from the others. Maxim, when putting on his boots, found that the stitching had given way, and that his bare toes protruded in what English children call a "potato." He and his brothers rolled to and fro with merriment at this unexpected appearance, but Maria shook her head and hastened to mend the hole with twisted reindeer sinew.

This morning there was plenty of time for such jokes, for it was still raining heavily, and there was little temptation to go out and be wetted to the skin, especially when there was nowhere where damp clothes could be dried. Meanwhile there was a good opportunity of studying the *choom*, which, for the benefit of those who have never seen one, I may briefly describe. A *choom* is a little conical-shaped tent about fifteen feet in diameter. There is one upright pole in the middle; and a number of more slender rods leaning in towards it, and tied together in a bunch at the top, support the cover. According to the weather, the smoke escapes, or does not escape, through the opening at the apex. The only inside fitting is a cross-bar which is lashed from one of the side poles to the centre upright, and from which hangs a wooden hook for the cooking-pot. The outside covering is made of skins sewn together. Indeed, so all-important is the reindeer to the poor Siberian native, that it is no wonder that it is difficult to buy good skins in Golchika. Fawn skins are plentiful enough, and only cost a rouble or two, but the larger hides are all used in the *chooms*. The Sotnikoffs had about three hundred reindeer under their charge, of which about half belonged to Prokopchuk. This, however, was not a large number for one family to own, for reindeer are delicate creatures, and in some years are subject to a form of epidemic disease which carries them off in hundreds. The Samoyede reindeer are smaller than those used by the Tungus, and judging by the head of one that I saw from Dickson Island, they are not so heavy as the wild deer. The draught reindeer are gentle and tractable. Seebohm says that on the Petchora, *haviers* are used in the sledges; but all those that I saw on the Yenesei carried fine horns, although of course at that season they were still in velvet. In winter a team will go a hundred and fifty versts in a day, but in summer they are in poor condition, and cannot travel more than thirty miles. Their scenting powers are wonderful, and when lost in the *pourga*, they will travel miles to find a *choom*, guided by the smell of the fire; but they have none of the homing faculty of dogs, and will run to a stranger's camp as readily as to their own. I once saw Joseph Gerasimvitch flay a newly-killed carcase within thirty yards of where a team were standing. Cattle under similar circumstances would have been driven frantic by the smell of blood, but the reindeer paid no attention whatever.

In the afternoon the skies cleared, and as I started on a solitary ramble up the valley, I saw the tundra under another guise. Last night we saw its dour side, its greyness, its loneliness, and seemingly under the scourge of the wind and the rain, its hopelessness. The frame of the land was just as the ice had left it. Its horizons lay in long, open curves, all angles planed away by the firm hand of the glaciers. Most likely the form of the swamps and the rivers had not changed since the mammoth lumbered over the frozen mudhills. But to-day I felt more clearly the promise of the tundra—its huge fertility, its immensity, its strange, indefinable magic. Nowhere, except in the Alps, may be seen such a profusion of flowers—forget-me-nots, lupins, saxifrage, pedicularias, and poppies—purple, blue, crimson, and orange—and in the hollows the willows were fragrant with bloom. On every hillock stood a plover in gold-studded livery, playing on his wild pipe, or malingering piteously to lead me from his hidden nursery. Down in the hollow, a pair of godwits whistled to one another in notes like the striking of flint on steel, and red-throated pipits dropped carolling among the flowers. As I walked quickly beside the river-bank, little waders ran before me down the sandy spits, too busy to be afraid, and a fine willow-grouse rose with a *whirr* and boomed away over the hill. Beside the ford, the gulls flew to and fro, and stooped at their own purple shadows on the sandbanks. And yesterday there had not been a bird to be seen, and all the flowers had hidden their rain-drenched heads! All this transformation had been caused by a little sunshine. It was like a resurrection. The river ran tranquilly, reflecting a clear sky. Yesterday the monotony of its broad, flat banks had oppressed us by its drabness and dreariness. But to-day, its very monotony lent it an added charm. It had no history:

it served no human purpose. It came out of nowhere, flowed a little way, bubbling contentedly in the sunshine, and then disappeared into nowhere. In some sort the river was typical of the tundra itself. The tundra is a land of the present. It has no past. No history was ever made there, and its people scarcely reckon the flight of years. It has no future. What can you do with a million square miles of lichen and moss, which for nine months of the year are frozen fast and deep? The life of the tundra is an eternal present. Thus it was an æon back; thus it will be an æon hence. It is one of Pan's pleasure gardens. Of which—alas!—there are so few remaining in this small and much-trodden earth.

To me, passing along the tops of the hills, flew a pair of golden plover, zealously feigning a broken wing. One was shy and kept her distance: I am ashamed to say that I think from her plumage that this was the lady. The other was a bold bird, and ran so close to me that, time and again, he might almost have been caught in a butterfly net. Presently I lay down to watch the couple. The male bird soon dropped his plaintive whistle, and began to pick up imaginary worms—which, to those who know Ploverski, is a reassuring sign; but his mate speedily discovered my whereabouts and told all the tundra about the espionage. However, by and by she had to go off to attend to a Buffon's skua who was trespassing too closely, and as soon as she had gone, her mate came back to the neighbourhood of the eggs. I watched him for over an hour, and finally, after marking him down, once or twice, I found the nest. It contained one newly-hatched chick and three chipping eggs. The old bird need not have made all that fuss about the skua, for without field-glasses he could never have found her treasure. Both eggs and young were tinted wisely. The chick was dusky and golden-green as the moss on which he crouched; the eggs, modestly marbled with umber and grey, were drab like the lichen. Each was a mighty successful piece of scenic painting in miniature, and quite invisible on the tundra. The cock bird was so tame that I determined to return the next day and photograph him at the nest.

The second night in the *choom* was much more comfortable than the first had been. It was dry, and not really cold if you stuck your feet into the ashes of the fire. The dogs came in to share the warmth. There were two of them—Malchik and Ouss. Both were trained to herd the deer, but while Ouss was quite a rising practitioner, Malchik was a fool. Ouss knew his superiority, and traded on it. He would not allow his brother to sit by the fire, scarcely would he permit him to enter the *choom*. They were both prick-eared, long-coated curs, with tails curled tightly over their backs like Chow or Pomeranian dogs.

I turned out early on the following morning, and went to call on the golden plover with my camera. It was a beautiful day, and under a cloudless sky, the tundra was for the first time buzzing with mosquitoes. The pests swarmed everywhere and turned photography into a regular martyrdom. It was impossible to focus the camera through a veil, and I speedily found that most of the decoctions which are recommended as preventives

Dotterel ♀ (Charadrius morinellus).

Grey Phalarope ♂ (Phalaropus fulicarius).

Temminck's Stint (Erolia temminckii)

were more of a protest than a protection against the attacks of the Siberian *Culex damnabilis*. Luckily, however, the male golden plover was a most obliging sitter. He even returned to brood his newly-hatched young while I was lying in the grass not five yards away, and by the use of a lens of 14" focal length, I exposed about two dozen plates upon him as he ran round the nest. This sort of "fluke" photography is often very successful as far as picture-making is concerned, but it is, or ought to be, as poor sport to the naturalist photographer as hunting a bagged fox is to a fox-hunter. Nine-tenths of the pleasure and profit of nature photography is derived from watching the bird under natural conditions. To lure an anxious creature within range of the lens by the *cheeping* of its own chicks seems to savour so much of seething the kid in its mother's milk that I always feel rather ashamed of having done so, and as if I owed the poor bird an apology. However, this plover is so excessively wary that to photograph it from the ordinary hiding-tent would be a long and difficult business.

When I returned to the *choom*, the rest of the party were at breakfast. Ouss was sitting in the family circle on the look out for titbits, but Malchik as usual was made to keep his distance. The men said that he was a fool—*dourak*. I had a fellow-feeling for him, because a pair of bar-tailed godwits had just shouted out the same thing to me when I could not find their brood among the rushes. I therefore called him inside, and told him that some day I meant to found a Sodality for Incompetent Fools, both human and canine. Ouss promptly rolled him over into the fire; but for once in a way the family took his part, and he received the scrapings of the cook-pot with abject gratitude. However, to show how unequal things are—two minutes afterwards, when Ouss looked insinuatingly at our plates, I found myself feeding him on choice morsels; and Malchik, who was too deprecatory to ask for any for himself, looked on hungrily and got none. Therefore the fool was dealt with according to his folly, and everything was as unfair as before.

The Dolgans were going out to shoot geese for Prokopchuk's larder, and invited us to accompany them. Vassilli took his ancient muzzle-loader and the little canoe, and we started out on reindeer sledges.

Up on the higher ground, the mosquitoes were less virulent than in the valley, but it was very hot, and from horizon to horizon, the whole country seemed to leap and quiver in the sunshine. Tennyson wrote of the Lotus-eaters' land, "where it is always afternoon." Out on the tundra it was like a perpetual Sunday morning. A Sabbath stillness brooded over the vast sunlit plain: one almost expected to hear the distant tinkle of church bells. Away from the river valleys there were no flowers among the reindeer-moss, and few birds except an occasional golden plover.

Here and there, however, we passed a small moss bog, which seemed to form a kind of oasis for birds. Little stints sprang up at our approach, and red-necked phalaropes — *koolik*, as the Siberiaks call them — shepherded their young out of the way of the sledges. We were crossing one such bog when a curlew-sandpiper

A SUMMER ON THE YENESEI

jumped up right in our path, and I caught sight of a downy youngster dodging through the grass. Without taking my eye from the spot, I leaped off the sledge, to the amazement of our pilot, Vassilli, who thought that I had suddenly gone mad; and after a short chase, succeeded in capturing a couple of young curlew-sandpipers in down, the first that, to my knowledge, have been taken by an English ornithologist. A little farther on, by some scrub willows, where the deer halted for a breather, I shot three ptarmigan, the only ones secured during the trip. They were very tame, and the report of the gunshot that sealed their comrades' fate only caused them to crane their necks inquiringly.

By and by we reached the bank of a small river. On the farther side was a bog, in the midst of which, like a gem in an ample setting, was a small lake—the goose nursery. Vassilli took the canoe, and drove the deer into the stream. They were glad enough to swim and drink, for the poor things were very hot; and Ouss, who had run all the way behind the sledges, was panting like a steam-engine under the weight of his thick pelt. Arrived on the other bank, we sprang on to the sledges and drove off at full gallop over the bog, in order to take the geese by surprise and cut them off from the water. At the other side of the lake was a slope of rising ground, and down this, three or four broods were already waddling to the lake. Nicolai tumbled off his sledge and, shouting to me to follow him, he ran off with Ouss scampering at his heels. He easily beat me in the race, for the shores of the mere were spongy with sphagnum, and I soon dropped into a breathless walk, as much the result of laughter as exhaustion. Nicolai, running on ahead, had floundered through the marsh, and had given hot chase to a family party of geese. The young birds, although they were not yet able to fly, were strong pedestrians, and they were adepts at dodging. Each time that their pursuer clutched at one, the gosling doubled under his arm like a football player and sprinted away in the opposite direction. Ouss, who thoroughly entered into the game, fastened into the pinion of an elderly gander, who was running with outspread wings before his progeny. The bird immediately sprang into the air, and sent the dog sprawling, with a mouthful of feathers, while the fluttering and cackling redoubled. In the end Nicolai and Ouss between them caught two birds. The rest beat them altogether, and reached the water. Here, however, they had to reckon with Vassilli, who had launched the canoe, and now pursued them with his fowling-piece, which made almost as much noise and smoke as a 45-cm. siege gun. It seemed cruel thus to shoot the birds in the nesting season, but it was necessary to take fresh meat back to Golchika, and the surviving goslings were old enough to look after themselves. All the geese that I saw at this place belonged to the white-fronted species (*Anser albifrons*). Between them, the Dolgans captured enough birds to load a sledge, but they professed to be disappointed with their bag, and said that if it had not been a late season the adult geese would already have been in moult, and unable to fly at all. As it was, only the goslings were taken; the old birds flew to and fro overhead, screaming imprecations upon the violators of their sanctuary.

On the following morning our provisions were finished, and as our hosts had none to spare, we were obliged to return to Golchika. It was with the greatest regret that we said good-bye to the little *choom* with its freedom, its friendliness, and its hospitality; and its inmates shook hands with us over and over again in their hearty native fashion. Before leaving, I bought his cap from Vassilli for the sum of three roubles. It is made of white wolfskin fringed with dog's fur, and is a perfect specimen of Dolgan beadwork. Maria was a notable worker, and each bead is sewn by deer's sinew into its proper place in the ancient pattern that is handed down from mother to daughter in the Dolgan race, and reduplicated again and again in every generation. It is before me as I write, and its faint, musty odour recalls, as nothing else can do, the memory of those two days spent in the little *choom* out in the tundra, and of its quaint and kindly owners.

CHAPTER XI.

Swerifskye—Its reputation—We go there—*Mnogie vino*—A stroll on the tundra—A night in the open air—Walk to Och Marino—Mirage—A search-party—Birds and men at Och Marino.

THE other day I took my old school atlas from the shelf, and turned up the map of Asia with greater interest than it received in the days when we learned in our geography primer that, *" Western Siberia, an immense region where a few dwarf Samoyedes dwell, and where miserable convicts are cruelly made to work in quicksilver mines, is watered by the Ob, Yenesei, and Lena Rivers, whose mouths are mostly frozen."* Four towns were marked upon the Yenesei —Krasnoyarsk, Yenesiesk, and Turukhansk of course, and then, right up at the top, in type covering a space which actually represented about three hundred miles, and challenged attention with the name of the river itself, was Swerifskye. Nobody knows what made the worthy cartographer introduce Swerifskye into his map. In the year of grace 1914 the place consisted of two balagans and three native *chooms* built upon a shingle beach. Even Golchika was a gay and populous place compared with it.

Swerifskye was on the other side of the Yenesei, and on a clear day you could see the stacks of firewood, and the smoke from the balagans, quite distinctly. But when we proposed to row over there, the Golchikans shook their heads. From their account, Swerifskye was of as evil report as the Cities of the Plain, and its inhabitants were thieves and murderers all. There was a legend that, during the previous summer, two men from the south had gone there to fish. Some days later they went on board Kutcherenkoff's steamer, and besought him to ship them home in any capacity, for they could no longer live with the people of Swerifskye.

However, instead of deterring us, this made us the more anxious to visit the place; and as at about the same time Madame Antonoff wished to go down to Och Marino to see how Hachenkoff's fishery was prospering, we agreed to join forces and hire Sylkin's boat to take us across the river. Sylkin was quite ready to go, because some Yurak friends of his were living in the Swerifskye *chooms*. However, he took it for granted that the outing was to include his family as well as himself; and when he brought the boat to call for us, it had already a full cargo of children and dogs. We were obliged to explain to him that we could not cross the Yenesei with either a Noah's ark or a kindergarten, and waited while he ejected all the dogs, and most of the children. Then, after picking up Madame Antonoff and Nill at the fishing station, we started off. Sylkin took the paddle, and his two boys were at the oars. The elder son, Nicolai, had been baptized in the Orthodox Church, and wore a Christian token round his neck, but the younger, Nerobi, was still unchristened. Possibly his father's experience with the ikons, which has been mentioned elsewhere, may have had something to do with his heathen state. At any rate, when Madame Antonoff tried to persuade him that if he would go to the pope he would receive "a nice Russian name and a nice new Russian shirt," he only glowered defiantly, and, retorting, "I want neither your nice Russian name nor your nice Russian shirt," he remained a pagan.

Madame Antonoff, who, naturally, had seen much of the natives and their ways, also told us another story, which, although irrelevant here, I cannot help repeating. A Samoyede came to her one day and, laying his hand upon his heart, declared that he had a worm inside him which would not lie still! She tried in vain to reason him out of this delusion, and at last, to humour him, she gave him some simple draught and sent him away. Half an hour later he came back and complained that her prescription had done him no good at all—he had drunk the medicine and laid the empty bottle inside his shirt, but the worm was still there!

It was a distance of only ten versts to Swerifskye, but before we arrived the wind began to rise ominously. By the time that we beached the boat before the balagans, we saw that it would be impossible to go on to Och Marino that night, as had been our previous intention. As the boat approached, excited figures reeled out of both huts and *chooms*, very much as tipsy wasps tumble out of an apple core, and we guessed that there was what Sylkin called *mnogie vino* (*i.e.*

much drink) in the place. Here was a kettle of fish, for the weather was too bad to return to Golchika, and a balagan during a carouse is not the most desirable lodging. To make matters worse, the most sober of the Siberiaks came forward with the news that Vassilli Vassillievitch Hachenkoff, whom Madame Antonoff had intended to visit at Och Marino, had left his fishing, and consequently his rent, to take care of itself, and had been living for a fortnight at Swerifskye, drinking hard all the time. There was nothing to be done but stay where we were and hope that the wind would soon go down. Fortunately there was not much vodka left for Sylkin and his sons. My companions, escorted by a jubilant crowd, went down to the *chooms*, while I went for a ramble over the tundra.

Swerifskye stood at the entrance to a broad, shallow valley, which had been planed out of the river-bank by some glacier of the older world. I explored this glen for some distance, and then struck out over the tundra, but it was late in the season, and I saw nothing of particular interest. The golden plover were already strong upon the wing, and the Lapland buntings had gone up to the higher ground to moult in privacy among the whortleberries. I saw no curlew-sandpipers, although in some spots the ground looked very suitable for them, and neither did I see, as I had hoped to do, any Buffon's skuas. I shot a couple of dotterels, a female and a young one just fledged, and at the end of three hours, as the wind was remarkably cold, and it began to rain, I returned to the fishing station. Sounds of high revelry came from the *chooms*, but none of our party were in sight. I tried the door of the nearest balagan, and found Vassilli Vassillievitch lying in a drunken slumber in one corner and Madame Antonoff keeping watch in the other. Nill lay across the door like a faithful dog; but when I came in he evidently thought that his guard was relieved, and lumbered out. It was dark and damp in the balagan, but at least it was warmer than the wet beach outside. Madame Antonoff and I sheltered there for some time, until, lulled by the snores of Vassilli Vassillievitch, we both fell asleep. About ten o'clock the remainder of the party turned up, very wet and very hungry. They had gone for a walk, and had fallen into a bog on the way home. We therefore made up an immense fire on the beach, and bivouacked there for the night. The sky was clear, and although the wind was as cool as an English November, the sand was quite dry, and we slept very comfortably in sheepskins. One of our party commandeered an empty fish barrel, and spent the night in this Diogenes-like dormitory. She declared that it was very cosy, but the rest of us preferred to creep under the lee of a piece of driftwood.

In the morning we made a fire and cooked breakfast, and during the meal we held a council of war. The weather was too bad for the boat to venture either to Golchika or Och Marino, but Madame Antonoff was anxious to take Vassilli Vassillievitch back to his home. It seemed that during his absence the girl had been left all alone in the house with the ailing baby. Twice she had sent messages by the natives, entreating him to return and bring food, for she had nothing but black bread and salt fish to give the child. In his maudlin way, Hachenkoff was fond of her, and between his drinking bouts he wept continually because he feared that the child would die, and that it would be buried under its mother's name and not under his own. By and by a message came that he was awake and sober, and Madame Antonoff sent word bidding him to come and speak to her. But Vassilli Vassillievitch had a guilty conscience, and presently he was seen slinking away to hide himself in the tundra. However, Nill, to whom his mistress' word was law, gave chase, and haled the culprit back to the camp. Whereupon Madame Antonoff gave the good-for-nothing creature a lecture, which left him with nothing to say for himself, and sent him back immediately to Och Marino under escort of the grinning Nill.

We decided to walk down the river to Och Marino and spend the night there, returning on the morrow to Swerifskye to pick up Sylkin and the boat. If the weather did not improve, we should have to remain where we were, and as we had brought only two days' provisions with us, we should have to depend for food upon the charity of the balagan people.

Snowdrifts were still piled up along the western shores of the Yenesei, for the mud-hills screened them from the sun, and although the water drip-dripped from their flanks, yet they never melted all the summer through.

Among these mud-hills, I stalked and shot a Siberian herring-gull, and also procured a couple of turnstones, the first that I had seen on the Yenesei. During this day, and for a day or two before and after it, small parties of these waders might be constantly observed. It was the second week in August, and probably these were non-breeding birds of the previous year, who migrated southwards before the nesting birds had reared their young along the shores of the Arctic Ocean.

This coast of the Yenesei, as I must call it, for it sounds inadequate to speak of the *bank* of a river which is fifteen miles in width, was in places spread to a depth of eighteen inches with a deposit of driftwood, pounded almost to sawdust by the action of the ice and the spring floods. This wet vegetable fibre was very tiring to walk upon, for at each step one sank knee-deep into the spongy mass. The beach was also strewn with pieces of graphite, and stones containing traces of copper-ore—tokens of the unexploited wealth of Siberia.

There is no such place as the Yenesei for mirage effects. Whatever the state of the weather may be, a distant coast-line, or even a boat a couple of versts away, seems to hang in the air with a bar of shining water beneath it. Moreover, even in cold weather, the whole skyline of the estuary seems to leap and quiver as if with heat, until it is almost impossible to distinguish the lines of a distant ship or beach through the telescope. Both appearances are probably due to the fact that the water, coming from the south, is much warmer than the air of the Arctic. Consequently a thin layer of atmosphere immediately overlying the surface of the river becomes heated; and, being of different density to the chilled air above, it plays curious tricks with the refraction of the light.

THE NESTING PLACE OF THE CURLEW-SANDPIPER.

SIBERIAN GULLS (LARUS F. ANTELIUS).

FOX TRAP ON THE TUNDRA.

The people of Swerifskye said that it was only eleven versts to Och Marino, but from the time that it took us to cover the distance, and the measurements of the map, it seemed a good deal more like twenty. Neither the natives nor the Siberiaks have any idea of distance. If they tell you that it is ten versts to a given point, it may just as well be five or fifteen. They are as vague about distance as they are about time, neither of which are of any account in their immense country. Several times we had to wait for Hachenkoff, who was in a sad state of collapse. He plodded along before us, with Nill, who guarded him like a detective, striding behind.

When we were half-way to our destination, we met a search-party that had come out to look for our prisoner. Such a pitiful search-party, trudging wearily over the sand! It was the poor young woman from Och Marino with her baby. For two weeks she had waited, hoping each day that the man would return to her, and at last, in despair, she had started out by herself to walk over to Swerifskye and drag him away from his boon companions. Her only friend was a little Yurak girl, who helped her to carry the baby. When Hachenkoff saw the two forlorn little figures hastening over the waste to meet us, he had the grace to hang his head, while the poor girl burst into hysterical tears of anger and relief. We left Madame Antonoff to make peace as well as she could, and walked on towards the house. When we had visited it before, the surrounding swamps had been impassable with snow, but now the grass grew green and luxuriantly round the pools, and the sandy shores were bright with flowers. Ringed plover, dunlin, and little stints ran through the herbage, and some Siberian river gulls were evidently breeding by the lakes where I had seen them more than a month before. The house was locked, so we sat down to wait for the owners, who were trudging along wearily behind us. Our consciences smote us for asking the poor woman for hospitality; but unwitting of the circumstances, we had brought nothing with us except some meat lozenges, which, although their advertisers claimed for them that each contained the essence of two and a half oxen, did not make a satisfactory supper after a fifteen-mile walk. However, the arrival of unexpected visitors makes less difference to the housewife in Siberia than in most other parts of the world; for there is always an abundance of fish, and as each balagan bakes its own bread in large batches, the larder is never empty. The guests, moreover, are not particular as to beds, and if their own coats are not sufficient for palliasse and blanket, a rug on the floor is all that is needed.

Nevertheless we could only admire the pluck of the poor little woman, who, when she returned footsore and heartbroken, instead of giving way to her fatigue and trouble, first smoothed her hair and washed her own face and that of the child before preparing the evening meal. She herself had more colour in her cheeks than when we saw her last, for she worked all day in the open air at sorting and packing fish; but the baby looked more sickly than ever, and was evidently fading fast. Hachenkoff, who in his weak way was fond of it, hushed it while his wife prepared the *samovar*; and as it pressed its face to his shoulder, there was something grotesque and, at the same time, tragic in the likeness between father and child. We were so hungry that the meal of black bread, salt fish, and "brick" tea seemed one of the most delicious that we had ever tasted. Afterwards I went out shooting in the marsh, being anxious, if possible, to procure a specimen of the downy young of the Siberian herring-gull. The birds were evidently nesting on the tussocky islands in the lake. I shot two adult birds, but persuaded myself that it was too cold and too far to swim out on the chance of finding eggs. A grey plover, a species that I had not noticed on my previous visit in July, was also breeding in the marsh. I watched her for a long time, and finally came to the conclusion that she must have young ones hidden somewhere among the herbage, for she would run to one spot and shuffle upon the ground to decoy me into following her, and then go through the same antics in a totally different place, as if she were trying to protect first one fledgling and then another.

There were a number of Yurak *chooms* pitched farther down the river, for there is quite a Yurak colony at Och Marino in the summer-time. Seebohm, writing on his visit to the Yenesei,[1] says that it is difficult to discriminate between the Samoyede and Yurak tribes, and came to the conclusion that the former is a general name for any native.

The word "Samoyede" is certainly used in a general sense to describe the tribes on the Yenesei; but the

[1] *Birds of Siberia*, p. 400.

dark race to the east of the river to which it is most commonly applied is distinct enough from the Yuraks, from which it differs in dress and language. On the western side of the river it is more difficult to discriminate, and it has been suggested that all the so-called "Samoyedes" of the tundras west of the Yenesei are really Yuraks. It must not be forgotten that in former days the Yenesei must have been a much greater barrier to intercourse between the different races than it is at present—a barrier as wide as the Straits of Dover; and it would not be surprising to find two distinct, though allied nations, sprung originally from a common stock, living on either bank. All the native races are very cautious in giving their names to a member of another *orda*, as they call a man of a different nationality, probably because they suspect that the inquirer may be an official on the search for information. Both Siberiaks and aborigines are careful what they divulge, lest it should be used against them later by the authorities, and made a basis for further taxation or inquisition. Even the most innocent questions about the fishing are answered guardedly, and it is possible that Seebohm was suspected of some ulterior motive for his inquiries: hence his difficulty in obtaining information.

That night at Och Marino was the most uncomfortable that we had ever spent, or hope ever to spend again. Mr. Hall and Nill slept on the floor in one corner of the kitchen, and the Hachenkoff family in the other. My two companions and myself shared the wooden settle with Madame Antonoff. Each hour, Vassilli Vassillievitch called for tea and vodka to steady his nerves, and when he was not drinking, he smoked cigarette after cigarette, as quickly as the native girl could roll them for him. Added to this, it was not long before other, and even less desirable, companions made their presence known, and their raids soon banished sleep. We were all heartily glad when morning came, and we could have a breath of clean air, and a cold splash in the river outside.

The wind had dropped completely, and we chartered a native boat and three Yuraks to row us back to Swerifskye. Our hostess came down to the beach to watch our departure. This morning the poor girl's face looked as radiant as it ever could look, because her man had come home to her. Vassilli Vassillievitch himself sat huddled sulkily beside the stove, and answered nothing when Madame Antonoff said good-bye, and hinted kindly but gravely that the patience of even the most long-suffering landlord must come to an end at last. But his wife flared up at once in his defence. She would not hear a word about his neglect of herself. He was too good for this work, she said, and other folks were jealous and carried slanders of him to Golchika. She would not even admit that she had been solitary all by herself while he had been carousing at Swerifskye. But all the same, her green eyes looked a little wistful as the boat pushed off, and left her standing all alone on the shore. Then the babe wailed for her fretfully, and she ran back quickly to the house.

CHAPTER XII.

A native postman—An invitation—We go to Kazachye—A midnight visit—Simeon Prokopchuk and his family—Mezenchyne—The long-tailed skuas—A night on the river-bank—The tragedy of the balagans—The flowers of the tundra—The return to Golchika—Appeasing Gerasim Androvitch.

ONE day, about the middle of August, a native who came to Golchika told us that one of the Samoyedes at a neighbouring fishing station had a letter for us. He said that the letter had been given to this man for delivery by one, Simeon Prokopchuk, a brother of Gerasim Androvitch, who lived with his family in a balagan about fifty versts higher up the river. Our informant said that he had tried in vain to persuade his friend to let him bring the letter. The Yenesei native looks upon a letter as a most sacred trust. He may carry it about with him for weeks before he has the opportunity of delivering it, but he will never lose it, and to no one but the addressee will he give it up—not even to his prince.

On the following morning, the man himself, Katya by name, came over and delivered an exceedingly dirty and ill-spelt document to Miss Czaplicka. While he was drinking tea, with the regulation thimbleful of *vino*, she read it, and found that it contained an invitation from Simeon Prokopchuk to visit him and his family. We were beginning to tire of the hut, but there were certain difficulties in the way of the excursion. The chief of these was the lack of a boat. The only one available was that of Prokopchuk, which was so large and heavy that it required two men to row it. Then someone suggested that Joseph Gerasim-vitch—the Giant, as we had nicknamed him—might be persuaded to go. The Giant was shyly amiable, but non-committal. The season was getting on—there was the firewood to be gathered in. Clearly further pressure was needed. Next day we called on Madame Antonoff and persuaded her to allow the two girls to come with us to Kazachye for the night. At the time the Giant made no remark when he heard that Nura Antonoff was to be one of the party, but on the following day, about noon, he arrived in the boat with his holiday shirt on and his curls well brushed. Evidently the business of the firewood was not so very pressing after all. We dared not ask whether he had obtained his father's leave to take the boat.

Nura and Tania were waiting at the fish station. With them was poor, depressed Marusia Prokopchuk. She looked so forlorn, returning all alone to her drudgery in the kitchen, that we persuaded her to come too. And it was worth while to offend Gerasim Androvitch five times over just to see her eyes light up with pleasure at the invitation. But we were not to start yet. There was a favourable wind, and the Giant, like all Siberiaks, was nothing if not resourceful. He went down to the shore and returned presently, striding along like Polyphemus with a young tree-trunk over his shoulder. In less time than it takes to tell it, the pole was transformed into a mast, and an old tarpaulin, purloined from the store, made a square sail. Not only that, but Joseph pressed into our service Micha, the chubby-faced youth from the fish station, who was only too glad to earn a holiday by taking an oar.

Once out on the Yenesei the wind freshened, and we were able to sail nearly all the way. Indeed, the river was more choppy than some of the party found quite pleasant; but the waves, which had looked so formidable on our voyage from Och Marino in Antonoff's canoe, seemed nothing at all in Prokopchuk's unwieldy *lodka*. Once or twice, as we luffed, some water slapped over the gunwale, but the only thing that was really wetted was Vassilli's coat. As he and his possessions were by his own care or good fortune generally exempt from the accidents which befell those of the rest of us, I looked to see what he was doing. He, however, was lounging in the bows of the boat, singing sentimental songs to himself and snugly wrapped up in the sheepskin of Joseph Gerasimvitch. For that was the way of Vassilli. The common misfortunes of other mortals never affected him. I believe that even the brimstone of Gomorrah would have run from him as water runs from off a duck's back. Under all circumstances Vassilli slipped into the warmest and driest place, and the astonishing part of it was that, sooner or later, you yourself began likewise to indulge him.

About eleven o'clock in the evening, Joseph put the helm over and turned inshore. A broad and shallow river flowed down from the tundra, and at its mouth, on a green slope, stood the wooden house of Simeon Prokopchuk. Evidently the family were all asleep, for nobody came out to meet us except a pack of dogs. We felt like a troop of housebreakers as we marched up in a body in the dead of night. Joseph Gerasimvitch and his sister entered first, and soon returned with their uncle. Simeon Prokopchuk was a short, thickset man, with neither the good manners nor the good presence of his brother, Gerasim. He had been a publican in Yenesiesk, and a number of empty vodka bottles on the roof showed that he still maintained the customs of the pot-house. His right hand was twisted and crippled, and he had one of the ugliest and most repellent countenances that we saw on the Yenesei. However, in spite of the rude way in which we had aroused him, he was all hospitality, and ushered us into the kitchen. A flickering candle sent our monstrous shadows dancing over the ceiling. Before the stove, just awakened from sleep, stood Mrs. Simeon Prokopchuk. She was a large-limbed woman, who, if she had not aged by much toil and child-bearing, would have been strikingly handsome. When she had shaken hands with us she went quietly to fetch the *samovar*, as if it were quite a matter of course that a party of ten should turn up unexpectedly in the middle of the night. As she worked she explained that she and the younger children had only just returned to the house. They had passed the summer in a balagan at Mezenchyne, a fishing station about eight versts farther up the river, where the eldest son, Nicolai, still worked.

This house, although not so well furnished as that of

Prokopchuk at Golchika, was incomparably more comfortable than the balagan at Och Marino. On a shelf stood a couple of tins of condensed milk and cocoa, which betokened a certain amount of luxury. Presently our hostess took us into the inner room, which was larger than the first, and well furnished. A heap of furs lay on the floor. She turned them back, and underneath was the prettiest sight—five little naked children, warm and rosy with sleep, nestled together, for all the world like a litter of kittens, with their fists crumpled into their eyes. The proud mother pulled the youngest out of bed in order to exhibit him, whereupon he opened his sloe-black eyes and yelled lustily, until she gave him back to his eldest sister, aged six, who cuddled him up and stifled his wails with the coverlet.

As soon as the *samovar* was singing, we hastened to prepare supper, with the help of the Antonoff girls. They had brought bread and a pot of fresh caviare, and as we had tea, sugar, sausage, and cheese, we soon had a good supper on the table. We sat down, a party of twelve, to eat it with much merriment, in spite of the usual shortage of cups and saucers. On all these excursions we found that although we seemed to have provided ourselves amply, yet somehow in the end there were more thirsty throats than there were cups to supply them. After supper Joseph Gerasimvitch declared that he meant to walk on to the fishing station and see his cousin, Nicolai. Micha offered to go too, and, to our secret relief, Simeon Prokopchuk said that he would accompany them. We none of us liked our host, whose notion of conversation it was to blacken the characters of his acquaintance, and we were very glad that he was to spend the night elsewhere. When they had gone, and we had washed up the tea-things, we spread our sheep-skins on the floor. Our hostess gave us an armful of splendid furs, and we slept comfortably in the kitchen, or rather the Siberian members of the party did. For my part, I had an inconvenient English hankering for fresh air, and could not sleep in the close atmosphere of the balagan. At 5 a.m. it became unbearable, so I went out to finish the night on the river bank, where, although chilly, the wind was at least cool and clean.

It was a beautiful morning, and we decided to walk on to the Mezenchyne balagan, whither the Siberians had gone overnight; for there were some Samoyede and Yurak *chooms* there, and our anthropological companions were anxious to visit them. The river bank here, as on each side of the Yenesei in this district, rose into a range of low mud-hills, which had been scooped into all kinds of bluff and grotesque shapes by centuries of flood and snowfall. A rough-legged buzzard or two, soaring over the tundra, and a few stray gulls, were all the bird life to be seen. The actual shores of the Yenesei are curiously lonely. I often used to think how much I should like to introduce a couple of oyster-catchers to dabble at the water's edge, or even a sandpiper or two, to give animation to the scene.

We reached Mezenchyne a little after midday. It was a typical summer station, with two small balagans and three *chooms* pitched close to the beach. Nets were spread out to dry everywhere, and heaps of fish offal lay on the sand. Joseph Gerasimvitch, with his uncle and Micha, were in one of the balagans. They were cooking fish, and invited us to join them. While we were taking cover in the smoke from the raids of the mosquitoes, Simeon Prokopchuk, who was almost as anxious to oblige us as was his brother at Golchika, told Miss Czaplicka that, about fifteen versts away, in the middle of the tundra, were the remains of a mammoth. The actual place was known only to one of the native Yuraks, who had discovered it. Miss Czaplicka had long wished to secure some specimens of mammoth bones, and therefore she most pluckily decided not to rest here, but to take the native as a guide, and push forward at once, accompanied by Mr. Hall. They therefore took a little food in their pockets and started out immediately, hoping to reach our base at Kazachye on the following day. The three girls seemed to find plenty of entertainment, judging from the peals of laughter that came from the balagan, where they had taken refuge from the mosquitoes and also from the eyes of their chaperons, as I am afraid they regarded us. Miss Curtis wanted to go to the *chooms* to sketch the Samoyedes, and we arranged that she and I should meet at the balagan at six o'clock and walk back to Kazachye together. The only drawback to the arrangement was that we should thereby be obliged to keep the boat out for a second night, and we none of us liked to think of what Gerasim Androvitch might say. However, he was fifty versts away, and, as they say in Ireland: *It is time enough to shake hands with the devil when you meet him.*

A pair of long-tailed skuas were flying between the shore and the tundra with suspicious regularity. I followed them for some distance up the dry bed of a watercourse, which harboured such myriads of mosquitoes that it was only by smearing myself with a lard-and-tar ointment that I could watch the birds at all. About a mile from the balagan I found the object of the skuas' care—a gross and awkward youngster. He looked so ugly, as he sat upon a hillock, squalling to be fed, that I did not much mind shooting him. In this, however, I was foiled by half a dozen of the native dogs, who kept me under respectful but vigilant surveillance. Curiously enough, the old skuas objected to the dogs much more than to the human intruder; but the fledgling was very wide awake, and never allowed me to come within range of him. Eventually I shot the cock bird, and the other two flew away. Afterwards I went up to the higher lying tundra, but as my canine retainers persisted in following me, and quartered the ground on either side as they went, I bagged nothing but a young ruff in the ruddy plumage of the year. I returned to the balagan with my attendant pack to find Miss Curtis waiting for me. She said that Simeon Prokopchuk had accompanied her down to the *chooms*, and while there had received some drink. He had incited the natives to all sorts of antics, and as he was now lying asleep in the balagan, we thought that it would be a good opportunity to make our escape.

It was a beautiful evening, with just that touch of crispness in the air that in England belongs to the first autumn frost. In its own way the fall of the year is as tonic as the spring, and carries no sadness with it. Then, as at all the great seasonal changes, we put our mistakes behind us and turn over a new leaf. This year pheasants will fly higher, and foxes will run straighter, than they ever did before. Therefore I like the autumn weather well, and put it second only to the spring in the mercies that are vouchsafed to us in this good world.

The sand by the waterside was hard and firm for walking, and we soon outstripped the Siberian girls. By and by we saw three figures following us in the distance. They could, we thought, be no other than the tipsy Simeon Prokopchuk, with Joseph Gerasimvitch and Micha, and we were annoyed to see that the three girls were lingering behind. We felt more or less responsible for the young Antonoffs, and had not much trust in their discretion. We also had a disquieting suspicion that a flask of cognac had been left on the table, and we hurried on quickly to put it out of sight before the master of the house came home. However, our fears were needless; for when half-way through supper the loiterers appeared, giggling and rather flushed, their escort consisted only of Joseph, Micha, and their cousin Nicolai Prokopchuk, a slender, good-looking boy of about nineteen years of age.

After supper the girls spread their beds in the inner room, and Miss Curtis and I were expected to do the same; but the thought of eleven people behind those hermetically closed windows daunted us, and as it was a fine night, we resolved to sleep out on the river bank in our sheepskins. We explained our intention to our hostess as well as we could do so in halting Russian; but she, poor soul, was much distressed, and poured out a long explanation, of which we could not understand a single word. We therefore smiled and said "Thank you," and "Good-night," which custom had taught us were the most intelligible words of our vocabulary, and then we went down to the riverside, where we made for ourselves a very comfortable bed between two trunks of driftwood. The darkness was never deeper than a soft twilight glow, and the mysterious shining spears of the *aurora borealis* mingled with the glamour of a night-long dawn. However, we awoke with one accord at four o'clock, and found that the rain was pattering down smartly. We sat up and agreed sleepily that we certainly ought to go indoors, and then turned round and went to sleep again. Two hours after, when we awoke for good, needless to say we were very wet, but any amount of rain was preferable to the air of the balagan.

As we entered the house for shelter, we heard heavy snoring from a small and noisome den which opened off the porch. We pushed open the kitchen door cautiously, expecting to find the floor encumbered by the sleeping forms of Joseph and his friends. Behold, there was no one in the room except Vassilli, who lay at his ease on the settle by the stove. It dawned upon us that through our mad English craving for fresh air, fate had once more played into the hands of our henchman. Madame Prokopchuk had taken our (to her) incomprehensible conduct as an extreme symptom of our distrust of the three young Siberiaks, and accordingly they had been banished to the bathhouse. Hence the mysterious snoring outside. But Vassilli had pointed out that, as our servant, he must be above suspicion; and therefore he had enjoyed the warm kitchen all by himself, while the rest of the party were either crowded into one room, or slept in the bathhouse or on the river-bank, as necessity or inclination drove them.

While we were wondering how to pass the time until breakfast, our hostess came into the kitchen. We were surprised to see her astir so early, and were still more surprised, and sorry too, to find that she had spent the previous day in making bread for us, and had come out at this hour to attend to her baking. In vain did we assure her that we had brought plenty of food for our party. She would take no refusal until we had breakfasted off the very best fish *pirog* that we ever tasted. We made her join us, but she had scarcely eaten a morsel before the children awoke, and her day's work began by the washing and dressing of all five.

The tragedy of the women in those Siberian balagans has still to be written. The lot of the overworked wife and mother in civilised lands is hard enough; but there at least she may sometimes have the luxury of a good grumble with a sympathetic neighbour. But these women in the wooden huts of the Yenesei never see another white woman from month's end to month's end, and the loneliness and monotony of their lives must be terrible. This woman had already five little children, all under seven years old, and a sixth would soon be born. In the summer-

BALAGAN FOLK.

time she worked at the fishing all day, and when the natives came to trade she worked at night as well.

The winter would soon come, and then the whole family would be shut up in two rooms for the greater part of the day; but indoors or out, summer or winter, she dared not spare herself. There was the bread to be baked; the house must be swept; the children must be clothed; and there was no one but herself to do all these things. Truly these women are *burnt up* in the cause of civilisation. In Siberia, as is said to be the case in so many of our own colonies, it is no uncommon thing to find a man of middle life who has outlived two or even three wives. Up on the hill behind the house stood a large wooden cross, with two little ones beside it. This was the grave of the first Mrs. Prokopchuk and her two infants. Each time that this poor woman stepped out of the door she could see the tomb of her predecessor, who had already gone the road along which she herself was travelling. What would she do when the child was to be born, we asked—was there any other woman near? No, she answered, but her man was a master at the work. He had received all the other children at their birth. (We thought of Simeon Prokopchuk, with his crippled hand, and of the vodka bottles on the roof.) In spite of the hereditary taint that they could scarcely hope to escape, these children were the healthiest that we had seen since we came to Golchika. In that country the climate is so so severe that it is very difficult to rear a child, and, besides, there is no milk. Most of the infants are weaned upon tea and bread. The result is that the women all suckle their babes until they are two or three years old, and both mother and child suffer in consequence. As soon as it was known that we had some condensed milk among our stores at Golchika, one woman after another came and asked to buy some for her children.

The girls and their squires still slept, and as the rain had passed away and the sun was shining, I went for a ramble up the valley, for there is a great fascination about those little lonely rivers of the tundra, up which no boat ever sails. In this bay the river-bank was more sheltered than at Golchika, and the flowers were scarcely past their prime. The slopes were starry with white saxifrage, lemon-coloured poppies, and forget-me-nots, and in the sunny corners blue larkspurs grew knee high. Here was even that beautiful orange ranunculus which grew so luxuriantly near Yenesiesk. In Siberia, where the summer is so short, the flowers run through a ridiculous season of six weeks—an epitome of a cycle which, in England, requires a whole year for its completion. In our country we begin decorously with the sober butterbur in January, and then follows a course of white and golden bulbous things. These give place to buttercups and daisies, forget-me-nots, iris, and rose, and these again to flaming gold and purple flowers — ragweeds, thistles, and marjoram. On the Yenesei it is true that a sort of Eastern butterbur raises its pallid head before the snow has gone, but in a day or two everything else crowds on to the top of it. The changes are rung quite correctly through white and yellow—cistus, garlic, and buttercups—to blue and saffron—poppies, lupines, and forget-me-nots—and lastly to purple and red—valerian and heath; but all the blooms chase each other through a space of six weeks, and you have no sooner realised their coming than they have gone again. It is just the synopsis of a summer, and already the whortleberry leaves were tinged blood-red with autumn. The only butterflies that hovered over the flowers were two species that were evidently nearly allied to the brimstones and tortoiseshells of our English waysides; and there was also a small day-flying moth, with wings prettily variegated with primrose and umber.[1]

But although vegetable life was at its heyday, the tide of bird life had already begun to ebb towards the south. The Temminck's stints, the last of the waders to breed, set their signs manual in the criss-cross patterns of their toes as they paddled over the mud, but the willow-grouse and the little stints and the ruffs were already strong on the wing. Young snow-buntings, bluethroats, and wheatears flitted along the river-bank, and a couple of long-tailed ducks chaperoned their broods out of the ken of a soaring buzzard.

Even the remnant of the mosquitoes could not disturb the Sabbatarian calm of the tundra. It was good to be alive and listen how the birds on the sandbanks gave thanks for the good weather that a kind Providence sends to the Yenesei in August to make amends for the storms that are to be. Even the Giant

---

[1] A specimen has been identified by the authorities at the British Museum as *Hyphoraia subnebulosa* (Dyer), which has been described from Alaska.

and his two companions felt the influence of the day, and occupied themselves idyllically in picking wild flowers. Of course the Giant's nosegay went to pretty Nura Antonoff.

About four o'clock in the afternoon, our two companions arrived on reindeer sledges. They were accompanied by a number of natives, and also by Simeon Prokopchuk, who had slept off his carouse. Miss Czaplicka, always tireless where there was work to be done, began at once to take measurements of the natives' skulls. The rest did mysterious business with Prokopchuk, and then sat down to an uproarious meal of tea and vodka. The difference between Simeon and Gerasim Androvitch was nowhere more seen than in their dealings with the natives. The latter never permitted the least familiarity, nor allowed them to take any liberties. Simeon Prokopchuk, on the other hand, indulged in horseplay with them, and encouraged them in all sorts of antics. There was, in particular, one big boisterous Samoyede, with a shock head of hair, who was evidently in the condition described in Ireland as: "not to say drunk, but he had drink taken." He gambolled about the beach, danced with our host, and was so far on the high road to get out of hand altogether that we were glad to take our leave. We promised to send our poor hostess some milk for her babies, and in turn she offered to sell some furs. If afterwards it was found that she had the best of the latter bargain—well, as the Malay proverb says: *If there are worms in the earth, why dig them up?*

We left Kazachye that evening, and as the wind

had fallen completely, we were obliged to row most of the way home. The two young Prokopchuks were both very uncertain what their reception would be, after their two nights' absence. Joseph was tempted to shirk the interview with his father by spending the night at the fish station. However, he was too generous to leave Marusia to bear the blame alone, and so, in the end, he went home with her.

The hut was quite quiet as we rowed up to it, but as the boat ran ashore, the door opened and the tousled head of Gerasim Androvitch looked out. He had very obligingly come down to sleep there during our absence, for a good deal of pilfering went on round the houses in the settlement when there was no one at home to look after the property. Marusia and her brother slunk home at once, but we persuaded Gerasim Androvitch to stay for an impromptu supper. This invitation, and a glass of cognac, softened his heart, and next day his son and daughter escaped without the scolding that they had expected.

CHAPTER XIII.

The fall of the year—The departure of the *chooms*—The arrival of the *Yenesiesk*—First news of the war—Packing up—A dinner with the Antonoffs—Church parade at Golchika—the *Turukhansk* and *Lena* arrive—Stormbound—News of home—The *Oryol* again—Joseph Gerasimvitch—Disappointed hopes—The English steamers—A native wedding—Nosonovsky Ostrov.

AUGUST the 14th, the day on which we returned from Kazachye, was the turning-point of the summer. It was difficult to say exactly wherein the change lay, but there was a subtle difference in the air, and on the following morning, as surely as if the great fiat had gone forth to the proclamation of trumpets, we knew that summer was over and autumn had begun. Those who live much alone in the wilderness are the first to discern the great seasonal changes, and act upon their warning. That very day the natives in the settlement began to repair their nets after the season's fishing, and cut up wood to build their winter sledges. Yet more promptly the birds responded to the change. Even the least observant of my companions remarked upon the sudden flux of feathered life on the mud-banks in front of the hut. All day long, turnstones, stints, and ruffs came and went in companies, and the divers left the tundra lakes and flew down to the river, screaming jubilantly as if in anticipation of their autumn journey.

And although we civilised folk were less sensitive to weather influences than either the birds or the Samoyedes, yet we too felt an indefinable *something*—perhaps a legacy from the days when our fathers were as simple as they—which made us long to pack up our things and likewise take our leave of Golchika.

At this time our plans were rather nebulous. Miss Czaplicka and Mr. Hall had arranged to travel back to Turukhansk by the *Oryol*, and from thence make their way into the tundra, in order to study the Tungus tribes. Miss Curtis and I were to return to England for the winter. We wished if possible to obtain a passage on one of the ships of the Siberian Steamship Company, which, each year, sends an expedition for trading purposes to the mouth of the Yenesei. This expedition was expected to reach Golchika at the end of August; but there was always some uncertainty about its arrival, owing to the condition of the ice in the Kara Sea, which in some years completely closes the Yenesei against shipping. If the *Angliski parahod* (English steamer), as the Golchikans called it, did not arrive, we could return to Krasnoyarsk in the *Oryol*, and from thence make our way overland by the Trans-Siberian Railway. Our hopes as to the punctual arrival of the steamer were a good deal dashed by the report of some Samoyedes who came to Golchika at the beginning of August. They had travelled up from the wild tundras which lay far away at the mouth of the river, and they said that, farther north, they had been unable to fish, for the season was so cold that the ice on the lakes had never broken up at all. However, in any case, we had to make all preparations for an early departure, for on 25th August the river steamers—*Oryol*, *Turukhansk*, and *Lena*—were expected to arrive, and we must be ready to leave for the south. There was plenty to be done. Specimens must be packed up, stores must be examined, and good-byes said.

And we were not the only people in Golchika who were making ready for an autumn flitting. One by one the *chooms* disappeared from the other side of the river. Almost every evening we could see against the sky the tangle of reindeer horns which told that the sledges were coming in from the tundra. It was quite sad to walk along the river-bank and see the blackened patches, now strewn with rubbish, which showed where a *choom* had once stood, and no longer meet the kindly brown faces which used to peer round the doorways and wish us " Good-day " as we passed.

On the 25th of August three of the remaining *chooms* were moved across the river, and pitched just above the house of Prokopchuk. Towards evening I was strolling up the valley, when far away I heard the strange long cries with which the natives urge their reindeer. Presently, across the marshes, came a score of sledges. The drivers dismounted on the opposite bank and turned the deer into the water. At first the leaders were reluctant, but one of the natives launched a canoe and headed them out into the stream. The rest followed docilely enough, and soon the whole herd of perhaps a hundred and twenty deer were grunting and splashing their way across the river. I thought that there was something familiar about the man who paddled his little

CHOOMS AT GOLCHIKA.

VASSILLI SOTNIKOFF AND HIS REINDEER.

craft to and fro so adroitly to hasten the laggards, and soon recognised the white wolfskin cap of our old friend Vassilli Sotnikoff from the *choom*. I greeted him and asked him where he was going.

He waved a vague hand towards the south as he answered in the naive fashion of his race: "*Daleko, daleko*" (far away, far away). That is all that you can ever learn from a native. He is going "into the tundra, far, far away." I asked after Nicolai and Maxim and the little old mother. Nicolai was here with the sledges, but the rest were waiting in the tundra. They had come here to buy tea and *soushki* for the journey. To-morrow they would all go south before the snow came. Already the nights were cold, and their warm clothing had been left behind them in their winter *choom* at the border of the forest. We said: "*Prastchai*" (farewell) many times, and wished each other luck in pidgin-Russ.

Next morning all the sledges had gone, and the river-bank was deserted. Cold embers and a litter of worn-out garments and cracked cooking-pots were all that was left of the summer settlement. The people had all gone "into the tundra."

This same morning—the 26th of August—was hot and still. Soon after midday we were returning from a walk, when we saw Vassilli gesticulating like a madman from the roof of the hut. There, just off the island, was a steamer at last. Robinson Crusoe was not more delighted than we, for a ship meant news of the outside world—the first that we had received for weeks. We tumbled pell-mell into the boat and rowed off in haste down the river; but as we reached Kutcherenkoff's fish station, we met a boat coming ashore from the vessel. A smart gendarme officer sat in the bows, and beside him was none other than our old friend, Mr. Christensen, from Krasnoyarsk. A minute later we were shaking hands with him on the bank.

I remember our first words, spoken laughingly: "Well, have you arranged for us to go home in the English steamer?"

But his reply struck all the laughter out of us.

"You *must* go home that way, for you cannot travel overland. England is at war with Germany."

We stood aghast.

"Yes," he went on, "and Russia and France and Servia and Montenegro are helping England, and Austria is allied with Germany."

It sounded like Armageddon! "But what are they all fighting about?" we managed to inquire.

"Because a Servian student murdered the heir of Austria."

That was all he could tell us. Even this news was out of date, for the steamer had left Krasnoyarsk three weeks previously, and had received no fresh tidings since passing Turukhansk. We could only stare at each other helplessly and exclaim: "War in Europe!" It seemed wonderful that in such a state of things the sun should continue to shine.

In the midst of our bemusement, the gendarme officer came up and asked leave to photograph us in company with the natives, because "it would make such an interesting group." As a matter of fact, we reflected afterwards that he did not so much want our portraits

A SUMMER ON THE YENESEI

for the sake of their intrinsic interest, as for the more practical purpose of identification; for the Russian Government has always a lurking fear that the opening up of the Kara Sea route will afford a means of escape to some of the Yenesei exiles. However, we were too much bewildered to refuse. I believe that, if at that moment he had asked to electrocute us, we should have submitted obediently enough. As it was, I remember being pushed into position between two very disreputable and awestruck Samoyedes, and if my expression was anything like those of my companions, I must have looked quite as miserable as the most despairing of political exiles.

Later on we had a long consultation with Mr. Christensen. He had heard that the two English ships had left Denmark safely just before the outbreak of the war, and unless any accident had befallen them on the way, they were due to reach the Yenesei at any moment. They were escorting three small tug-boats, which had been bought by the Russian Government from a Hamburg firm for trade on the Yenesei. Mr. Christensen himself had chartered the *Yenesiesk* and the *Ob*, two small river steamers, and had brought down eight lighters loaded with the cargo destined for Europe. He had left these lighters at the appointed rendezvous at Nosonovsky Ostrov—one of the Breokoffsky islands—and had come down to Golchika in the *Yenesiesk* to look out for the English ships. Our mails were following in the *Oryol*, which was only a day's run behind. He had arranged that we were all to go together in the *Oryol* as far as Nosonovsky, a distance of about two hundred versts to the south. Here Miss Curtis and I were to disembark and live on one of the lighters until the English expedition arrived.

Since we might have to leave at any moment, we spent the rest of the day in a whirl of packing and preparation, but on the following morning, instead of the *Oryol*, the *Turukhansk* and, later on, the *Lena* appeared. They stopped only for a few hours at Golchika, for they were both going on to the Sopochnaya to take up a cargo of fish. The *Yenesiesk* lay where she was, for she had not enough coal to take her to the river's mouth.

On the third morning, however, there was still no *Oryol*, for a boisterous easterly wind held her stormbound about fifty versts up the river. Perhaps the week that followed was the most trying that we spent in Siberia. The gale raged without intermission for six days. Each evening we expected the wind to drop, but morning after morning it roared over the tundra and lashed the river into foam. Most of our goods were packed up, and as at any hour we might have to start in a hurry, we did not like to open the boxes. Each meal we hoped would be the last that we should eat in the hut. We partook of it, figuratively speaking, as the Israelites ate before the Exodus, with our loins girded and our staves in our hands. We began to run very short of food also; and as five people cannot live for an indefinite time on condensed milk and sardines, we were reduced to buying salt beef from the Prokopchuks. Besides this, we were very anxious lest the continued storm should blow the ice into the river's mouth, and so prevent the arrival of the English steamers. Thus we all felt unsettled, even Vassilli, who had begun to hanker for the fleshpots of Egypt, and said daily that he was anxious to return to his " morning cup of chocolate and his daughter at Krasnoyarsk."

But during this week of waiting, we were able to greet some old friends who had returned in the *Lena*. Chief of these were Anastasia Ivanowna, and, more welcome still, Michael Petrovitch. One evening, kind Madame Antonoff, who guessed perhaps that our larder was getting low, asked us to dinner to enjoy the good things that her husband had brought from town. It was characteristic of those people always to share a delicacy with their neighbours. Dinner was at six o'clock, and on arrival we found the little room so full of guests that a kind of overflow meeting had to be held in the bedroom. First there was Michael Petrovitch himself, as stout and jolly as ever. With him he had brought a pale shy student from the Petersburg university. This luckless young man had got into trouble owing to his political opinions, and had been exiled to the Yenesei for three years. This winter, the last of his banishment, he had obtained leave to stay at Golchika, in order to study the language and customs of the Samoyedes. There was also a young cousin of Madame Antonoff, who, with his wife and child, had just travelled all the way from Little Russia. In time he was to take Hachenkoff's place at the Och Marino fishery. The third guest was an elderly priest, who had come from Dudinka in order to hold the annual services at Golchika. The dinner was a very grand one of three courses, with a dessert of nuts and chocolate creams. We had *stchee* and macaroni pudding, and lastly a blanc-mange made of fruit juice. The feast was notable, because nobody was expected to speak. Unless he really had something to say, he could keep silence, and was under no obligation to manufacture such small talk as passes current at European dinner-parties. We were very grateful for this custom, for Madame Antonoff was too busy for conversation, the exiled student was painfully shy, and none of us dared to open a discussion with the pope, whose cassock and spectacles were both rather awe-inspiring. However, towards the end of the meal, the latter leaned forward and inquired whether we came from London. We answered that we did, whereupon he wanted to know how large London was. Was it, for instance, larger than Ostend? He had heard so, but could scarcely believe it, and was it really built on both banks of the Thames?

We told him that London was rather larger than Ostend, and drew an elaborate diagram on the table-cloth to show its exact relation to the Thames. The pope seemed agreeably surprised, and remarked: " I have always understood that the English nation was very cold and stiff, but these women surpass even the French in vivacity!"

On the following day, which was Sunday, the pope held a service in the church. Gerasim Androvitch made it his business to collect a congregation. Early in the morning he went over to the remaining *chooms*, and by dint of bribes and threats, he gathered together about a dozen natives of all ages, and drove them off to church. Sylkin tried to cry off by pleading a sore back, but Gerasim would have no malingering, and about midday we saw a string of depressed figures wending their way across the island. Anything more ridiculous than this enforced attendance of the natives can scarcely be imagined. They know nothing whatever of the doctrine, and neither they nor the Siberiaks understood a word of the service, which, of course, was conducted in the old Slavonic tongue. Something of the spirit in which the worship was held may be realised from the following custom. At the close of the ceremony, a collection was made for the benefit of the pope. Those who gave half a rouble had an altar candle credited to them, but those who gave a whole rouble had the honour of hearing their names shouted aloud by the congregation. We were told that the pope sometimes received as much as fifty roubles at a single service.

While the people were at church, the gendarme went out to search for vodka. Almost the only evidence of the war at Golchika were the effects of the Russian Government's magnificent crusade against alcohol. Only those who have visited the country can have the slightest idea of what the suppression of the drink traffic means to the Yenesei. Surely a nation which can thus make war upon her own besetting sin has already achieved a victory mightier than any that her armaments can win! Only two days previously this officer had seized 2000 roubles' worth of vodka at one haul. The law was carried out without any distinction of persons. Our friend, Michael Petrovitch, had bought a few bottles of cognac for his own use, but these were confiscated with the rest. The officer also searched Prokopchuk's house, but needless to say he found nothing, for the wily Gerasim Androvitch had already placed his stock of vodka in a safe hiding-place in the tundra.

During those last days our relations with Prokopchuk were rather strained. We had agreed to pay him for the repairs, etc., of the hut, but the bill when presented was made out for twenty roubles more than the sum agreed upon. Vassilli was sent to point out the "mistake," and as the result of his negotiations, Gerasim deleted the objectionable items without demur. He had not expected us to pay them, and would have despised us if we had. It was just his way of doing business. He invited himself to supper in the evening, and his dignified geniality was such that it was impossible to turn the cold shoulder to him, fraud though we knew him to be.

Joseph Gerasimvitch was a more serious problem. At first he had been too shy to visit us uninvited; but since the expedition to Kazachye, he frequently called in the evening as he returned along the river-bank from his work at Kutcherenkoff's fish station. For the first day or two he sat silent in the corner, then gradually he spoke out his mind.

Like most big and simple-minded people, the Giant was extraordinarily patient and slow to wrath; but equally, when it was kindled, his anger was fierce and deep. Now it flamed up red-hot against his father's treatment of his mother. Mrs. Gerasim Prokopchuk and her husband had never been on the best of terms, and the constant interference of her sister, Anastasia, had not made for peace. The climax had come two years before, when, during the winter, the poor woman had developed scurvy. Her condition killed what little remained of her husband's affection, and several times he ill-treated her brutally before her son. In the summer she had gone to the south for medical treatment, and was now living at Achinsk with the younger children. Meanwhile, Anastasia Ivanowna had usurped her place at Golchika, and although, to do her justice, she meant to do her best for her nephew and niece, yet, as we had ample opportunity of observing, she treated them simply as unpaid servants. During the previous winter, while her father and her aunt had gone together on a trading expedition into the tundra, Marusia had lived alone in the dreary little house with only the man, Michael, and his witless wife for companions. Only those who have lived at such a place as Golchika can have the faintest idea of the severity of those arctic winters, when for two months the frozen land sees no daylight, and the *pourga* howls over the tundra. And how greatly must the terrors of the solitude increase when there are no books and little society to occupy the mind! After such an experience the wonder was, not that the girl looked listless and depressed, but that she kept her reason at all. However, this autumn, her father had consented that she should go to Achinsk to see her mother and learn dressmaking. She was to leave in the *Oryol*, and the Giant was trying to make up his mind to accompany her. It was a wrench, for most of his twenty-four years of life had been spent at Golchika, and of the world which lay beyond the Yenesei he knew as little as any English schoolboy of half his age. He talked the matter out in his slow, persevering way, and it was almost midnight before he left the hut. Vassilli came in half an hour later with the news that Gerasim Androvitch had come out to meet his son, and abused him roundly for some fancied neglect. "I would not speak to a dog as he spoke to Joseph Gerasimvitch," said Vassilli virtuously, "but Joseph did not answer a single word."

We found the situation rather a delicate one, for while we sympathised heartily with the Giant in the wish to escape from his miserable home and participation in the very doubtful transactions of his father, yet we did not like to appear to influence his decision. However, on the following evening, when Joseph went past the door with the slow, dignified step that was peculiar to him, he did not stop, but merely bowed good-night with a stately inclination of his curly head and passed on. It was just as well that he did so, for shortly afterwards our door opened without a preliminary knock, and the two old Prokopchuks entered. They asked for cigarettes, and made a few uneasy remarks as they smoked them, while we wondered what this visitation might portend. However, they took their leave without saying anything, and it was not until afterwards that we realised that the worthy couple had paid us a surprise visit in order to find out whether Joseph was spending the evening at our house.

The gale blew itself out on 2nd September, and at

midday news was brought that the *Oryol* would be in at daybreak. In the evening, Joseph told us that he had made up his mind to leave Golchika on the next day. We feared that when his father heard of the intention, he might, in his anger, refuse to allow Marusia to leave home. We tried to persuade Joseph to let her start safely with us in the *Oryol* while he himself followed a few days later in the *Lena*; but the Giant refused to do this. He replied that Nura Antonoff was going to Yenesiesk in the latter steamer and, as he said simply :

"It would spoil her name for ever among these people if she and I left Golchika together."

We had always noticed Joseph's love and reverence for Nura; and it touched us the more that at present the girl was a flighty little minx, and not nearly good enough for the honest Giant.

Meanwhile the *Yenesiesk* was still lying off the island, and in the evening we saw Mr. Christensen. He was anxious about the arrival of the English steamers, which were now more than a week overdue. The *Lena* had brought up a bundle of newspapers, in one of which was a little paragraph stating that three German torpedo boats had captured some English merchantmen off Trondhjem. Mr. Christensen was afraid that these German warships might have interfered with the expedition. He therefore advised us to give up the idea of returning by the Kara Sea, and to go straight to Krasnoyarsk in the *Oryol*.

We awoke early on the following morning, and ran straight to the window. There at last was the *Oryol*, and a few minutes later, Joseph Prokopchuk knocked at the door with a huge packet of letters—the first that we had received since we left England at the end of May. I felt just like a child with a stocking full of toys on Christmas morning, as I sat up in bed and tore open letter after letter. Of course they had all been written before the war had broken out, and our joy in reading them was somewhat tempered by our anxiety to know what was going on now in Europe.

Before we had time to open them all, there was a clank of oars outside, and the Prokopchuks appeared, ready to row us and our luggage to the steamer. Hence we left in such haste that we had no time to say a sentimental farewell to the little hut which had been our home for two months. The Giant was wearing his fur cap, and had put on his best shirt under his old white *sakoōy*. We could not help looking at him, but he only stared at his boots as he tugged at his oar in his patient, ox-like way. The only fear was that Vassilli should give away the plot. Our henchman dearly loved to hug a secret, and he cast such meaning glances, and smiled such knowing smiles, that if Gerasim Androvitch had not been the worse for liquor, he must have suspected that something was afoot, even if he had not already guessed it from the woebegone expression of little Michael, the servant, who, like everybody else in Golchika, loved Joseph Gerasimvitch.

Ten minutes later, and we were on the *Oryol* again, feeling as if it were only yesterday that we had left it. There was Captain Ello, and his wife, as benevolent as ever. Nicolai, the waiter, with his hat as usual on the back of his head, beamed at us in the saloon; but the cook and most of the sailors had been taken for the war. Russia needed every man, and from Yenesiesk alone a thousand men had been sent to the front.

Everyone from Golchika was on board, whether southward bound or not. There was the chubby Micha, who had eyes for nobody but Marusia Prokopchuk, the Jew, Cherniavinsky, from the fish station, and my acquaintances from the Kuria balagan. They were all going to Yenesiesk, as also was the pope. Old Sylkin and his boys had come to see the steamer, and also Anastasia and Nill. Here, too, we took leave of Michael Petrovitch and his wife. Their unfailing kindness and fun are among the pleasantest of my Siberian recollections. It was sad to say good-bye to all these good friends, and know that we might never meet them again. However, in almost every case we left them prosperous. Anastasia was so relieved that her Nill would not be taken for a soldier that there would be no more domestic tiffs for a long time. The Antonoffs had rebuilt their house and were looking forward to a busy and cheerful winter. Nura was to go to a situation in Yenesiesk, but little Tania, much against her will, was to remain behind and finish her schooling. However, with the matchmaking instincts of our sex, we thought that Tania would not find her studies with the exiled student as irksome as she expected!

The only family whose affairs did not run smoothly were the Prokopchuks. The Giant was fully resolved to brave his father's anger and go out into the world, but unfortunately Anastasia Ivanowna had guessed his plans, and had hidden all his clothes. Consequently he had left home with nothing but what he was wearing, and had not a kopeck in his pocket. He had not even brought his sheepskin, lest, as he proudly said, "they should say that he was a thief who took what was not his own."

When he told Gerasim Androvitch of his intention, the old man wept tears of mingled grief and vodka, but the Giant remained firm. Afterwards they called Joseph into the cabin and tried to stupefy him with alcohol, but he was shrewd enough to see their purpose, and refused to drink. We could not but feel a little vexed with Marusia. Instead of helping her brother, she did nothing but weep because she must leave her father. Gerasim Androvitch possessed a strange magnetism for affection. He had been a neglectful, and sometimes an unkind, father to the girl, and yet she grieved bitterly at parting from him. She would have preferred to stay with him, rather than with her indulgent mother. But that was his way. No matter who it was, nor how badly he had treated them, nobody ever bore a grudge against the charming old sinner—nobody, that is, except his big, silent son, who leaned against the rail and watched the dusk creep over the tundra.

It was all very tragic, and yet for the life of me I could not help feeling as if we were looking on, not at a bit of real life, but at some rather trite melodrama. Here were the old stock characters—the jealous stepmother, the weak father, and the handsome disinherited son. The sunset helped out the illusion. It was as red as fire, and against the flaming sky the hooded figures of the natives, and the bearded heads of the Siberiaks, were limned clear and black, like dark silhouettes cut out and pasted against the glowing orb of a lamp. In fact, the effect was so theatrical that the onlooker almost expected to see the limelight operator in the "wings"; and unconsciously I found myself approving the attitude of the Giant, who stood moodily beside the gangway with his arms folded under his *sakoōy*. Anastasia Ivanowna stepped into the boat without a farewell, but as she pushed past him, she dropped her shawl. Joseph picked it up and gave it to her courteously.

Old Prokopchuk was weeping maudlin tears, and as he went down to the boat he said to his son:

"Are you going?"

"Yes," said the Giant laconically.

"Will you not even come as far as the shore with us?"

"No," said the Giant. He knew that they would not hesitate to drag him by force from the boat, and detain him until after the steamer had sailed. Then the canoe pushed off, and we watched it disappear into the dusk. I almost expected to hear the bell ring for "curtain."

The comic element was as usual supplied by Vassilli, who had a fine idea of drama. He listened eagerly to the duologue between father and son, and then cried out delightedly:

"Madame, did you hear them? The old one asked him whether he would go back, and he said that he would not do so!"

"Vassilli, *nye govorit*,"[1] hissed Miss Curtis fiercely; and Vassilli, who had a wholesome awe of our "Artist Mees," as he called her, subsided into the crowd.

But just then something occurred which took our attention away from the Prokopchuks. Captain Ello called us up on to the bridge to look at a faint smudge, which might have been smoke, on the northern horizon. The English steamers! Our hopes immediately rose high. Presently a second wreath appeared beside the first, and we were jubilant. But when a third came into view, we became suspicious, and soon, to our disgust, the whole northern horizon was dotted with smoke puffs. What we had seen was nothing more than the birth of a flock of little cumulus clouds from the surface of the Yenesei. One by one they floated away into the sunset, and as they rose, our spirits sank.

We went below, and invited Marusia and her brother to supper in the saloon. It was not a cheerful meal. The young Prokopchuks were silent and depressed. We were uncertain about our future plans, and were besides full of anxiety as to what was happening at home. Suddenly the captain called us again: "Ship in sight!" Upstairs we rushed, binoculars in hand. Yes, there was not a shadow of doubt this time. On the horizon, just where we had seen the first "smoke wreaths," were two vessels. In the glamour of the sunset, they seemed to be uplifted above the water, and float in the air like the wraiths of

[1] Do not talk!

ships. They might have been two of the fleet of the Flying Dutchman. Fascinated, we watched their slow advance, and as night drew on, saw the twinkling lights kindle at their mastheads. Then came the pronouncement that shattered our hopes for the second time that evening. Those, said the wise men of the *Oryol*, were not the English ships at all. They were nothing but the *Lena* and the *Turukhansk* returning from the Sopochnaya. The captain said so; the pilot said so; everyone said so except Joseph Gerasimvitch, who maintained that the lights were too bright to belong to either of the river steamers. My companion and I were depressed beyond words. Before us lay a tedious, uncomfortable, and eminently difficult journey over two continents seething with war. Behind us was the estuary of one of the noblest rivers in the world, guarded as by mighty gates by the twin promontories of Och Marino and the Sopochnaya. Beyond, lay the tremendous skyline of the Arctic Ocean, and the seas that no man has sailed:

"*Gazing hence we see the water that grows iron round the Pole,
From the shore that hath no shore beyond it set in all the sea.*"

The *Oryol's* siren hooted her melancholy farewell to Golchika, already hidden in the gloom, and we slowly moved southwards. I cannot tell with what feelings of disappointment I turned my back upon the North. Seebohm had once, Popham had twice, failed to make the passage of the Kara Sea. I had hoped that I, more fortunate than they, might have followed the course of the great river down to the ocean. The immense horizon, splendid with sunset, lay behind us like a land of enchantment, filled with all the mystery and magic of the north. Sadly we turned away from it and went below. Disappointed hope is a bad bedfellow.

. . . . . .

At seven o'clock next morning came a call : "Come up quickly; the ships are in sight." The *Oryol* was rolling along in a choppy sea, and there, not ten versts away, were the vessels at last. There was no room for uncertainty this time. Here were two big steamers with three little tug-boats between them, all keeping station as they steamed steadily southwards. The English expedition had reached the Yenesei. We joined hands and danced round the bridge, singing, "Hurrah for the Kara Sea!"

All day we puffed up the river, but towards evening the wind rose again and obliged us to lie to. There was a balagan on shore, and about midnight a boatload of people came off to the *Oryol*. Presently the pope came in to tell us that he was about to celebrate a native wedding. Should we like to see it? Of course we went, and were given the seat of honour beside the captain's wife at one end of the saloon. The bridegroom was an Ostiak, and the bride was a half-breed—the daughter of a Yurak by a white woman. Their relations, in various degrees of inebriety, crowded into the room. The pope, in the gaudy robes of his order, put a little table in the middle of the room, and arranged thereon all the ikons that he could collect. As the woman, who did not look more than seventeen years of age, had already borne two children, prayers of purification were read over her before the marriage service proper began. The couple were supported on either side by two more half-breeds, and all four bowed and crossed themselves continuously. If they stopped for a moment, the pope broke off to say, *sotto voce*, "Cross yourselves—cross yourselves." We were, of course, not able to understand the prayers, but presently the pope took two small ikons from the table, and after blessing them, instructed the bridesmaids or best men (I confess that their sexes puzzled me) to hold the holy images in position on the foreheads of the wedded pair. We found it difficult to keep our gravity as we watched the attendants' efforts to support the ikons at the proper angle during the ensuing genuflections. The ceremony concluded by a procession three times round the table. The pope walked in front chanting prayers, and the bride and bridegroom followed him, while their supporters struggled after, still holding the ikons upon their heads. As the ship was rolling considerably, and the congregation were, many of them, the worse for drink, the whole thing looked much more like a football scrum than part of a religious service. The proceedings concluded by both bride and bridegroom kneeling down to touch the ground three times with their forehead before the principal ikon. The bride accomplished the feat successfully, but the bridegroom was not so supple, and the pope paused to admonish him contemptuously:

"What sort of a *Samoyede* are you that you cannot bow before the ikon?"[1]

[1] On some parts of the Yenesei the name Samoyede is used as a term of derision or reproach.

I never saw a more lamentable parody of Christian ceremonial than at this so-called wedding. The people seemed to have no idea of the meaning of what they did, and in any case they would have been too drunk to understand the rite. The pope, however, was quite pleased, and said to us complacently:

"Now you have seen a real Russian marriage."

All the next day we crawled up the coast against the wind, stopping here and there to take cargo on board. We were anxious about the future of Joseph Gerasimvitch, who seemed to have no idea of what he was going to do after he arrived at Krasnoyarsk. Meanwhile, as the third-class passengers were expected to provide their own food, he had nothing to eat but what his fellow-travellers were charitable enough to allow him. Perhaps it was the strain of knight-errant Polish blood in him which sent him out to open the world-oyster with nothing in his hand nor in his pocket but his Sunday cap and his clasp-knife. It was easy enough to imagine Joseph setting fox-traps or hewing wood at Golchika; but how would he fare when he reached the towns, and brains as well as muscle were needed? He did not lack shrewdness of a certain kind, but he was so simple, and so diffident, that it was doubtful whether he would be able to push his way among other men. When urged to tell such and such a possible employer that he was a skilful workman, all he would say was, "But how can I say such a thing of myself, when there are scores who are better than I?"

Poor Giant! As I write these lines I remember his slow good-nature, his handsome face, and his

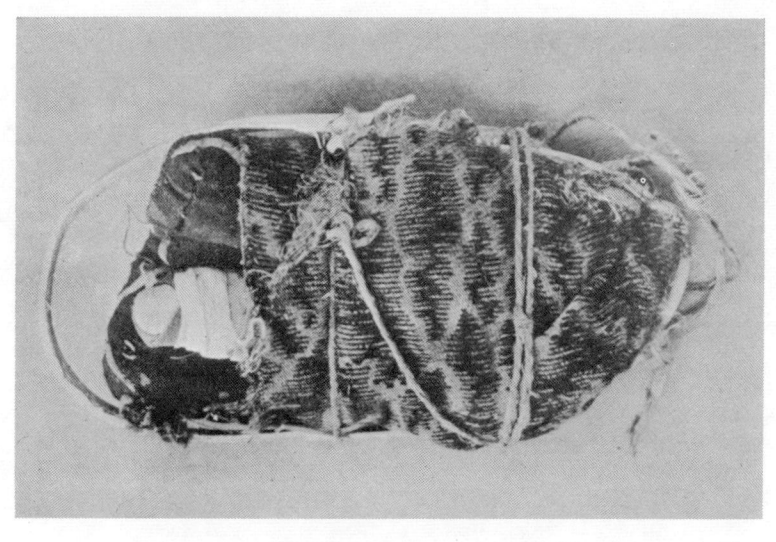

A Samoyede Coll.

A Yurak Grave.

A SUMMER ON THE YENESEI

honesty, and wonder whether the world treated him kindly. That when he reached Krasnoyarsk he would be claimed for military service can scarcely be doubted. Russia, who needed all her men for the titanic struggle in the West, was not likely to overlook one so fine as Joseph Prokopchuk.

Early on the morning of 5th September we reached Nosonovsky Ostrov.

CHAPTER XIV.

Nosonovsky Ostrov—The English expedition—Our party is broken up—The *Ragna* and the *Skule*—A cosmopolitan crew—A heavy cargo—Homeward bound—The last sight of Golchika—Dickson Island—In the ice—A narrow escape—Wireless news—A Government scandal—Novaya Zemlya.

NOSONOVSKY OSTROV is the most easterly island of that great flat archipelago called Breokoffsky, which represents the first delta of the Yenesei. Here the river widens out into a vast basin forty miles in width. You cannot even see from one side of the delta to the other. The eastern arm alone is fifteen versts from shore to shore. Nosonovsky has no permanent dwellings upon it, but it is a not unimportant fishing station in the summer, when several Siberian families, and a number of Yuraks, camp on its shores. But in the month of September, 1914, Nosonovsky was the scene of such bustle and activity as its flat marshes had not witnessed since the old Yenesei floods laid them down, thousands of years before. It was the first place on the river which afforded good anchorage and shelter to shipping, and consequently it had been chosen by the Siberian Company for the rendezvous where their English expedition was to meet the cargoes which had been brought down from Krasnoyarsk for shipment to

Europe. The two large ships, *Ragna* and *Skule*, were lying about half a mile off shore. Around them were moored eight lighters loaded with goods, and five small steamers, including the *Ob* and the *Yenesiesk*. Dinghies were hastening from one vessel to another; whistles were blown; chains rattled; donkey engines roared; and coal-sacks and bales rattled and bumped from hold to hold. After two months spent in the peace of Golchika, all this noise and activity seemed as wonderful and as bewildering to us as it must have done to the natives, who paddled their clumsy boats round the island, and stared at the *Angliski parrahod*, as they called the little Anglo-Norwegian squadron.

As soon as the *Oryol* had cast anchor we went on board the *Ragna*, which was, so to speak, the flagship of the fleet. Here we were introduced to Mr. Jonas Lied, the managing director of the Siberian Company, and asked whether he would consent to take Miss Curtis and me back to Europe through the Kara Sea. At first there were some difficulties in the way, for the *Ragna*, which was chartered to carry only one passenger, was already booked to take three —Mr. Lied himself, and two scientists who had spent the summer on the Yenesei. The *Skule* had more passenger berths, but these were already occupied by the German crews of the new steam tugs, who, owing to the war, were obliged to return to Europe by sea, instead of by the overland route through Russia. But with the greatest good nature, everybody agreed to crowd a little closer in the already crowded saloon.

The captain even gave up his own cabin to our humble but intrusive selves, and for the rest of the voyage he slept in the charthouse on the bridge. Miss Curtis and I felt that we could not be sufficiently grateful for a kindness which thus spared us the danger, difficulty, and tedium of the journey across Europe, although, as it turned out, our voyage through the Arctic Ocean was not lacking in incident either.

Having arranged the matter with Mr. Lied, we heard that the *Oryol* was spending a few hours longer at Breokoffsky in order to pick up some fish cargoes. We therefore all four went ashore together. There were two or three balagans, whose occupants were all preparing to leave in the steamers *Lena* and *Turukhansk*, which were expected to pass in a day or two; and there were also seven or eight Yurak and Samoyede *chooms* beside the beach. Miss Czaplicka and Miss Curtis went to call upon the natives in their extremely dirty dwellings, while I walked along the shore with my binoculars; for it was the time of the autumn migration, and the bird life of the Yenesei delta was likely to repay observation.

Nosonovsky Ostrov is a low-lying island, about six versts in breadth. Most of the land is swampy and overgrown with yellow willow bushes. These willows, although none of them are more than five feet high, seemed like a regular forest after the stunted knee-deep scrub at Golchika. During floods, the island is sometimes entirely swamped, and even now most of the low-lying ground was so wet as to be almost impassable. The covert was so thick that it was difficult to see any birds, especially as it was the mute season, and their voices did not betray them. Wheatears were common, and so many of them were flitting along the shore that it was impossible that they could have all been reared at the island. They were probably on passage from the north, and their gay white tail-coverts, flitting among the sandbanks, gave a touch of liveliness to a scene that otherwise was sombre and desolate enough. A few Lapland buntings were lying in the grass, and I put up a solitary turnstone beside a pool. But on my return I found a very interesting bird, and one which had been overlooked on my previous visit to Breokoffsky in June. This was the mountain accentor (*Accentor montanellus*), a little bird akin to the hedge-sparrow of our English waysides. Several of the birds were flitting about the bushes; but, unlike the hedge-sparrow, they frequently took wing and flew a short distance with a jerky pipit-like flight, while they uttered a shrill triple call.

Presently I rejoined my companions, and we walked back along the shore to the balagans. We were all rather silent, for it was sad to think that the summer's trip with all its work and its little adventures was over, and that our small party was to break up. Miss Czaplicka and Mr. Hall were about to embark on a very serious undertaking, for to brave the severities of a Siberian winter in a native *choom* in the *taigà* is to take a big risk. Miss Curtis and I were going home by a route, which even the most modern appliances and safeguards cannot make anything but uncertain, to a state of things about which we all had the gravest forebodings. Vassilli trudged along behind us. I think that he, too, was sorry that the summer was over.

When we reached the balagans, there was still no sign of the boat from the *Oryol*, and a thin rain began to drift over the island. By way of filling up the time, we went into one of the huts. With ready Siberian hospitality, the family brought us tea, bread, and excellent fresh caviare. It was a tiny little room, and an unlimited number of people seemed to live in it, but they all appeared unusually healthy. The women here were dressed like men, and very sensible and neat they looked in their loose Russian shirts and long boots and breeches. They were just making ready to return to Yenesiesk for the winter, after an unusually successful fishing season. One seine net alone had brought them in seven hundred pouds of omul. We had scarcely finished when the boat was seen at the beach, and we had to take leave of our companions. Good luck to them both, and their plucky adventure into the twilight and frost of an arctic winter!

We watched them go on board the *Oryol* and saw the steamer slowly depart on her fifteen-hundred-mile journey to the south. Then, feeling very much of a pair of waifs and strays, we went back to our new quarters on the *Ragna*.

The *Ragna* was a steamship of 2250 tons. Both she and the *Skule*, her consort, flew the Norwegian flag. Both had been fitted up with ice-bows for this expedition, and were also provided with wireless telegraphy. At supper we learned how it was that the ships had arrived at the meeting-place a week later than was expected. They left Cuxhaven at the end of July, just four-and-twenty hours before the port was closed by the authorities. Thence they went to Aalborg, where they took on board a cargo of cement and machinery. They had under their convoy three tug-boats which had been bought by the Russian Government from a Hamburg firm for service on the Yenesei. These were manned by German crews and flew the German flag. This was the explanation of the rumour that German torpedo-boat destroyers had captured two merchantmen on the Norwegian coast. The "destroyers" were the three tugs, which followed the larger vessels to the Yenesei. However, at Tromsoe, when the expedition put into that port, the German consul claimed all three crews. They were required at once for military service —all, that is, except seven of the officers and engineers, who were over the age limit. New crews had to be found at a day's notice, and then the vessels had proceeded safely to the Kara Sea. They reached the mouth of the Yenesei on 1st September. Here, in the harbour of Dickson Island, they found the explorer, Captain Swerdrup, in his ship, the *Eclipse*. He had come out to look for two Russian expeditions which had been lost in the Kara Sea, and was now fast aground himself. The English expedition spent two days in salving his ship, and he then proceeded along the coast to the north-east. Now that the expedition had reached Russian waters, there was some technical difficulty with the remaining Germans on the tug-boats. As soon as they entered the river, the ships became the property of the Russian Government, and the Russian flag was hoisted. As Russia and Germany were at war, it was impossible for a German officer to command a Russian ship; therefore these had to resign their commands and be transferred as passengers to the *Skule*. Here they remained until they left the Yenesei, for the moment that they set foot on shore, they rendered themselves liable to arrest as prisoners of war.

It would not have been possible to find a more curious gathering than that on the ships at Nosonovsky. In the first place, at least half a dozen nationalities were represented—English, Russian, Jewish, Norwegian, Swedish, and German, to say nothing of the Yuraks and Samoyedes who frequently came on board to sell fish. Then on the *Ragna* we had two live bears, two wolves, a sackful of mammoth bones, a murderer, and the carcase of a polar bear. The young bears and wolves had been brought from Krasnoyarsk by Mr. Christensen for shipment to Norway, but they suffered so much in confinement that in the end they had to be shot before we left the river. The murderer lived on one of the lighters which was moored alongside the *Ragna*. He came from one of the balagans on shore, where he had stabbed a neighbour in a drunken brawl. He was a tall, dreamy-looking man, who looked much more gentle and inoffensive than the *gendarmes* who guarded him. Miss Curtis and I were sorry for him because he looked so quiet and melancholy, and occasionally gave him cigarettes. He was to be tried for his crime in Yenesiesk, but the Russian law is merciful to the drunkard, and he expected to escape with a light sentence. The polar bear had been shot on Dickson Island by Mr. Lied. We had a steak for supper one night. It tasted like good beef, but I am told that the hams only are fit to eat, for the flesh of the rest of the body is interlarded with blubber.

During the fortnight that we lay at Nosonovsky, the party in the saloon, besides our two selves, consisted of Mr. Lied, the captain, the ice-pilot, a Russian gentleman—a geologist from Petersburg—and a Swedish pastor, Herr Enander, who was a botanist and a special student of the family *Salix*. He must have found plenty of opportunity to study willows at Breokoffsky, for the islands produced nothing else. Besides these, Mr. Christensen, who superintended the discharging of the cargo, used to come in to meals, and sometimes Captain Gundersen of the *Skule* paid a visit. Captain Johansen, the ice-pilot, was a fine old man who had sailed in the arctic regions since boyhood. In 1878 he had accompanied Nordenskiöld on the famous voyage of the *Vega* through the North-East Passage, and was the first captain to take a steamer up the river Lena. His brother was that Captain Johansen who discovered and named Lonely Island, to the north of the Taimyr Peninsula; and he himself at one time had owned the sloop *Gjöa*, until he sold her to the explorer Amundsen, who made his famous voyage through the North-West Passage in her.

Miss Curtis and I were the only two people on board who were idle, and we used to feel quite ashamed of our inability to haul baulks of timber about the deck or handle bales of tow, when we watched the furious activity of everybody else. For trade with the Yenesei cannot be carried on in the same leisurely way that is permissible in the south. The mouth of the river is open only during a few weeks of the year, and by the end of September the polar ice again drifts southwards, and closes the estuary as if by frozen gates. Therefore every man on board worked against time, for each day's delay lessened the chance of accomplishing the return journey safely.

With so much work going on, Miss Curtis and I were not able to go ashore much, for whenever the weather was fine enough for a boat to land, every man was needed to help with the cargo. I was sorry for this, for I had hoped to make some observations on the autumn migration at Nosonovsky. As it was, my notes were too scanty and disjointed to be of much value. The waders had all disappeared by the second week in September. The last seen were a turnstone and a ruff. One day a couple of little merlins hawked round the ship. I did not observe this species north of Pustoy. Wheatears were the last of the passerine birds to go south, and, like the waders, they had all disappeared by 12th September. The geese, ducks, and divers were seen up to the day of our departure; but perhaps owing to the cold spring, they were said to have lingered later than usual. Sometimes a flock of swans went up the river. It was magnificent to see the great birds, with their wings outspread white and cruciform against the sky, barking solemnly to one another as they flew southwards.

But the time spent on the ship was never irksome, for there was so much to see. Eight lighters had come down the river from Krasnoyarsk. They had originally been brought through the Kara Sea from Europe in 1905, and were of the type that is used for trade on the Rhine. Two of them lay on either side of the *Ragna* all day long; and as fast as one was emptied, it was towed away and another took its place. It was a never-failing interest to see the hatches taken off, and look right down into the hold of the ship whence dusty cement casks coupled together were drawn by rattling donkey engines, and swung over the side into the lighter. The greater part of the cargo consisted of cement for use on the Siberian railways. But 15,000 casks of cement cannot be handled in a day, especially as the stuff is spoiled by the damp; and a shower of rain means that hatches must be closed until the skies are clear. The cargo that replaced the cement was more varied, and consisted chiefly of timber, hides, and tow. At the eleventh hour Mr. Christensen had shipped twenty tons of butter, which, considering the price of provisions during the first days of the war, was expected to fetch a good price in Europe. The timber was Siberian cedar, and the history of the great logs that bumped and banged their way into the hold of the *Ragna* is one of the romances of commerce. They came from the heart of the forest, some hundred and fifty versts south of Yenesiesk, where a Government concession has been obtained to cut timber. The wood that grows close to the waterside is apt to be rotten at the core, and therefore these trees were felled two or three miles inland. Sixty horses, and more than a hundred men, are employed at this lumbering station, and the work begins in April; but in the year of which I write the snow was so soft that the horses fell through the surface, and most of the wood had to be drawn by human haulage. The logs were squared roughly on the river-bank, and then loaded into the lighters for shipment to Nosonovsky. Between them, the *Ragna* and the *Skule* carried five thousand of the logs; and as they were worth on an average £2 or £3 apiece, they were a valuable freight to risk among the ice in the Kara Sea.

At first we found it strange to hear English spoken again, and to have our meals prepared for us, instead of having to cook the dinner and then wash up afterwards as we had done all the summer in the hut. Indeed, life in the ship seemed so luxurious and up-to-date, and the shipping around made the place appear so populous and civilised, that it was hard to realise that we were still living beside one of the vastest wildernesses in the world. In fact, the crew, most of whom had never visited the country before, were sometimes slow to understand that the Yenesei is not a place where risks may be taken lightly. The two young wireless operators, who had no duties to perform while the ships lay at anchor, took the little motor-boat one morning, and went over to shoot on the mainland, about fifteen miles away. They did not return at night, and on the following morning there was a good deal of anxiety felt on their account, for the river was choppy, and blizzards were sweeping over the tundra. Mr. Lied took out a search-party in one of the tug boats and looked for them all day, but without success. Towards nightfall, however, they regained the ship. They had tried to return on the previous evening, but the motor-engine broke down and obliged them to take to their oars. They rowed until midnight, and then, being unable to make any headway against the stream, they had put ashore again. For eight hours they lay in a hollow in the tundra, with nothing to cover them from the snow, and nothing to eat but a willow-grouse, which they plucked and cooked as well as they could over a fire of driftwood. Next morning, they set out again, and by dint of rowing for eight or ten hours, they reached the ship at last, completely worn out, but otherwise none the worse for what might have proved a very dangerous predicament.

On 11th September, the *Lena* came up the river and stopped for an hour at Nosonovsky. Her decks were crowded with passengers, among whom, although we could not distinguish her, was doubtless Nura Antonoff. The *Lena* was the last of the southward-bound steamers, and when she hooted thrice and steamed away, those melancholy coasts seemed the sadder for her going. She took off the remaining fisher-folk, and a couple of days later the natives also packed up their *chooms* and went—"*daleko*, into the tundra." It was indeed time to flit, for the weather grew colder day by day, and the mainland was already sugared over with snow. The crew, who were unprepared for an arctic climate, shivered in the bitter wind, and most of them swore openly that they would never come to Siberia again—for which decision, looking at the bleak shores of the island, and bleaker waves on the river, it was impossible to blame them.

However, all the cargo was on board at last, and we left Nosonovsky Ostrov on 19th September. There was a grand meeting in the *Ragna* in the forenoon, and the success of the enterprise was drunk in champagne. We took leave of Mr. Christensen here, and also of poor Jest, whom he was taking back with him to Krasnoyarsk. The *Ragna* weighed her anchor at six o'clock in the evening, and by that time not only the hold, but the decks also, were stacked with timber. The *Skule* followed half a mile astern. The little *Yenesiesk* piloted the two ships from their anchorage, for on either side of the channel lay dangerous shoals and banks. Then when she had led the way past the islands, she blew a long farewell blast and turned out of our course. We saluted her as we passed, and two minutes later were steaming northwards alone.

As soon as darkness fell, we lay to until dawn, for the estuary of the Yenesei is full of uncharted sands, and with the season so far advanced, it would never have done to run aground in the river and risk being caught in the ice outside. At 10 a.m. on the following morning, we passed Golchika. With the help of glasses we could make out all the buildings distinctly. We distinguished the light-coloured raw wood on Antonoff's new house, and beyond, the weather-beaten walls of Prokopchuk's homestead. There was our little hut beside the Golchika, and Sylkin's tiny balagan on the mainland behind the island. We could even persuade ourselves that we saw the Antonoffs, with Nill and Anastasia, watching us from the river-bank, as indeed they were certain to be doing, for news flies apace at

Golchika, and such an event as the passing of the English steamers would certainly set the whole place in a flutter. It was curious thus to see from a distance a place that we knew so well. In some sort, it gave one the same sensation that the dead may be imagined to feel if they are able to revisit scenes they knew in life. On the other side of the river, we saw the balagans of Swerifskye, all deserted now, and grey with snow. An hour later, and we came abreast of Och Marino, where the inhabitants came out to point at the ships as they steamed past. There was Vassilli Vassillievitch, and beside him the green apron of the girl, in front of the dark *sakoōys* of the natives. My last impression of Siberia was of that terrible little house, surrounded on three sides by grey water and on the fourth by the snowy tundra. Its windows stared at us like blank, unseeing eyes as we rushed past it into life—into danger, into misery, into battle of all we knew—but still into life. We left it astern as if it had been a house of the dead. Was Vassilli Vassillievitch still drinking—drinking—smoking—smoking himself to death? Was the baby, with its dreadful eyes, still wailing day and night? And the girl—we did not like to think of her, and wondered rather what the winter would bring to the rest of our Siberian acquaintance. It was melancholy to think that we might never see so many of them, quaint or kindly as the case might be, again. We had turned the page of the Yenesei, and were now going to write a new one across the Arctic Ocean.

All that day we steamed northwards beside the low, bleak shore. Even Och Marino is not the uttermost spot to which man will adventure, for one or two families spend the winter below the Sopochnaya in order to trap white foxes. To the west we saw no land at all, for the noble estuary was more than fifty miles wide at this point.

At seven o'clock on the following morning we reached Dickson Island. Between Golchika and Dickson the temperature of the water had fallen 10°, and it was easy to guess the reason why, for Vega Harbour was now packed with ice. This was disappointing, for if the ships had been able to enter, Mr. Lied proposed to go ashore there to see whether there were any traces of the two Russian expeditions of which Captain Swerdrup was in search. Dickson is a low, flat island of the same formation as the neighbouring tundra, from which it looks as if it had been wrenched not so very long ago. On a knoll at the western arm of the harbour, a post has been set up to mark a coal dépôt, which was placed there in 1901 for Baron Toll's expedition. Nothing lives on the island except wild reindeer, bears, and foxes, and for ten months of the year the harbour is choked with ice. Its low, rocky shores—our last sight of Asia—soon sank below the horizon behind us.

Now we began to pass floating cakes of old ice, worn by much knocking about in the water, and with them were many logs of driftwood, which for months had rolled to and fro in the estuary. By and by, we came to what is called a *slam*, *i.e.* a mass of floating snow. The water here was dull green and thick like soup. The waves, stirred by the ship's passage, heaved sullenly, as if oil had been poured on to the sea, and little shining flinders of ice rippled from our bow. The sky became more overcast, and the *slams* were more frequent. We seemed to force our way through an ocean of thick honey. Gradually the dull surface changed, and became dimpled over with spots like innumerable raindrops. At first these pock-marks were no bigger than a man's hand, but gradually they became as large as plates, and then the plates drew together into cakes as wide as carpets. Miss Curtis and I sat on the deck timber and watched larger and ever larger "pancakes" glide past. By the evening some of them were as big as lawn-tennis courts, and the engine-room bell rang sharply for "half-speed ahead."

We had supper as usual, and then went on deck again, for the sight fascinated us. The grey fog, which had lain above the northern horizon all day, now closed down completely. Again the engine-room bell tinkled —this time for "slow." We could hear the lip-lap of the water against the ship's sides as the floes drifted softly by. Everybody was on deck watching the ice, but no one spoke. We seemed to be entering into some solemn places where we had no right to venture. Grim entelechies, beyond man's invocation, wrestled together behind the mist. It was as if some unseen powers strode southward, and the floes were only the print of their feet upon the water. The sea was very calm, but a thin wind was singing little evil songs to itself round the mast, and a heavy rain distilled from the fog and fell into the water with an incessant *hush-hush* like the heaving of enormous sighs. Then, quite suddenly, the mist parted ever so slightly, and right under our bows, stretching away into the dimness as far as the eye could see, was a packed ice-field. It is a curious game—to play chess with the Arctic on the board of the Kara Sea, chequered by alternate patches of ice and open water, and here for the first time our invisible opponent, throned at the Pole, said: Checkmate.

The *Ragna* shivered as the ice ground along her bow, and then the threefold bellow of her siren split the silence. Scarcely had the sound echoed away into the night, than the *Skule* took up and answered the blast with a shriller roar. We saw her dark hull and haloed lights looming through the mist a cable's length away. The two ships lay side by side for a little while. They seemed like two forwandered and frightened animals, calling to one another in the dusk. And all the while the ice stole past on its journey to the south. Then a lead opened up ahead, and the *Ragna* crept along it with the edge of the floes tickling her sides. The *Skule* followed—you would almost have said that they went a-tiptoe. Then the ice closed again. "Stop!" roared the *Ragna's* siren, and—"Stop!" screamed the *Skule* in reply.

So we advanced hour after hour, and when morning came we lay in the middle of a sea of ice, which stretched unbroken from horizon to horizon. The only way to force a passage was by ramming the floes. Both ships were prepared for such an emergency, and had an ice-bow of stout oak planks, but in the *Ragna's* case, the dimensions, which had been well enough when the vessel carried a heavy cargo of cement, were not low enough below the waterline when she was loaded with timber. Consequently she met the shock of the ice, not on a wooden buffer, but with her naked plates. The *Skule*, whose bow was better protected, had not sufficient engine power to drive her through the newly formed ice, which was already five inches thick. In two hours, we advanced about a quarter of a mile. Every now and then there was a shout from Captain Johansen, our ice-pilot, who was up aloft in the crow's nest. His signal was answered by the rumble of the steering gear or else by the siren's bellow to the *Skule*—the long blast and a short for full speed astern, or the five long blasts which were the sign that wireless communication was needed. The weather was still and foggy, and there was no open water to be seen. We had left all the gulls behind us at Dickson. A pomatorhine skua—a bird of the year—was the only living thing besides ourselves that moved over the desolate waste.

Towards evening the ice became more open, but the ominous white " blink " along the horizon showed that the field was a vast one. Several times we steamed down a channel which looked as if it might lead to safety; but each time it proved to be a cul-de-sac, and we were obliged to put about and try for another opening. It was like wandering in a maze. The *Skule* was following us along the path that we carved through the ice, when the two sides of the floe gradually closed up before her. She was seen to stop altogether, and then came a wireless message : " *Stand by, in case we have to take to the boats.*" The state of affairs was serious, for if the ice tightened its grip, the ship would have been crushed like an egg-shell in a mailed fist. Fortunately, however, the *Skule*, like the *Ragna*, had a deck cargo of heavy timber. The donkey engines were started, and by dint of swinging the logs overboard in the cranes, the ice around was smashed sufficiently to relieve the pressure, and the ship ultimately struggled out. Her pilot was so much upset by this experience that he sent a despairing marconigram: "*For God's sake steer south, or we shall all be frozen in.*" When this appeal was communicated to Captain Johansen in the crow's nest, he chuckled mightily. Before leaving Tromsoe, our good ice-pilot had consulted a wise woman who based her predictions upon the forms taken by the "grounds" in a cup of coffee. She had assured him that all would be well on the voyage, and as Captain Johansen had great faith in her prophecies, he did not doubt but that we should come through safely. It would have been awkward, to say the least of it, if an accident had occurred at this point. There were neither the equipment nor the stores necessary for a winter in the Arctic Ocean, to say nothing of the fact that an iron ship could not withstand the grinding of the floes. Besides, we were at least five hundred miles from any human habitation, and two hundred miles from communication with any wireless station. Therefore the *Skule* had a lucky escape.

For the rest of the evening, we forced our way through tightly packed "pancake" ice. The effect was most curious, for there was no open water to be seen, and the ship seemed to be steaming over a boundless white shingle beach, strewn with stones and pebbles and boulders of all shapes and sizes.

S.S. Skule in the ice.

"Pancake" ice in the Kara Sea.

September 23rd, although clear, was the coldest day we had yet known. In spite of the stove, the portholes in the saloon were covered with frost ferns, and an unfortunate pigling, one of a couple who lived in a hutch on the after-deck, was frozen to death during the night. All the forenoon we passed through fields of "pancakes" of every size, from a mere spot of ice no bigger than a handkerchief, to sturdy blocks which were as large as a croquet ground and stood two feet out of the water. Some were curiously crimped at the edges; others bore, as it were, blossoms of white rime, and as the *Ragna* pressed on her course and set the whole mass rocking in her wake, she might have been passing through a lake full of water-lilies. Here and there were larger blocks of old ice, which had been carved into all sorts of fantastic shapes in the course of their summer's wandering through the Kara Sea. Some were spiked almost like a porcupine; others stood like monumental slabs upon two pillars, green as malachite. Here was a floating grotto, surrounded by frost sculpture and filled with yellow water; there was a block besmirched with mud-stains from the beaches of Novaya Zemlya. And very slowly, the whole icefield was drifting southwards. For two hours we coasted along its outermost edge and saw a frosty scum spread into the surrounding water, just as grease rises on the surface of a cooling pipkin and congeals into opaque flakes. Gradually the mass was eating like a canker into the open water, and before the long winter night set in, the whole sea from horizon to horizon would be bound down into utter silence and stillness. Sometimes the ice was new and rotten, and the bow of the *Ragna* crumpled and tore the floes as easily as a knife cuts through a sheet of cardboard, opening up a lane of open water. Others, however, were stronger, and the ship grazed their flanks with a bumping jar that made her shiver from stem to stern. Between the ice, the water was black and oily—such a surface as you may sometimes see in a wood where the pool is much overhung by trees. It seemed strange that such dark, forbidding water could lie under such a clear sky.

As we were thus watching the war of the ice with the bow of the *Ragna*, we heard half a dozen strange but very happy voices, and over the floes came a flock of ivory gulls out of the north. Their wings, built to battle with the gales that blow over the polar seas, met this little wind with a contained strength that gave their flight a curious butterfly buoyancy. Their voices, which reminded me of the talk of the common terns on our English dunes, were gay and careless as the wind they conquered. Rising and falling in sport they crossed our bow, and disappeared over the floes to the southward.

At noon we drew clear of the ice, and were soon steaming full speed ahead. All the following day, the weather was fair, and as we approached Waigatz Island, bird life increased. On 24th September four fulmars hawked round the ship, half a dozen scoters rushed across our bows, and a few immature kittiwakes appeared. The next day, 25th September, was a red-letter day, for in the evening our wireless operator succeeded in calling up the Marconi station on Waigatz, whence we hoped to hear news of the war. But in this we were disappointed. The telegraphist on the island knew nothing of the European turmoil except that the name of Petersburg had been changed. We were obliged to take what comfort we could from the fact that the town had been renamed Petrograd, and not Wilhelmstadt, or something equally ominous; and resign ourselves to wait for news until we reached Norway.

This poor telegraphist and his fellows had been sent to Waigatz during the previous summer. They had been under-supplied with provisions, and were also suffering from scurvy. The Russian Government, who take great interest in the modern attempts to open up Captain Wiggins' old route, undertook to establish three wireless stations in the Kara Sea—at Waigatz, at the Yugor Strait, and at Moré Salé, in order that incoming ships should have news of the condition of the ice in the straits, and shape their course accordingly. However, it caused such a scandal that the unfortunate operators should have been sent out so badly equipped, that questions were asked in the Duma, and the matter was put right.

Late in the evening we sighted the coast of Novaya Zemlya, and lay-to for the night to wait for the *Skule*, whose engines were less powerful than ours, and was constantly falling behind. It was strange to stand on the bridge at dusk, and look over to the dim purple smear under the mist on our starboard bow which represented Novaya Zemlya. It is a place that every schoolboy has heard of, but which, by the tricks of common speech, has as little reality to most people as Timbuctoo or Jericho.

I remember that on the same evening, the laughing suggestion was made that as Mr. Lied was a Russian subject, and Miss Curtis and I were Englishwomen, that we should therefore go to the Austrian territory of Franz-Josef Land, which lay about five hundred miles to the north, and take possession of it in the name of the Allies! Miss Curtis and I were in love with the North: I believe that if the Pole itself had been proposed, we should have been all the better pleased.

CHAPTER XV.

The Kara Gates—Sir Hugh Willoughby—The magic of the Arctic—Captain Wiggins—The Kara Sea route—Ingoe—A storm—Bird passengers—Midnight off North Cape—Hammerfest—Rumours of war—Tromsoe — Sidelight on German mobilisation — From Bergen to Newcastle—War-fever—London again.

EARLY next morning we entered the Kara Strait. Narrow as the passage appears on the map, it is in reality some fifty miles wide, and as we skirted along the coast of Novaya Zemlya, we could see nothing of Waigatz Island, which lay to the southward. The older expeditions generally entered the Kara Sea through the Yugor Strait, which lies to the south of Waigatz. It was supposed that the more northerly passage was perpetually choked with ice, and it was from this idea that it took its name of the Iron Gates. However, of late years ships have used the Kara, in preference to the Yugor, Strait.

To the north lay the cliffs of Novaya Zemlya, ribbed with newly fallen snow. From the broad tundras behind them, a perpetual stream of bird life poured southwards. During migration times, Waigatz probably plays the part of an immense bridge, spanning the channel between Novaya Zemlya and the mainland. Even as we steamed through the strait, I saw some evidence of this. All day long, divers crossed our bows in small parties. Some flew high and some low, but they were all heading for Waigatz. In the course of an hour, more than a hundred must have passed the ship. Mr. H. L. Popham tells me that some years ago he watched a similar stream of divers from Novaya Zemlya. The fulmars, of which species we had seen only four birds in the Kara Sea, now increased in numbers, and a pair of glaucous gulls, in the mottled brown plumage of immaturity, followed us. Brünnich's guillemots became common, and several small flocks of scoters passed, all flying to the south-west. The strait also seems to be a fairly definite dividing line between the two tides of birds, which, during the migration times, sweep, one down the east, and the other down the west, coasts of Novaya Zemlya. For instance, I did not see a single diver to the west of the Kara Strait, nor a single kittiwake to the east of it. We know very little of the way of migration in these regions; but it seems most probable that when the bird stream reaches the mainland, it divides, and allows one battalion to proceed southwards along the valley of the Ob, and the other by that of the Petchora.

Watching these bold travellers returning from their summer in the north, set us speaking of other adventurers of our own race. It is well enough to venture into the Arctic Ocean in steam-driven ships, with wireless telegraphy and all the rest of it; but how much more honourable were those explorers who dared the ice that we ourselves had barely escaped in sailing vessels which were altogether dependent on wind and tide. I have sometimes wondered wherein the magic of the Arctic lies

A SUMMER ON THE YENESEI

—a magic exceeding that of the rest of the five seas. It has a terrible charm all its own. If, as legends say, the spirits of the dead linger round the places that they loved when in the flesh, then not only would the polar waters be thronged with phantoms of ancient shipping and ghosts of bygone navigators, but its shores would also be filled with the wraiths of all the dreamers who have watched the *aurora* flicker in the north, ever since the days of brave Sir Hugh Willoughby. He, the first Englishman who sought the North-East Passage, landed on this very coast of Novaya Zemlya three hundred years ago, on a voyage that he fondly hoped would take him to the land of Cathay. Instead, the ice carried his ship southwards to the Kola Peninsula, where he and his crew perished miserably in the snow.

It is as far a cry from poor Sir Hugh Willoughby in his bluff-bowed galleon, to the *Ragna* with her 1000-horse-power engines and wireless antennæ, as it would be from the golden sands of his mythical Cathay, to the sober Siberian timber upon our decks, but the same restless, irrational Spirit of the North hailed both ships when they entered the Kara Gates. Our chief engineer, a stolid, stout Norwegian, who spent his time in a mysterious roaring oily place in the bowels of the ship, where you might only trespass by especial favour, was the most notable victim. He went to those in authority and begged that if a similar expedition went to the Yenesei in 1915 he might be permitted to join it. He had taken a liking for these parts, he confessed with a half-shamefaced grin, as he blew upon his cold fingers.

It would take too long to tell of half the captains who sailed into these waters and lost their ships, if not their own lives, there; but there is, above the rest, one name which is imperishably connected with the conquest of the Kara Sea, and that is the name of Captain Joseph Wiggins. It is usual to call this great English seaman a *pioneer*. A pioneer he certainly was, in as far as he opened up this north-eastern trade route to British shipping; but he may also claim the not less honourable title of a link with the past. For he was of the order of Hawkins, Drake, and Frobisher, and the mariners of the Elizabethan age, part explorer and part merchantman, whose voyages have shed a little of the purple of romance over the fustian-grey of commerce. Wiggins began his work in the 'seventies, and for thirty years he tried to establish regular trade with the Ob and the Yenesei. During the 'nineties his example was followed by others, both Russian and English, the most notable among the latter being Mr. Leyborne Popham. But after the action of the Russian Government, who no longer allow goods to enter the river duty free, the sea route to Siberia fell into disfavour for a time, nominally on account of the uncertainty of clearing the ice in the Kara Sea. Against this it has been pointed out that in none of his voyages was Wiggins obliged to return because of ice.

The present promoters of the scheme maintain that there are four entrances to the Kara Sea, and that under no weather conditions can all four be blocked at once, for if the ice is packed in one part of the Novaya Zemlya bight, the rest is sure to be open. Hence the

A SUMMER ON THE YENESEI

wireless stations round the Kara and Yugor Straits. The routes by the Matochkin Strait, and the north of Novaya Zemlya, are too uncertain for ordinary use. In 1913 the s.s. *Correct*, chartered by the Siberian Company, made a successful trip to Breokoffsky — an account of which has already been published by Doctor Nansen.[1] In the future the company expect larger developments, and are taking more precautions. A dépôt of stores is to be placed on Bieliy Ostrov, and the ships will carry a winter equipment of clothing, a hut, etc., in case, by any accident, the crew are obliged to abandon the vessel and take to the ice. It has even been suggested that a useful adjunct would be a pilot in a waterplane, who could fly over the floes and find out the open leads. Whether modern science can do what pluck and seamanship failed to accomplish in the last century, and overcome the natural difficulties of navigation in these waters, remains to be seen. At least the energy and enterprise of Mr. Lied, and the other promoters of the present attempt, deserve all success in their undertaking.

I think that everybody breathed more easily when Novaya Zemlya lay astern. The Kara Sea, especially in its eastern waters, is charted only approximately, and shipping insurance premiums rise mightily if the destination of a vessel is known to lie east of the Petchora. On 27th September we had hoped to hold wireless communication with the station at Ingoe on the Finmark coast; but, alas, the operators there could give us little or no reliable news of the war, and we

[1] *Through Siberia*, by Fridtjof Nansen.

were obliged to curb our impatience until we reached Hammerfest.

Next morning I was awakened at 4 a.m. by a heavy roll of the ship, which swept every loose object in the cabin, including my own person, into a heap on the floor. At breakfast out came the fiddles for the first time on the voyage, and the meal was eaten under difficulties. It was a fine clear morning, and the *Ragna* was wallowing westwards through a mammoth swell. Overhead a couple of hundred kittiwakes followed the ship, and about a score of pomatorhine skuas—passengers from Novaya Zemlya—followed the kittiwakes. Now and then, when they spied some piece of jetsam in the water, two or three birds swooped down to squabble over it, but, for the most part, they hung above us in a cloud. When the ship forged ahead, as at a given signal the whole host moved forward in order to keep station over the mast. I cannot tell how it was, unless perhaps it may have been the influence of so many watching eyes all fixed upon us, but after a while there seemed to be something ominous in this immense flock of birds with their straining but motionless wings silhouetted against the sky, and beautiful as they were, I felt that I almost hated them and their watchful escort.

At noon the wind freshened, until by sunset a regular gale was blowing. The *Ragna* took little water over the side. She was, however, making a good deal of water in her forehold, for her plates had been badly strained while ramming the ice. By and by, the deck cargo began to work loose. The mate and two seamen went down and tautened the chains that secured it, but it was soon knocking about as badly as ever. The *Skule* had dropped so far astern that she was out of sight, and as efforts to get into communication with her by wireless proved ineffectual, some concern was felt for her safety, for she carried even more deck cargo than did the *Ragna*. However, before nightfall, our telegraphist called up the station at Ingoe, which reported that the *Skule* had telegraphed that she was weathering the storm all right, but that her operator was not able to communicate with us because he had collapsed with sea-sickness! The people at Ingoe added a rider to the effect that the storm now raging round the coast was the worst within the memory of man.

The gale was at its height at eight o'clock when Miss Curtis and I went on to the bridge. The ship was rolling to an angle of 30° to 35°, and the waves towered so high above the decks that it seemed as if they must infallibly swamp her. But how can a plain pen write of those grand seas that hurled themselves unbroken upon us out of the dimness, and then thundered away to leeward? In the ice all had been still except for the grinding of the floes, but here there was storm music enough. The creaking of timber, the rumble of the stearing-gear, the howl of the wind round the mast, and through it all the whirr and hum of the dynamos in the charthouse—all blent into a roaring groan which might have been the voice of the ship herself as she wallowed into the trough of the sea and then rushed up the giant shoulder of the next wave. Now and then, in the twilight, I saw a dozen moth-like fulmars, who, through all the uproar, skimmed eternally round and round the ship, never hastening and never rising more than a few inches above the combers, chasing us ceaselessly through the gale like spirits of the storm. Just before midnight the wind increased, and for a minute or two the *Ragna* rolled so heavily that to a mere landlubber like myself it seemed wonderful that she should ever right herself again. Then Miss Curtis cried out suddenly that the timber was going overboard, and, sure enough, half a dozen great logs flew over the side as if they had been no heavier than matches. That clinched the matter, and the captain altered our course lest any more of the cargo should be lost.

The gale moderated at daybreak, and the sea, although still very choppy, was much calmer. My friend and I found life quite stale and unprofitable now that there was neither ice nor wind to give our interest a fillip; and we had nothing more exciting to do than to pay a call upon the galley cat, who had a litter of kittens during the storm. But it was also very amusing to watch the sea-birds round the ship. The fulmars pleased me most. They had followed us faithfully through the storm, and their thick bodies and rapid flight, with the odd marbled markings on their upper wings, made them look something like giant hawk-moths. It was very pretty to see them alight on the water, poised daintily upon their outspread wings in the attitude of the angels out of one of Gustave Doré's pictures; and the worst seas had no terrors for them, for they could swim unconcernedly up wave-slopes as steep as the roof of a church. A few Brünnich's guillemots were still to be seen. They popped up suddenly in front of us and flung themselves along the surface, splashing ludicrously in their efforts to take wing and escape the bows of the ship. The storm had blown away all the pomatorhine skuas, but it brought other bird guests to the *Ragna*. At noon a purple sandpiper—a passenger from Spitzbergen or Franz-Josef Land—came on board, and during the day we saw both a snow-bunting and a mealy redpoll. Some small wader also fluttered round for a while. I think it may have been a dunlin. The sandpiper was tired, and consequently very tame. I tried to photograph it, but owing to an impending blizzard and the roll of the ship, the result was not very successful.

Hammerfest was our first port of call. We had expected to reach it on 29th September, but the installation of the wireless apparatus in the charthouse behind the wheel had affected the working of the compass. We were something out in our reckoning, and as the coast was hidden by driving snowstorms, we were not able to take our bearings, and had to lie to for the night.

For the first time we saw the *aurora borealis* in great splendour. To the south the snow-clouds were piled along the cliffs of North Cape. Half-way to the zenith the wind tore them apart, and between their ragged edges, the stars shone, polished with frost. But in front of the stars, and lighting the whole firmament and the sea with their soft shifting radiance, the spears and shafts of the *aurora* spanned the sky. The broken edges of the storm-clouds caught the glow, until it seemed as if the light of heaven was shed faintly upon the earth—and under the Pole Star hung a splendid comet like a sword. The whole spectacle of *aurora*, comet, and starlight was so amazing and so rare that it suggested the fantastic idea that here the earth was symbolised in the skies. To the north, under Corona Borealis, lay the arctic lands where no man may walk, vast and pure in the first grasp of winter. To the south, behind the cloud-pack, was a continent seething with evil passions and filled with the din of war. . . . Much as we longed for home, I think that we were both sorry that the voyage was over. To-morrow we should reach Europe again, and what news should we hear?

. . . . . .

At noon we sighted land, and presently entered Hammerfest fiord. Its rocky islands and capes were dimmed with snow. Sometimes the clouds drooped until their driving skirts hung like a curtain in front of the cliffs; and at other times they parted to show fierce headlands that butted into the surf. Once or twice a gleam of sunshine burst upon tiers of snow-mountains. It was very beautiful, and the scenery seemed perhaps even more than usually overwhelming and grand after the infinite blankness of the tundra.

Hammerfest itself lay in the midst of these *sea-mountains*. Steep cliffs rose up behind it, and the grey houses harmonised so closely with the grey rock around that the town was almost invisible at first sight, and even afterwards, one was constantly realising odd little outcrops of buildings that had been overlooked before. Part of Hammerfest was burnt down about fifteen years ago, and much of it has been rebuilt. Now it has 3000 inhabitants, and churches of both Catholic and Reformed Churches. It was the first city in Norway to use electric lighting. Even in the dusk, we could see the thin waterfalls—the so-called "white coals" of Norway—from which the power is derived. Thirty years ago you could probably have bought the strength of all the streams in the country for ten shillings. To-day you could not buy it for ten thousand times that sum. The Norwegians — business-like race — are thoroughly aware of the value of their waterfalls in the future, when electric dynamos will supersede steam-boilers as the world's motive power.

We went ashore in the dusk, glad of the opportunity to stretch our legs. The chief thing that struck us was the absence of public-houses. There were only two in the place, both of which were closed owing to the war. Hammerfest does not publish a paper of its own, but the news is telegraphed from the south, and then issued in printed bulletins. We were very jealous of the rest of the crew, who could read these bulletins in their entirety, whereas we had to put up with such scraps of information as we could tease out of our acquaintance. Accordingly we remembered a treat which we had planned weeks before at Golchika, when a diet of fish, bread, and tea was beginning to pall, and which we had gloated over in anticipation during the voyage. We walked shamelessly into a pastrycook's shop, and I do not think that I have ever taken such an unholy delight in tarts since my schooldays, when we held night orgies in the bathroom with biscuits and chocolate.

Meals on the *Ragna*, excellent though they were, sometimes recalled the feast of the stalled ox; and during the crises of the ice and of the storm, when everybody was busy and anxious, we felt doubly bound, as supercargoes, to be on our best behaviour. Besides, the change from our free-and-easy feasts at Golchika to the order and civility of meals in the ship's saloon was a little difficult at first. It took quite three days to reaccustom oneself to use an especial knife for the butter. These meals used to remind me of the table-talk in the " Soliloquy in a Spanish Cloister " :

> " Not a plenteous cork crop: scarcely
> May we hope oak galls, I doubt:
> What's the Latin name for parsley?
> What's the Greek name for swine's snout?"

Our " swine's snoutishness " took the form of tarts, in which we indulged to the extent of five apiece. We looked guiltily down the street as we left the shop, and hoped that if seen we should pass unidentified, lest we should bring discredit on the ship. But all the while we knew that this was a vain hope, for in a place like Hammerfest, everyone knows everything about everybody else, and the shopkeeper had already remarked " Engelske " and " Yenesei " to three deeply interested customers in succession.

After this satisfactory kick over of the traces, we returned on board. The *Ragna* waited until midnight for the *Skule*, who had been obliged to lie to after the storm in order to restow her deck cargo, most of which was hanging over her side. I employed the time by trying to take a photograph of the town by night, and, in order to do so, lashed the camera to a stanchion for an hour. However, the swing of the ship to the ebbing tide was not taken into consideration, and on development the famous arc lights of Hammerfest were presented in a cloud of streaks and bars like a photograph of fireworks.

It was at Hammerfest that we first heard the famous rumour of the scheme for shipping Russian troops from Archangel to the coast of France *via* Great Britain. Of course we had seen nothing of any such movement, for our course lay to the north of the coastwise shipping. Moreover, the idea sounds so fantastic that we were surprised to find out later what excitement it created in England. The harbour of Archangel, kept open artificially, could play an important part in relieving the congestion in Russian export trade caused by the closing of the Baltic and Black Sea ports; but it is another matter to convey transports across the mine-spangled North Sea, especially at a time when Russia herself needed every man upon her western frontiers. Nevertheless, when once started, the hare ran a long way, and I know of one dear old lady who believes in it to this day, for did she not once give a tract to a soldier at a railway station and hear him reply: "Thankyouvitch." Which proves conclusively that he *must* have been a Russian!

We took a pilot on board at Hammerfest, and reached Tromsoe at midday on 1st October. Blizzards drove across the fiord at intervals, and the mountains were already ribbed and wealed with snow. Four or five German ships were moored in the harbour. They had lain there ever since the beginning of the war, when their crews were called away for military service. Although they flew the German flag, they carried cargoes consigned to English firms in Hull and Sunderland.

As soon as possible, we went ashore, and, oddly enough, in all our travels we never came nearer a ducking than on this occasion, for the mate, being in a hurry to go ashore, forgot to plug up the boat. Before we had gone a hundred yards, our feet were awash, and after having successfully weathered the Yenesei shoals, and the ice and storms of the Arctic Ocean, we had to bale for dear life, and row too, in order to escape foundering ignominiously in Tromsoe Harbour.

At Tromsoe, the *Ragna* changed her destination, for owing to the dangerous state of the North Sea, her owners would not take the risk of bringing her over to Aberdeen, as at first they intended. Therefore Miss Curtis and I had to cross over to England by another route, and we arranged to leave two days later for Bergen. Afterwards we walked about the town, until, at the hotel, we found a great prize—a copy of the *Times* only ten days old! No newspaper was ever devoured more thoroughly than that one. From it we learned of a threatened attack upon Antwerp, of the sack of Louvain, and of the bombardment of Rheims. But it all seemed so vague and so far away—we, fresh from places where the change of the weather and the catch of fish were the events of importance, could not realise it at all.

Early in the morning of 3rd October we were

obliged to leave the *Ragna*, and during the day she and the *Skule* left for Bergen, where they were to go into dock for the winter. The mail-boat to the south did not leave until midnight, so we had more than sufficient time to see the sights of Tromsoe, which, to tell the truth, as it was snowing heavily and the streets were filled with slush, were quickly exhausted. The principal "lion" was a Customs official who had been to the South Pole with Roald Amundsen; but when we had seen this hero, and also a party of Lapps who were wandering about the town in their picturesque national dress, there was nothing to be done but go back to the hotel and read the *Times* all over again.

A little incident at Tromsoe may give some idea of the extent to which Germany was mobilising her forces at this time. It will be remembered that there were on board the *Skule* seven German officers, who had commanded the little steamers as far as the Yenesei. Six of these could unquestionably claim exemption from military service on account of their age, but the seventh was more doubtful, for he did not look much past forty years. However, when the German consul had claimed the rest of the crews in Tromsoe six weeks before, he asserted so strenuously that he was above the age limit, that he was allowed to proceed on his voyage. Poor man, no amount of equivocation can escape the lynx eye of German officialdom. Now, on his return to port, he was met with the news that the Hamburg authorities had telegraphed a command that he was to return and report himself at once in Germany, where he would run a good chance of being shot as a deserter.

We left Tromsoe at midnight in the mail steamer *Finmarken*. Mr. Lied accompanied us as far as Trondhjem, whence he went by rail to Petrograd. The southward voyage took four days, and most of the time we passed through some of the most beautiful scenery in Europe, but we were both too anxious to pay it all the attention that it deserved. At each stopping-place we rushed ashore to buy papers, but needless to say, as these were all printed in Norwegian, their perusal did not make us much wiser. The only item of news that we could translate with any degree of certainty was a frequent telegram to the effect that another English ship had been blown up in the North Sea. There were also wild rumours that Zeppelins were dropping bombs upon London, and that India and Egypt had severally declared their independence. At the first declaration of war, the Norwegians feared that they would be drawn into the conflict by Sweden, to whom they are bound by treaty. Sweden, who is always fearful lest Russia should cast a covetous eye on one of the northern ports, was disposed to throw in her lot with Germany. Now, however, the alarm was over, and the Norwegians, like the thoroughly efficient and practical race that they are, were preparing to act the part of the little dog who, when the two hounds were quarrelling, ran off with the bone. In other words, Norway hoped to annex some of the European trade while the Powers were all at loggerheads.

We reached Bergen early in the morning of 7th October, and secured berths on a boat which left at midday for England. At first we believed that our destination would be either Peterhead or Aberdeen, as it was rumoured that new mine-fields had been laid down in the North Sea, but in the end we went to Newcastle. This second-rate little steamer had now become of international importance. She carried all the mails from England, not only to Scandinavia, but also to Russia, China, Japan, and the Far East. In fact, during the last three weeks, no less than 120 extra clerks had been sent to the Bergen post-office, for the local staff was quite overwhelmed by the flood of mails and telegrams.

In spite of all sinister rumours, our journey across the North Sea was the most uneventful section of the journey. Secretly we had looked forward to adventures of some kind, and we were quite disappointed that the weather was halcyon, and no ship appeared on the placid horizon. The only sign that anything unusual was expected was that the boats were slung outwards from the davits, so that they could be lowered at once if any accident occurred. We spent most of the voyage in reading the papers, for the captain, hearing what Rip van Winkles he had among his passengers, kindly lent us a parcel of newspapers that he carried as a gift to any British warship that might hail us. Here we read of the plight of Antwerp, of the torpedoing of the *Aboukir*, *Hogue*, and *Cressy*, of the retreat from Mons, and of the battle of the Aisne; and from a chance allusion here, or a quotation there, we began gradually to piece together the opening events of the war.

It was not until we reached home waters at Berwick that we saw any shipping, but along the Northumbrian coast, trade seemed to be proceeding much as usual. It was well guarded. Off the Tyne a cruiser kept watch at the river's mouth, and a couple of submarines foamed past us. Hard after them came a picket-boat: Where did we hail from? Where bound for? Had we seen anything of the enemy? The enemy!—off the Tyne!—such a thing had not been heard of in England for a hundred years; and as the pilot came on board, a pair of lean dark destroyers stole seawards through the mist. Passengers were sent below as we entered the river, but from the porthole one might mark the bustle and clangour of the shipwrights' work upon hulls where already the familiar red of commerce was overlaid by the sinister grey of Admiralty. Beside the quay were more officials to examine passports and detain German subjects. We reached the station at last. Men in khaki in the streets; men in khaki on the platform; men in khaki on the train. On the walls flamed patriotic posters; patriotic songs were on everybody's lips. Signs everywhere that the British lion was beginning to wake up at last, and was going to make up for lost time in his own stupid, blundering, heroical way. There was war-fever from end to end of the country, and here were we, two practical, educated Englishwomen, and we knew less about it all than even the newsboy who sold us a paper. We read everything, from the *Times* to the *Daily Sketch*. "And what on earth is it all about?" we said at last. At first sight it is a far cry from the murder of an Austrian archduke to warships in the Tyne.

Luckily there was a fellow-traveller ready to

enlighten us—there are always such. He discoursed at some length. It was, of course, a bad business, but there was no doubt that the Allies would be at Berlin by Christmas. Of course we were opposing 300,000 men to a force of a million, but that would be all right, because everyone knows that one Englishman is worth four Germans, and besides, it did not take more than three months' training to make a soldier, and Kitchener's army would be ready by Christmas, and so forth, and so forth—the optimistic platitudes of the average railway-carriage Briton. Finally, however, he became mistrustful of our simplicity and suspected a hoax.

"But where d'ye come from that you let on not to know all this?" he demanded sarcastically. "North Pole, I suppose!"

"Well, from somewhere that looked not unlike it," we admitted humbly, as the train rolled into King's Cross Station.

INDEX

Abba. See Willow-grouse.
Accentor montanellus. See Mountain accentor.
Alexis Petrovitch, 164, 169.
Amundsen, Roald, 287, 317.
Anabara River, 49.
Anas c. crecca. See Teal.
— *penelope.* See Widgeon.
Anastasia Ivanowna, 94, 157, 173, 263.
Angara River, 10.
Anser albifrons. See Goose, white-fronted.
— *fabalis.* See Goose, bean.
— *finmarchus.* See Goose, lesser white-fronted.
Anthus cervinus. See Pipit, red-throated.
Antonoff, Michael Petrovitch, 61, 65, 168, 263, 271; his dog sledge, 72; at Och Marino, 75 *et seq.*; his family, 91 *et seq.*; and Prokopchuk, 104; in *pourga*, 178.
— Madame, 66, 93, 229.
— Nura, 66, 241, 269, 291.
Archangel, 315.
Arctic Circle, 41; as breeding-ground, 121–123; migration in, 121–122; flora of, 252; avifauna of, 147; spell of, 305.
Arenaria i. interpres. See Turnstone.
Asio f. flammeus. See Owl, short-eared.
Aurora borealis, 249, 311.

Barentz, Willem, 1.
Bear, 286.
Bei-kem River, 18.
Beluga, 60.
Bergen, 316, 318.
Bieliy Ostrov, 307.
— Pesok, 53.
"Birdland" camera, 140.
Bluethroat (*luscinia s. gaetkei*), 12, 41, 58, 253; migration of, 162.
Brambling (*fringilla montifringilla*), 35.
Brenta ruficollis. See Goose, red-breasted.

Breokoffsky Islands, 48, 56 *et seq.*
Bunting, Lapland (*calcarius l. lapponicus*), 50, 52, 58, 71, 81; on the tundra, 146, 158; nests of, 189, 194; note of, 158; migration of, 158, 161, 283.
— little (*emberiza pusilla*), 32, 41, 46.
— snow (*plectrophenax nivalis*), 71, 157, 161, 253, 311.
— yellow-breasted (*emberiza aureola*), 14, 21, 24.
Buteo l. lagopus. See Buzzard.
Buzzard, rough-legged (*buteo l. lagopus*), 146, 155, 253.

Calcarius l. lapponicus. See Bunting, Lapland.
Carduelis l. linaria. See Redpoll, mealy.
— *h. exilipes.* See Redpoll, Coues'.
Cedar (*pinus cembra*), 16.
Charadrius apricarius. See Plover, golden.
— *d. fulvus.* See Plover, Eastern golden.
— *h. hiaticula.* See Plover, ringed.
— *morinellus.* See Dotterel.
Chelidon lagopoda. See Martin.
Cherniavinsky, 163.
Chiff-chaff, Siberian (*phylloscopus c. tristis*), 33, 50, 51, 58.
Choom, 26, 80, 104, 218, 258, 282.
"Chorna chika." See Skua.
Christensen, Mr. Gunnar, 6, 260, 261, 269, 287, 292.
Clangula hyemalis. See Duck, long-tailed.
Cockroaches, 68, 69.
Colonisation in Siberia, 44, 116–118.
Correct, s.s., voyage of, 307.
Cossacks, 4.
Cuckoo (*cuculus canorus* and *c. optatus*), 21, 35, 36, 37.
Curtis, Miss Dora, 3, 9, 166, 167, 246, 247, 248, 257, 274, 282, 286, 287, 295, 302, 309, 310.
Cygnus bewickii. See Swan, Bewick'.
Cypselus pacificus. See Swift, Siberian.

INDEX

Czaplicka, Miss M. A., 3, 4, 9, 101, 166, 167, 210, 257, 283; as organiser of the expedition, 3; as a physician, 113; on Samoyede names, 160; finds a mammoth, 246; her energy, 254.

Dafila acuta. See Duck, pintail.
Dgiotu. See Goose.
Dickson Island, 191, 219, 287, 294.
Disease among natives, 113–114.
Diver, black-throated (*gavia arctica*), 22, 58, 150, 190; call of, 151; nest of, 199.
— red-throated (*gavia stellata*), 45, 52, 58, 85, 190; nest of, 191; young of, 151–154; migration from Novaya Zemlya, 304.
— white-billed (*gavia adamsii*), 151.
Dogs, towing boat, 25; in sledges, 72 *et seq.*; eating stints, 140; at choom, 222–223.
Dolgans, geographical distribution of, 104; beadwork, 227; choom, 206 *et seq.*; shepherd, 190, 206 *et seq.*
Dotterel (*charadrius morinellus*), 146, 147, 231.
Dresser, Mr. H. E., 27 *note*, 33.
Dryobates m. major. See Woodpecker.
Duck, long-tailed (*clangula hyemalis*), 50, 52, 58, 81, 89, 148–149, 177, 189, 253.
— pintail (*dafila acuta*), 38, 160, 191.
— tufted (*nyroca fuligula*), 41.
Dudinka, 49–51, 191.
Dunlin (*erolia a. alpina*), 145, 189, 311.

Eclipse, s.s., 285.
Eggs of long-tailed duck, 117; of white-fronted goose, 196; of grey plover, 201; of little stint, 137; of curlew-sandpiper, 127; of black-throated thrush, 27; of dusky ousel, 47; of pale thrush, 35; of peregrine falcon, 192; of grey phalarope, 131, 189.
Eider, King (*somateria spectabilis*), 149, 160.
Ello, Captain Otto, 17, 61, 62, 270.
Emberiza aureola. See Bunting, yellow-breasted.
— *pusilla.* See Bunting, little.
Eremophila alpestris. See Shore-lark.
Erolia a. alpina. See Dunlin.
— *ferruginea.* See Sandpiper, curlew.
— *m. maritima.* See Sandpiper, purple.
— *m. minuta.* See Stint, little.
— *temminckii.* See Stint, Temminck's.

Falco p. peregrinus. See Falcon, peregrine.
— *r. regulus.* See Merlin.
Falcon, peregrine (*falco p. peregrinus*), 155, 192.
Fieldfare (*turdus pilaris*), 33, 41.
Fish, 53–55, 181, 191, 196, 284.
Fox, 157; traps, 155; skins, 156.
Franz-Josef Land, 302.
Fringilla montifringilla. See Brambling.
Fulmar (*fulmarus f. glacialis*), 300, 309.

"Ga-ga." See Eider.
"Ga-garra." See Diver.
Gallinago g. gallinago. See Snipe, common.
— *media.* See Snipe, great.
— *stenura.* See Snipe, pintailed.
Germany, news of war, 260; German crews, 281, 316; mobilisation, 317.
"Gillissy," 1.
Godwit, bar-tailed (*limosa l. lapponica*), 119, 120, 145, 155, 160.
Golchika, arrival at, 60; description of, 60, 70, 71, 90; birds of, 119–121; character of country, 145; last view, 292.
Goose, bean (*anser fabalis*), 154.
— lesser white-fronted (*anser finmarchus*), 34.
— red-breasted (*brenta ruficollis*), 55, 154; migration of geese, 154; native name for, 160; hunting, 225–226.
— white-fronted (*anser albifrons*), 154, 196, 198.
Grave, Yurak, 82.
Grosbeak, pine (*pinicola en. enucleator*), 34.
Guillemot, Brünnich's (*uria l. lomvia*), 304, 310.
Gull, common (*larus canus*), 21, 42.
— glaucous (*larus glaucus*), 304.
— ivory (*pagophila eburnea*), 300.
— Siberian (*larus f. antelius*), 81, 148, 181, 190, 233, 237.

Hachenkoff, Vassili Vassillievitch, 75 *et seq.*, 229, 231 *et seq.*
Hæmatopus ostralegus. See Oystercatcher.
Hall, Mr. H. U., 3, 7, 11, 13, 64, 87, 166, 246, 257, 283.
Hammerfest, 312–314.
Harnessing reindeer, 208.
Hazel-hen (*tetrastes bonasia*), 24.
Hyphoraia subnebulosa, 253 *note*.

INDEX

Ibis, 27, 47, 119, 130, 155, 152, 162, notes.
Ice, on banks of river, 52; at Och Marino, 80; formation of, 294; in Kara Sea, 294–300; rammed by ship, 295; bar to navigation in Kara Sea, 306–307.
Igarka, 42.
Ikon, 66, 108, 276, 277.
Ilia, Saint, 179.
Immigration into Siberia, 117.
Ingoe, 307, 309.

Jest, 7, 56, 73.
Johansen, Captain, and Amundsen, 287; belief in prophecy, 298; his brother's voyage to Solitude, 287.

Kamin Pass, 21.
Kara Sea, 1; possibilities of navigation in, 304; wireless stations at, 301; expeditions to, 304–307.
Kara Strait, 303, 304.
Katya, the Samoyede, 240.
Kazachye, trip to, 240 *et seq.*; family at, 243.
Khatanga River, 49.
Khua-kem River, 18.
Kitmanoff, 17.
Kittiwake (*rissa t. tridactyla*), 300, 304, 308.
Krasnoyarsk, 6 *et seq.*
Krestova, 51.
Krestovskiy Islands, 120.
Kropotkin, 144 *note*.
Kureika, 9, 36; graphite at, 41; birds at, 36 *et seq.*; lost in forest, 38 *et seq.*
Kuria, family at, 182 *et seq.*, 271.
Kutcherenkoff, 15, 99, 169, 170–171.

Lagopus albus. See Willow-grouse.
— *rupestris.* See Ptarmigan.
Larus f. antelius. See Gull, Siberian.
— *canus.* See Gull, common.
— *glaucus.* See Gull, glaucous.
Lena River, 209.
Lena, steamer, 171–172, 262, 291.
Lied, Mr. Jonas, 281, 287, 290, 294, 307.
Limosa l. lapponica. See Godwit.
Lukovoi Protok, 55.
Luscinia s. gaetkei. See Bluethroat.

Machetes pugnax. See Ruff, Reeve.
Magpie (*pica leucoptera*), 13.
Mails, 25, 270.
Malchik (dog), 223.
Mammoth, 156, 246.
Mangaseya, 31.

Markova, 27, 28.
Martin (*chelidon lagopoda*), 54.
Medical missions, 114.
Merlin (*falco r. regulus*), 288.
Mezenchyne, 243, 245.
Micha, 163, 271.
Migration, down river, 121; at Breokoffsky, 288; at Golchika, 160–162; from Novaya Zemlya, 303.
Mirage, 234.
Monastir, 30, 31–32.
Monastirskiy, 21.
Moré Salé, 301.
Moscow, 5, 6.
Mosquitoes, 13, 21, 177, 222.
Motacilla a. alba. See Wagtail, white.
— *c. citreola.* See Wagtail, yellow-headed.
Mountain accentor (*accentor montanellus*), 59, 283.
Muksun, 53.

Nansen, Dr. Fridtjof, *cited* 44, 51, 53 *note*, 307.
Nasimorokoya, 20.
Nerobi, the Samoyede, 156, 229.
Nerotova, Madame, 49, 114.
Nicolai, the Samoyede, 229.
Nicolai, the steward, 18, 270.
Nill, 74, 93, 229, 232, 271.
Norway, 312 *et seq.*
Nosonovsky Ostrov, 261, 279, 280, 282, 292.
Nyavoie. See Duck, pintail.
Nyctea nyctea. See Owl, snowy.
Nyelma, 53, 176.
Nyroca fuligula. See Duck, tufted.
Nyrpe. See Seal.

Ob, 191, 238, 293.
Ob, steamer, 261, 281.
Och Marino, 75 *et seq.*, 235 *et seq.*, 293.
Œnanthe œ. œnanthe. See Wheatear.
Oidemia n. nigra. See Scoter.
Omul, 53, 176.
— (motor-boat), 51.
Oryol, steamer, 15, 16, 67, 257, 269.
Ostiaks, ethnological position of, 26; *chooms*, 25, 26; in forest, 37.
Ouss (dog), 223, 225–226.
Owl, snowy (*nyctea nyctea*), 155, 162.
— short-eared (*asio f. flammeus*), 21.
Oyster-catcher (*hæmatopus ostralegus*), 27.

Pagophila eburnea. See Gull, ivory.
Peacock, Mr., 9, 64–65.
Petchora River, 219, 304.

326 INDEX

Phalarope, grey (*phalaropus fulicarius*), 81, 119, 120, 123; nest of, 131, 189, 190; note of, 131; habits of, 131–133; courtship, 130; protective resemblance, 132; migration, 133, 161; photographing, at nest, 131.
— red-necked (*phalaropus lobatus*), 50, 52, 58, 71, 133, 199, 224; nest of, 194; feeding habits, 133; migration, 133, 161.
Phylloscopus b. borealis. See Warbler, Eversmann's.
— *c. tristis.* See Chiff-chaff, Siberian.
— *s. superciliosus.* See Warbler, yellow-browed.
Pica leucoptera. See Magpie.
Pinicola en. enucleator. See Grosbeak, pine.
Pipit, red-throated (*anthus cervinus*), 50, 58, 159, 161.
Pirog, 54.
Platina, 45, 48.
Plectrophenax nivalis. See Bunting, snow.
Plover, Eastern golden (*charadrius d. fulvus*), 81, 119, 120; nest of, 142; flocking, 143; migration, 145, 161; native name, 161; photographing nest, 221–222.
— golden (*charadrius apricarius*), 143.
— grey (*squatarola squatarola*), 119, 120, 161, 197, 199 *et seq.*, 237.
— ringed (*charadrius h. hiaticula*), 36, 52, 146, 161.
Popham, Mr. H. L., 2, 171; and black-throated ousel, 27; on nesting habits of wood sandpiper, 34, 42; and cuckoos, 37; and dusky ousel, 47; and redpolls, 52; and red-breasted goose, 55, 154; on birds of Golchika, 119; on curlew sandpiper, 124, 127, 129; on divers, 150; on biuethroats, 162; at Golchika, 188; on migration at Novaya Zemlya, 304.
Popham, Mr. Leyborne, 306.
Potapooskoye, 170.
Pourga, 178.
Prokopchuk, Gerasim Androvitch, 61 *et seq.*; house of, 96 *et seq.*; methods of business, 105, 110, 266; on birds, 154, 162; and fox, 157; reindeer, 206; at church, 264, 268.
— Joseph Gerasimvitch, 63, 66, 175, 219, 241 *et seq.*, 266 *et seq.*
— Marusia, 94, 174, 241 *et seq.*, 267.
— Nicolai, 243, 247.
— Simeon, 240, 243, 247, 254.

Protyvik, 15, 70, 91, 100.
Ptarmigan (*lagopus rupestris*), 119, 120, 225.
Pustoy, 162, 288.
Pyasina River, 44, 191.

Rabchik. See Hazel-hen.
Ragna, s.s., 281, 284, 289, 308 *et seq.*, 316.
Redpoll, mealy (*carduelis l. linaria*), 41, 43, 51, 58, 158, 311.
— Coues' (*carduelis h. exilipes*), 52.
Redwing (*turdus musicus*), 21, 27, 33.
Reeve (*machetes pugnax*), 145, 189. See also Ruff.
Reindeer, 205, 208, 212, 219, 258.
Religion, of Siberiaks, 115; of natives, 108.
Riparia riparia. See Sand-martin.
Rissa t. tridactyla. See Kittiwake.
Road, Krasnoyarsk to Yenesiesk, 14.
Ruff (*machetes pugnax*), 50, 57, 161, 253, 288.

Samoyedes, 103, 106 *et seq.*, 113, 180; names for birds, 160; anecdote of, 230; name of, 237; wedding, 277.
Sanders, Mr. Armytage, 140.
Sand-martin (*riparia riparia*), 9, 10.
Sandpiper, common (*tringa hypoleuca*), 24, 36.
— curlew (*erolia ferruginea*), 123 *et seq.*; nest and eggs of, 127; breeding habits of, 127 *et seq.*; flocking of, 128; call of, 129; migration of, 130, 161; young of, 224–225.
— purple (*erolia m. maritima*), 311.
— terek (*terekia cinerea*), 41.
— wood (*tringa glareola*), 33, 34, 38, 42.
Schwanenburg, 170–171.
Scoter, common (*oidemia n. nigra*), 300.
Scurvy, 177.
Seal, 89.
Seebohm, 2, 19, 70, 171, 219; at the Kureika, 38; on dusky ousel, 47; visits Breokoffsky, 57, 59; on birds of Golchika, 119, 151; on note of grey plover, 201; on native tribes, 237.
Seld, 53.
Shammanism, 108, 109.
Shore-lark (*eremophila alpestris*), 145, 158, 161.
Siberian Company, 7, 257, 280, 307.
Skua, arctic (*stercorarius parasiticus*), 191–192, 155.
— long-tailed (*stercorarius longicaudus*), 155, 194, 199, 247.

INDEX 327

Skua, pomatorhine (*stercorarius pomarinus*), 54, 119, 297, 308.
Skule, s.s., 280, 284, 292, 297, 301, 309, 316–317.
Sledge dog, 68, 72 *et seq.*
Sledge, reindeer, 206–207.
Sloika, 206.
Smallpox, 105.
Snipe, common (*gallinago g. gallinago*), 54, 59.
— great (*gallinago media*), 52.
— pintailed (*gallinago stenura*), 27, 33, 54.
Somateria spectabilis. See Eider.
Sopochnaya, 75, 294.
Sotnikoff family, 206 *et seq.*
— Vassilli, 259.
Squatarola squatarola. See Plover, grey.
Starling (*sturnus vulgaris*), 21.
Stercorarius. See Skua.
Sterna paradisæa. See Tern, arctic.
Stint, little (*erolia m. minuta*), 71, 81, 134, 189; photographing, 135; habits of, 134–136; migration of, 136, 161; nest of, 193, 194, 253.
— Temminck's (*erolia temminckii*), 51, 58, 71; nest of, 137; courtship of, 137; photographing, 137–139; habits of, 140; migration of, 161.
Sturgeon, 53.
Sturnus vulgaris. See Starling.
Svyato-Troitskiy, Monastir, 31.
Swan, Bewick's (*cygnus bewickii*), 59, 81, 150.
Swerdrup, Captain, 285.
Swerifskye, 228 *et seq.*
Swertzoff, 123.
Swift, Siberian (*cypselus pacificus*), 161.
Sylkin, the Samoyede, 102, 108, 111, 178, 188 *et seq.*, 229, 271.
Syphilis, 113.

Taigà, 45, 46.
Tannykka. See Gull.
Tartary, Sea of, 1.
Tatars, 54.
Teal (*anas c. crecca*), 41.
Telegraph, in forest, 28; at Golchika, 106.
Terekia cinerea. See Sandpiper, terek.
Tern, arctic (*sterna paradisæa*), 43, 50, 148, 161, 194.
Tetrastes bonasia. See Hazel-hen.
Thrush, black-throated (*turdus atrigularis*), 26, 27.
— dusky (*turdus fuscatus*), 47, 52, 58.
— pale (*turdus obscurus*), 35.
— Siberian (*turdus sibiricus*), 27, 33.

Tilyokko. See Plover, Eastern golden.
Timber, Siberian, 289–290.
Tringa hypoleuca. See Sandpiper, common.
— *glareola.* See Sandpiper, wood.
Tromsoe, 285, 315 *et seq.*
Trotzska, 10.
Tufek. See Godwit.
Tulloni. See Eider.
Tundra, 186, 205.
Tungus, 48, 219.
Tunguska Rivers, 18, 21.
Turdus atrigularis. See Thrush, black-throated.
— *fuscatus.* See Thrush, dusky.
— *musicus.* See Redwing.
— *obscurus.* See Thrush, pale.
— *pilaris.* See Fieldfare.
— *sibiricus.* See Thrush, Siberian.
Turnstone (*arenaria i. interpres*), 161, 199; migration of, 234, 283, 288.
Turukhansk, 31, 32, 33 *et seq.*, 172.
Turukhansk, steamer, 162, 262.

Uria l. lomvia. See Guillemot, Brünnich's.

Vassilli, 7, 8, 10, 24, 35, 39, 74, 86, 188 *et seq.*, 242, 250, 268, 274.
Vassilli, Saint, 31.
Vega Harbour, 294.
Verkne Imbatskaya, 25.
Vino, 195.
Vorogovo, 20, 21, 102.
Vostratine, Stephan Vassillievitch, 11.
— Vassilli Vassillievitch, 11–15.

Wagtail, white (*motacilla a. alba*), 10, 71, 157, 161.
— yellow-headed (*motacilla c. citreola*), 33, 50, 52.
Waigatz, 300, 303, 304.
Warbler, Eversmann's (*phylloscopus b. borealis*), 33, 50, 54.
— yellow-browed (*phylloscopus s. superciliosus*), 21, 33.
Warsaw, 3.
Wheatear (*œnanthe œ. œnanthe*), 146, 158, 161, 253, 283.
Widgeon (*anas penelope*), 21, 41.
Wiggins, Captain, 103, 111, 171, 301, 306.
Willoughby, Sir Hugh, 305.
Willow-grouse (*lagopus albus*), 147, 160, 162, 193, 194, 253.
Witherby, Mr. H. F., 37.

Women merchants, 49.
Wood, drift, 42.
Woodpecker (*dryobates m. major*), 21, 24.

Yenesei, ancient names of, 1, 18; size of, 18; breaking up of ice, 19; fisheries, 53, 55; storm on, 85 *et seq.*; barrier to migration, 238; birds on, 245; trade with, 287.
Yenesei, steamer, 163.
Yenesiesk, 10, 11, 12, 14, 15.
Yenesiesk, steamer, 261, 281, 292.
Yugor Strait, 301, 303.
Yuraks, 31, 79, 82, 185, 229, 246; distribution of, 103, 237, 238.

RUSSIA OBSERVED

AN ARNO PRESS/NEW YORK TIMES COLLECTION

Adams, John Quincy.
The Russian Memoirs of John Quincy Adams: His Diary from 1809 to 1814.
Edited by Charles Francis Adams. 1874.

Atkinson, Thomas Witlam.
Oriental and Western Siberia. 1858.

Atkinson, Mrs. Thomas W.
Recollections of Tartar Steppes and Their Inhabitants. 1863.

Baedeker, Karl.
Baedeker's Handbook for Travelers: Russia. 1914.

Baerlein, Henry.
The March of the Seventy Thousand. 1926.

Bechhofer, C. E.
In Denikin's Russia. 1921.

Bourke, Richard Southwell.
St. Petersburg and Moscow: A Visit to the Court of the Czar. 1846.

Bryant, Louise.
Six Red Months in Russia. 1918.

Bryce, James.
Transcaucasia and Ararat. 1896.

Buchanan, Sir George.
My Mission to Russia and Other Diplomatic Memories. 1923.

Buchanan, James.
James Buchanan's Mission to Russia: 1831-1833. 1908.

Buchanan, Meriel.
The Dissolution of an Empire. 1932.

Burnaby, Fred.
A Ride to Khiva. 1877.

Bush, Richard J.
Reindeer, Dogs, and Snow-Shoes. 1871.

Cantacuzène, Princess (Countess Speransky, née Grant).
Revolutionary Days. 1919.

Chamberlin, William Henry.
Russia's Iron Age. 1934.

Chappé D'Auteroche.
A Journey into Siberia. 1770.

Clark, Rev. Francis E.
A New Way Around an Old World. 1901.

Clarke, Edward Daniel.
Travels to Russia, Tartary & Turkey. 1811.

Cochrane, John Dundas.
Narrative of a Pedestrian Journey Through Russia and Siberian Tartary. 1825.

Coxe, William.
Travels in Poland and Russia. 1802. (3 volumes in one)

Craven, Lady Elizabeth.
A Journey Through the Crimea to Constantinople. 1789.

Curtin, Jeremiah.
A Journey in Southern Siberia. 1909.

Dallas, George M.
Diary of George Mifflin Dallas, United States Minister to Russia, 1837-1839. Edited by Susan Dallas. 1892.

Dobell, Peter.
Travels in Kamtchatka and Siberia. 1830.

Dorr, Rheta Childe.
Inside the Russian Revolution. 1918.

The Englishwoman in Russia: Impressions of the Society and Manners of the Russians at Home. 1855.

Erman, Adolph.
Travels in Siberia. 1848. (2 volumes in one)

Francis, David R.
Russia from the American Embassy: April, 1916-November, 1918. 1921.

Frederic, Harold.
The New Exodus: A Study of Israel in Russia. 1892.

Gautier, Théophile.
Russia. 1905.

Gilliard, Pierre.
Thirteen Years at the Russian Court. 1921.

Graves, William S.
America's Siberian Adventure, 1918-1920. 1931.

Guthrie, Mrs. Katherine Blanche:
Through Russia: From St. Petersburg to Astrakhan and the Crimea. 1874.

Hapgood, Isabel F.
Russian Rambles. 1895.

Hard, William.
Raymond Robins' Own Story. 1920.

Haviland, Maud D.
A Summer on the Yenesei. 1915.

Hawes, Charles.
In the Uttermost East. 1904.

Von Haxthausen, Baron Franz August Maria.
The Russian Empire. 1856.

Hill, S. S.
Travels in Siberia. 1854.

Holderness, Mary.
New Russia. 1823.

Hume, George.
Thirty-Five Years in Russia. 1914.

Johnston, Robert.
Travels Through Part of the Russian Empire and the Country of Poland. 1816.

Kennan, George.
Tent Life in Siberia. 1910.

Kitchin, George.
Prisoner of the Ogpu. 1935.

Knox, Major-General Alfred William Fortescue.
With the Russian Army, 1914-1917. 1921. (2 volumes in one)

Knox, Thomas W.
Overland Through Asia. 1870.

Kohl, J. G.
Russia. 1844.

De Lagny, Germain.
The Knout and the Russians. 1854.

Lansdell, Henry.
Russian Central Asia. 1885.

Lansdell, Henry.
Through Siberia. 1882.

De Lesseps, Baron Jean Baptiste Barthélemy.
Travels in Kamtschatka. 1790.

Littlepage, John D. and Demaree Bess.
In Search of Soviet Gold. 1937.

Loubat, Joseph Florimund.
Gustavus Fox's Mission to Russia in 1866. 1873.

Lyall, Robert.
Travels in Russia. 1825.

MacGahan, J. A. **Campaigning on the Oxus and the Fall of Khiva.** 1874.

Marye, George Thomas.
Nearing the End in Imperial Russia. 1929.

Masson, Charles Francois Philibert.
Secret Memoirs of the Court of Petersburg. 1802.

Maynard, Major-General Sir Charles C.
The Murmansk Venture. 1928.

Meakin, Annette M. B.
A Ribbon of Iron. 1901.

Meakin, Annette M. B.
Russia, Travels and Studies. 1906.

Monkhouse, Allan.
Moscow 1911-1933. 1934.

Murray's Hand-Book for Northern Europe: Finland and Russia. 1849.

Nansen, Fridtjof.
Through Siberia. 1914.

Nevinson, Henry W.
The Dawn in Russia. 1906.

O'Donovan, Edmond.
The Merv Oasis. 1882.

Oliphant, Laurence.
The Russian Shores of the Black Sea. 1854.

Pallas, Peter Simon.
Travels Through the Southern Provinces of the Russian Empire. 1803.

Palmer, Francis H. E.
Russian Life in Town and Country. 1901.

Parrot, Dr. Friedrich.
Journey to Ararat. 1846.

Paul of Aleppo.
The Travels of Macarius.
Selected and Arranged by Lady Laura Ridding. 1936.

Pinkerton, Robert.
Russia. 1833.

Richardson, William.
Anecdotes of the Russian Empire. 1784.

Rigby, Elizabeth (Lady Eastlake).
Letters from the Shores of the Baltic. 1842.

De Rulhière, Claude Carloman.
A History or Anecdotes of the Revolution in Russia. 1797.

Scott, John.
Behind the Urals:
An American Worker in Russia's City of Steel. 1942.

De Ségur, Count Louis Philippe.
Memoirs and Recollections
of Count Louis Philippe Ségur. 1826-1827. (3 volumes in one)

Soutar, Andrew.
With Ironside in North Russia. 1940.

Spottiswoode, William.
A Tarantasse Journey Through Eastern Russia. 1857.

Staehlin, Jakob Von Storcksburg.
Original Anecdotes of Peter the Great. 1788.

Stevens, Thomas.
Through Russia on a Mustang. 1891.

Von Strahlenberg, Captain Philip John.
Russia, Siberia and Great Tartary. 1738.

Timbres, Harry and Rebecca.
We Didn't Ask Utopia: A Quaker Family in Soviet Russia. 1939.

Tooke, William.
View of the Russian Empire. 1800. (3 volumes)

Vambéry, Arminius.
Sketches of Central Asia. 1868.

Vambéry, Arminius.
Travels in Central Asia. 1865.

Vigor, Mrs. William.
Letters From Russia. 1777.

Wenyon, Charles.
Across Siberia on the Great Post-Road. 1896.

Wilmot, Martha and Catherine.
The Russian Journals of Martha and Catherine Wilmot.
Edited by the Marchioness of Londonderry
and H. Montgomery Hyde. 1934.

Wilson, William Rae.
Travels in Russia. 1828.

Wolff, Joseph.
Narrative of a Mission to Bokhara. 1845.